Praise for *The Devil in the Kitchen*

"Tantalizing." —*Vogue*

"The British star is still throwing punches." —*Men's Journal*

"A fascinating, exhilarating look into the life of a culinary genius and living legend." —**Amazon.com**

"Juicy." —*Milwaukee Journal Sentinel*

"Marco is a gift to humanity, with more passion per pound than anyone else I have ever met. His story is genius, his voice his own, and the tale retold is just as much fun as it was watching the whole chaotic conundrum evolve the first time around. His sophisticated cooking came out of nowhere but inside his rock-star head, and this autobiography makes it all clear in the juiciest and most delicious way. After all these years, Marco is still my hero." —**Mario Batali**

THE DEVIL
in the
KITCHEN

SEX, PAIN, MADNESS, AND THE
MAKING OF A GREAT CHEF

MARCO PIERRE WHITE
with JAMES STEEN

BLOOMSBURY
NEW YORK · LONDON · OXFORD · NEW DELHI · SYDNEY

*To Leticia Rosa, Luciano, Marco
and Mirabelle, and to the
grandmother they never knew*

Bloomsbury USA
An imprint of Bloomsbury Publishing Plc

1385 Broadway
New York
NY 10018
USA

50 Bedford Square
London
WC1B 3DP
UK

www.bloomsbury.com

BLOOMSBURY and the Diana logo are trademarks of Bloomsbury Publishing Plc

First published in the United Kingdom in 2006
by Orion Books under the title *White Slave*
First published in the United States by Bloomsbury USA in 2007
This paperback edition published in 2008

ISBN: HB.   978-1-59691-361-5
          PB: 978-1-59691-497-1
          ePub: 978-1-59691-932-7

Library of Congress Cataloging-in-Publication Data has been applied for.

20

Typeset by Westchester Book Group
Printed and bound in the U.S.A. by Berryville Graphics Inc., Berryville, Virginia

To find out more about our authors and books visit www.bloomsbury.com.
Here you will find extracts, author interviews, details of forthcoming
events and the option to sign up for our newsletters.

Bloomsbury books may be purchased for business or promotional use.
For information on bulk purchases please contact Macmillan Corporate
and Premium Sales Department at specialmarkets@macmillan.com.

Contents

Another Day, Another Dinner

C AN'T STAND FLYING. Hate it.
The fear stems from my inability to understand how planes
stay in the sky and the knowledge that some of them don't. I have
agreed to attend business meetings abroad, and then cried off because
I couldn't bring myself to board the plane. I surprised even myself
when I agreed to come to the U.S. for a book tour in May 2007. This
wouldn't be a simple return trip from my comfort zone in London to
New York. The eighteen-page itinerary had me flying all over the
place, from San Francisco to Miami and lots of places in between.
During the first three days of the seventeen-day trip I'd managed nine
hours of sleep and had turned into an exhausted, jet-lagged beast,
stumbling from book signing to radio show to airport, being overfed
and plied with too much alcohol along the way.

I don't want to sound like a moaning British git—there are far
worse things than being given too much food and drink and staying in
nice hotels. What I should point out—and this is important—is that I
fell in love with America. It's an extraordinary place. When it comes to
food and gastronomy, it reminds me of my early days in the industry
(Britain back in the 1970s and early '80s), when people still got excited about Michelin, and chefs wanted to be great cooks and win
awards, rather than become famous. The restaurant scene in the
United States is just more exciting than in the UK, where Michelin-
starred restaurants are patronizing to customers and the staff dictates

how you should eat your food, all the while reminding you that you're lucky to have even gotten a table. I didn't get any of that in the States. The dining experience in America is much more democratic.

In Chicago, I enjoyed both the technical brilliance of a ten-course meal by Grant Achatz at Alinea and the most delicious hot dog of my life at Hot Doug's, where I waited in a queue for twenty minutes just to get inside.

In New York, I was reunited with my old friend Mario Batali, the celebrated chef with whom I worked at the Six Bells, in Chelsea, London, in the mid-eighties. Up until then, the last time he'd seen me was just as I was chucking a pan of hot risotto in his direction. He's since forgiven me.

Mario met me at my hotel and said he would take me on a quick sightseeing tour on the way to lunch at one of his restaurants. We stepped out of the hotel, and he handed me a motorbike helmet—no visor, no strap—and said, "Put that on. Let's go." He then pointed at a parked Vespa to which I said, "Mario, it's great to see you after all these years, but there's no way the two of us are going to fit on that thing." He's a big man, and I'm not small, either. "Marco, put the helmet on," he said. Somehow we managed to squeeze onto the saddle and we zoomed off.

I found myself on the back of that Vespa for a good portion of my stay in New York, stopping to enjoying tripe and spaghetti with bottarga at Mario's legendary restaurant Babbo; marveling at the live frogs, eels and fish in Chinatown; taking in the view of the city's skyline from the Brooklyn side (note to the reader: the view is better enjoyed when one isn't jet-lagged, stuffed to the gills with food and wine and suffering from the onset of hypothermia); and, of course, teaching the good people of New York City about a drink I call "the house cocktail." The house cocktail consists of a large shot of sambuca, which you set on fire before slamming your hand down onto the glass. The aim is to get the glass to stick to your palm, and then suck the air and sambuca out of it in one quick shot. Halfway through one of my tutorials, someone knocked the flaming drink onto me, shattering the glass and causing shards to bury themselves in my hand. All in a day's work.

It's been quite a year. In addition to "discovering" America, one of the biggest changes in my life has been my decision to step back into the kitchen for the first time since 1999. A few weeks after the publication of the hardcover edition of this book, I received two offers of work, which, if accepted, would mean that I would have to put on the apron again and return to the kitchen.

I accepted both invitations.

The first job seemed uncomplicated enough and, given my experience, undemanding. I was asked if I would go to France to do a cooking demonstration for fifteen ladies in the kitchens of Sir Rocco Forte's hotel, Chateau de Bagnols, which is just outside Lyon. The women were all guests at the hotel. Their husbands would be spending the day wine-tasting at the Montrachet vineyard, while I would be at the stove doing my demonstration. When I arrived at the hotel, a smartly dressed man dashed up to me, held out his hand for a shake and said, "Hello, Darko."

I was a bit irritated that he couldn't get my name right and said, "No, it's Marco."

Again he said, "Hello, Darko."

Again I said, "No, it's Marco. It's Marco with an 'M.'"

"No," he said, "I'm Darko, Marco. I'm the host." I felt a bit of an idiot (and after that I was very polite to Darko), but not half as stupid as I did the following day, when it was time to do the demo.

The plan was to cook three dishes in one hour, or rather, rustle up three dishes that each took a mere twenty minutes to make. These dishes had to be quite effortless and easy to cook at home. I decided to serve grilled lobster with parsley and chervil and a bearnaise mousseline; turbot with citrus fruits, a little coriander and some fennel; then sea bass à la niçoise. It was while cooking the last one—the sea bass dish—that I came unstuck . . . or rather stuck to a plate.

Sea bass à la niçoise is a simple dish in which the tomatoes are put under the grill so that the water content evaporates under the heat. You're getting rid of the acidity, basically, and bringing out the sweetness. Once grilled, the tomatoes are thrown into a pan that contains olive oil, lemon juice, coriander and basil. During the grilling process, I somehow got dragged into a bit of chitchat with the ladies, which was disastrous because the distraction caused me to lose my timing. There I was, bantering, laughing and cracking jokes, when suddenly I remembered the plate of tomatoes under the grill. As I grabbed the plate, I felt the most excruciating pain in my hand and realized that the searing heat of the dish had welded my thumb to the porcelain. My entire body must have flinched. Yet the gaggle of smiling ladies—my happy pupils—didn't seem to notice that their cookery teacher was being cooked.

I told myself I had two options: first, I could either be professional and pretend nothing was happening, even though I could not remember the last time I had had so much pain inflicted upon me; second, I could succumb to the agony, cave in, drop the plate and scream so loud and for so long that I would shake the foundations of Rocco's chateau.

I went for the first option. In my head there was this mantra: *take the pain, take the pain, just take the bleeding pain.* I must tell you, that plate came out of the grill faster than any plate has ever come out of a grill. Normally, I would have got a spoon and scraped the tomatoes from the plate and into the pan, but because of the agony I was enduring there wasn't time for the spoon. I found myself tossing the sliced tomatoes from the hot plate into air, and it just so happened that they landed neatly in the pan, on top of the herbs, the olive oil and lemon juice. It looked like a circus trick. Afterwards the kitchen chef came up to me and said, "Wow, you are so quick." I should have said to him, "It helps if you're handling a plate that feels like molten lava." But I didn't.

While learning how to live with a grilled thumb back in London, I got my second offer to return to the kitchen. It was a call from the *Hell's Kitchen* people, asking me if I'd like to do their TV show in Britain. In this memoir, you'll find me giving an opinion about chefs who would rather be in front of the camera than behind the stove. As far as I'm concerned, if someone is paying a huge amount of money to come to your restaurant and eat your food, then you have a duty to be in the kitchen. When I was a lad working at Le Gavroche, if Albert Roux wasn't there for the service, you noticed the difference. Having said that, was it hypocritical of me to do *Hell's Kitchen?* No, I don't think so because I haven't been a chef at my restaurants since retiring.

I do not claim to be in the kitchen, and when customers come to my restaurants they do not expect me to see me behind the stove. All clear on that? Great.

Now, this wasn't the first time I'd been approached to do television. Over the years I'd said no to a number of TV production companies, knowing that invariably the projects hadn't been right or the timing was wrong. This time things just clicked, and the idea of stepping back into the ring began to appeal to me. I realized that I missed the adrenaline of the kitchen and the joy of serving great food. Sometimes in life we have something to prove to ourselves. I wanted to prove to myself that I'm not over-the-hill and that I still have a lot to give to my industry. So I accepted the deal and spent two very crazy weeks teaching ten celebrities how to cook (the format of the show is slightly different in the UK).

I think it was good for my kids to see me working in that environment—something to remember their dad by; an insight, in a crazy way, into my world—and I loved being reunited with some of the guys from the old days at Harveys and Canteen. It was only a TV program, but I treated it as a restaurant opening and looked to inspire those involved, rather than impress those who weren't. The truth is, I would never have agreed to do *Hell's Kitchen* if it weren't for *The Devil in the Kitchen*. The process of writing this book helped me to leave behind the baggage that was weighing me down and allowed me to move forward with my life. I like to think that I've developed, for the best.

And can I board a plane without trembling? You bet.

ONE

Off My Trolley

T**HE CHEESE TROLLEY** was just on its way out when I spotted It. This was in the mid-nineties, one evening shortly before dinner service. I was standing at the passe—the counter where the plates are collected by the waiters—in my kitchen at the Restaurant Marco Pierre White at the Hyde Park Hotel in London. The trolley was on its way out to the dining room and six or eight cheeses were on it. There was nothing wrong with any of them—they were all beautifully ripe, plump and oozing—but I had a rule in the kitchen, and as the trolley was being wheeled past me, I noticed the rule had been broken.

The rule was simple: the cheese had to be the right size. In the afternoon, after lunch service, we would take a look at the cheese on the trolley and a decision was taken as to whether it needed replacing. If a particular cheese was substantial, the size of a dinner plate perhaps, and half of it had been eaten during lunch, then the remaining half would still be large enough to merit staying on the trolley, and before we opened for dinner, it would be trimmed up, ready for serving.

However, if a cheese was small to begin with, the size of a saucer, say, and half of it had been served at lunch, then the rule dictated that it would be taken off the trolley. So we would always have backup cheese, which we would take out of the fridge to ripen up between lunch and dinner. As cheese is traditionally the responsibility of front of house, it was the maître d'hôtel's task to replace the ones that had been hit hard over lunch.

The point was that I wanted to present a generous cheese trolley. If the presentation is not correct, then it looks mean and should not go out into the restaurant. It must be grand and generous rather than a mess of lots of little cheeses, and it had to be particularly grand and generous in my restaurant because I was Britain's highest-paid chef and running what was considered to be one of the nation's finest restaurants in what was certainly one of the world's most luxurious hotels.

But on this particular night when I was at the passe, I saw the trolley going out carrying a cheese that was too small. My easy-to-obey rule had been broken by the maître d', Nicolas. There was a cheese on that trolley that was two-thirds eaten. That is when I flipped.

I stopped Nicolas in his tracks and pointed at the trolley. "Where are you going with that?" I asked.

He knew something nasty was coming. I could see it in his eyes. "I'm taking it through, Marco."

"No, Nicolas. No, no, no, no, no, no. Fuck, no."

"Sorry, Marco."

"Not right, Nicolas. Not correct, not right. The fucking cheese is not fucking right."

"Sorry, Marco."

I picked up the first cheese. "Not right!" With all my might I threw it against the wall. It stuck to the tiles. I picked up the second cheese. "Not right!" I chucked it at the wall. Like the first, it was so wonderfully ripe that it splattered onto the tiles and remained glued to them. Then I hurled the remaining cheeses, one after another, at that wall. Splat after splat after splat—six or maybe eight times. The trolley was now empty, except for a cheese knife.

Most of the chefs looked down, carrying on with their work as if nothing had happened. Nicolas and a couple of cooks raced over to the wall, ready to pry off the cheeses and clear up the smelly mess. I shouted, "Leave them there. *Leave them there.* Leave them fucking there all night. No one is allowed to touch them." The cheeses had to stay on that wall all night so that whenever Nicolas came into the kitchen, he would see them glued to the white tiles (except for the Camembert, which snailed down to the floor). And he would never, ever make the mistake again.

It was extreme behavior, I accept that, but I was driving home a point, and if it's OK with you, I would like to put the incident into context. My restaurant at the Hyde Park Hotel was probably the most expensive restaurant in Britain. If you had the Foie Gras Surprise followed by the Lobster aux Truffes and then a pudding, you were looking at £85 for a three-course dinner. If you wanted the Sea Bass Caviar, you would have to pay a £50 supplement. How serious is that?

I had spent twenty years of my life building my reputation, and people—the customers, in other words—were paying for my knowledge. By then I had won three Michelin stars, and was the only British chef to have them, and my great belief was consistency. A three-star restaurant has to get things right, otherwise there's no point in doing them at all. How often have you been out for dinner and had a great starter and a great pudding but a weak main course?

I could not allow you to endure any weakness at the Hyde Park Hotel. Whatever it was, from the bread to the amuse-gueules, the starters to the fish course, the main course to the puddings, the coffee to the petits fours, the chocolates to the cheese, it all had to be consistently of the highest standard.

Everything had to be right. Even the taste and temperature of the soup had to be checked. It had to be hot, which might sound like an obvious point, but how many of us have ordered a soup that comes out tepid? I'm not happy with that and I don't think you would be. If you're not consistent, you'll never go from one to two stars or two to three.

The cheese on the wall sent out a message to everyone working that night, from the youngest boy in the kitchen carrying food and serving bread to the maître d' bringing in an order. Every single member of the kitchen staff had to look at the cheese, glued to the wall by its ripeness, whenever they came to the passe. An eighteen-year-old commis—an assistant chef—walks into the kitchen to collect a tray, he walks past it, he sees it and it's imprinted in his memory forever. You have to deliver the message that they must never take a shortcut. You can't just say, "Come on, boys, let's try to get it right." That just won't work. If you are not extreme, then people will take shortcuts because they don't fear you. And to achieve and retain the very highest standards, day after day, meal after meal, in an environment as difficult and fast and chaotic as a restaurant kitchen, is extreme, well, in the extreme.

Looking back, I don't think I could have done it any other way. My pursuit for excellence went way beyond a passion for food. I was a man obsessed. I had to be the best and in order to do that I would have to win three Michelin stars. To explain: the *Michelin Guide* is the little red book that was first published by André Michelin in 1900 in France and today is updated every January. To every great chef in Europe— and since 2006, New York City—it is known as "the bible"; its rating can make or break careers, restaurants, even entire towns. Three stars, the guide's highest rating, means that your place serves "exceptional cuisine" and is "worth a special journey," but that's an amazing understatement. A restaurant with three Michelin stars is a monument to the highest—the most *extreme*—expression of the art of cooking. At the time of writing, only fifty-four restaurants in the whole of Europe have three stars. When I won mine, I became the first British chef—and the world's youngest—ever to achieve such an accolade.

It was my dream, and I didn't get there entirely by throwing cheese on the wall. And unlike many of the other winners in the Michelin lottery, I didn't get there through Paris, France. My story begins a couple of hundred miles north of London, in Leeds, where I was born on December 11, 1961. Don't be fooled by the first two names. I am neither from Italy nor France, but a Yorkshireman born and bred.

TWO

Blue Skies over Leeds

DAD WAS A chef too, and the son of a chef. I can't tell you much about the old man's abilities because I never saw him cook in a professional kitchen, but at home we always ate well. We'd have steak and kidney pie, shepherd's pie, boiled beef and dumplings. It was good traditional English comfort food. For tea on Friday, Dad would serve us pork chops and treat himself to a steak. We rarely had tinned food in the house because back in those days it was expensive, very much a middle-class thing. The usual sort of tinned foods—baked beans, soups, mushy peas—we made ourselves. Rhubarb crumbles would be made from the fruit in our tiny garden. The mint for mint sauce, again, came from the garden rather than a shop. Dad had lived through wartime food rationing, which had lasted into the fifties, and as a result I think his obsession was to ensure that we were fed well. When I was a hundred yards from my house, I could have closed my eyes and followed the smell of cooking to get me home. We might not have had much of anything else, but we always had lots of food.

As a professional, the old man would have had a good apprenticeship at the Griffin Hotel in Leeds, the hotel where he had met my mother back in the fifties. He had also worked at the Queens Hotel, that landmark beside the Leeds railway station. He would tell me stories of a brilliant French chef, Paul La Barbe, who worked in that kitchen but had trained in the grand restaurants of Paris. In the stories, Paul was a gifted chef who worked with speed and had that lightness of touch. I don't remember specifics about Paul's abilities but I was left with the feeling that cooking could produce passion. Other fathers might have told their kids impressive stories about American superheroes but I got the stuff about the French supercook and I loved hearing about him.

How do I think Dad would have fared in the kitchen? Well, he was organized and routined in his daily life; cooking being an extension of the person, I'd say that in his day he was probably a highly competent, disciplined cook. He would not have been a creative man; creativity wasn't a requirement in those days. Chefs rarely moved away from buffet work. In every professional kitchen there was that tiny book, *Le Répertoire de La Cuisine,* containing six thousand brief, concisely written recipes from hors d'oeuvres to pastries. There are no pictures in *Le Répertoire* to help the cook know how to serve a dish, but its recipes are invaluable. Written by Louis Saulnier and inspired by the great French chef Auguste Escoffier, *Le Répertoire* told you, for instance, dozens of ways to serve potatoes, from Algerienne (puréed sweet potatoes, mixed with chestnut purée, thickened with egg yolk, shaped into a quoit, dipped in egg and bread crumbs, and then fried in clarified butter) right through to Pommes Voisin (layers of sliced potato, bit of clarified butter, into the oven to cook and for color, out of the oven, grated cheese on top). Chefs did not stray from the recipes and were rarely adventurous. In Dad's time most restaurants served the same food: *Répertoire*-type dishes like lamb cutlets and kidneys with mustard.

After the Queens he'd become the canteen manager at Jonas Woodheads in Leeds, and sometimes I would go to meet him with my brother Clive. His cooks and waiters would be quietly working away to feed hundreds of people every day. The place was always spotless and clean, the tables were lined up beautifully and not a single chair was out of place. It was regimented and perhaps, in this respect, he was a perfectionist.

WE LIVED—MY father, mother, two brothers and I—in a two-bedroom, semidetached house on a housing estate in Moor Allerton, about five miles outside the center of Leeds. It was predominately Jewish and working class, with a warm community spirit—one of those places where the women would stand outside the shops chatting about the latest developments in Britain's favorite TV soap, *Coronation Street*. Hundreds of small houses lined the roads that were mostly named Lingfield something-or-other. If I came out of my house and turned left, I'd come to Moor Allerton golf course and, beyond that, the woods of the Harewood estate. If I came out of my home, turned right and strolled down to the bottom of the road, I'd reach the parade of shops on Lingfield Drive. There was the newsagent shop, which was run by two women who had lost their husbands in the war. There was the Jewish bakery and Tom Atkins, the veg man. There was the fish man and the butcher, whose afternoon custom was to sweep up the sawdust, wash the floor and then, and only then, give his dog a bone to chew on the pavement outside. The off-license was run by Harry Baker, and like other kids on the estate, I would sneak to the back of his shop, pinch the empties from crates and then go in through the front door with the bottles and reclaim the deposit. The parade is shabby today, but then it was the hub of our community.

We would take family holidays to Bridlington, the seaside resort in Yorkshire, which was windy and damp but heaving with people who couldn't afford to go abroad for a break.

My mother was Italian. She was tall, beautiful and elegant. She spent her days cooking and making patchwork quilts with her cherished Singer sewing machine. She was one of those women who always looked good. If she was wearing cutoff jeans and flat-soled shoes, she still seemed chic. When she got dressed up, she'd wear a cameo brooch in her lapel.

I had holidays with my mother in Genoa, where her side of the family lived and where she had grown up—before coming to England and being chatted up in the bar of the Griffin Hotel by a young chef called Frank White. I have happy recollections of those Italian vacations, picking fruit from the trees, fishing in the streams, making early-morning walks to collect goat's milk from a nearby farm. I remember sitting in the kitchen at home in Moor Allerton, watching her cook simple but delicious pasta dishes: sweating onions in olive oil, adding tomato purée, adding a little more olive oil—the comforting scent warming the room.

At lunchtime she'd collect me and my best friend, Geoffrey Spade, from school and take us back to our place for lunch. She'd make us treats of chunky banana sandwiches and then treat herself to well-sugared Camp coffee, the closest thing to espresso that England had to offer. She was a compassionate woman, a good mother.

IT WAS, I suppose, a childhood just like anyone else's: neighbors, family, food, sport, the outdoors. If it had gone on as it started, I might not have grown up tough enough to excel in the kitchen, and you might not be reading this book. But it didn't. One Saturday, February 17, 1968, when I was just a lad aged six, things changed and life would never be the same.

Dad and I had spent that morning in St. James's Hospital. A few weeks before, I had run into the door handle at the newsagent's just down the road and cut myself near my eye. We'd had the stitches removed and gone back home. We were sitting there in the front room when Mum came in, complaining that she felt unwell. Ten days earlier she had given birth to her fourth son, baby Craig, and up until that moment she had seemed fine. There had been no noticeable symptoms, no obvious signs. Now, suddenly, her head was splitting and she could hardly stand. My father called for an ambulance. What followed remains a vivid picture in my mind. I remember it better than I remember yesterday.

. . . I am standing at a windowsill in our council home. My brother Clive, six years my senior, is at my side and we are looking through the glass, down onto the pavement below.

The ambulance is parked. And there is my mother, a blanket is wrapped around her and she is sitting in a wheelchair. She is being put into the ambulance. An ambulance man turns to my father and says, "Bring the baby." A baby needs a mother.

My father is standing there, dressed smartly in a gray suit. He is holding Craig, the youngest of the family. Ten days old.

Crisp, blue sky. Bright sunshine.

"Bring the baby," the ambulance man repeats. "He'll need feeding." My father climbs in with Craig, who looks very snug and warm, wrapped up in a cozy white blanket.

Bang! Doors close, engine starts. The exhaust pipe pukes a dark cloud. The ambulance drives away, up the hill, out of sight.

EVERY NIGHT FOR the next few nights Dad would give us our dinner before heading off to the hospital to see Mum. After the visit he'd return quite late, bringing bags of sweets for his boys and telling us, "These are from Mum." She'd had a brain hemorrhage, but if he knew she was going to die, he never let on.

On February 20, the Tuesday after she had been taken to the hospital, the doctors turned off the life support machine. That night Dad came home and he woke us all up and told us to climb out of bed and to go downstairs. We gathered in the front room, where a few days earlier Mum had said she hadn't felt right, and Dad sat in his chair. I stared at his face and the tears on his cheeks. Then he told us, "Your mother died tonight." His words came thundering at me. Our mother had gone. Maria Rosa White—my father called her Maro—the woman who gave me so much more than my Italian name, was only thirty-eight years old.

After the funeral I don't think I went home to play or be with my family. Instead I was dropped off at school and stayed in the playground with my friends. I had a toy car, a gift from someone or other, and my classmates were enthralled by it. It wasn't a Matchbox car but something quite substantial and to me it was like a trophy. I think I was in the playground for about ten minutes and collected by I-don't-know-who and taken to a strange house, where I stayed for two, maybe three days. I still don't know where I went. It was a strange house with strange people who were obviously helping out Dad and who had kids the same age as me. It was as if I had been taken from my world into this other world.

THREE

Gambling, Greyhounds and Grief

A FEW DAYS after my mother's funeral, I returned home, home to a different way of life. I'd find my dad sitting up late at night, drinking along with a Shirley Bassey record. He rarely spoke of my mother's death but just got on with things, trying to cope with his damaged brood and apparently ignoring his own pain. But the bitterness of it remained with him. When he was a kid, his parents had separated and divided up their four children, and he seemed determined not to let that happen to his family. Somewhere along the way I learned that he had made a promise to my mother to raise her sons, rather than put us in a children's home. If he had put us in a home, it would have been acceptable, even expected, in the late sixties. For Dad it was totally unacceptable. He'd have hated finger-pointing people saying, "Poor Mr. White, lost his wife, had to put his kids in a children's home."

He was a disciplinarian, born in the twentieth century but raised with Victorian principles and values. He may not have been a religious man but he programmed me and my brothers religiously and he was a stickler for standards. He was punctual as hell. Each morning he would wake the family at six forty-five and we would get up, dress and have breakfast in time for his departure right at seven thirty to catch the seven forty bus that took him into Leeds city center. Off he'd go to work, wearing a smart suit, a trilby, and shoes that were polished with military precision. Even if he was feeling unwell, he would still head off for the bus stop, saying, "Never call in sick."

The thing about Dad is that he was a one-dimensional man, and like most one-dimensional men, he believed in correctness. On those occasions when I could neither conform nor live up to his high standards, he could not contain the impatience.

"Put on these clothes," I remember him saying once after I had answered back on a day when he was lacking patience. I looked at the pile of garments that he was pointing to, and they were my Sunday best. I changed into the clothes. Then he packed me a suitcase, took me to the front room, pointed at the sofa and said, "Sit there and wait."

I asked, "Why, Dad?"

"The taxi is coming to take you to the children's home," he replied.

Petrified, I sat waiting and thinking, am I going to be the next one to be taken away? But there was no taxi. It was simply Dad's method of punishment. The old man's failings were outweighed by the goodness and decency within him, but it would take me a long time to realize that. It's a demanding job, being a single parent.

MY FATHER THOUGHT, deep down, that he was an extremely unlucky man, and my mother's death only reinforced that opinion. But if you met him, you got a bloke, the working-class Northerner with a dry wit who talked betting nonstop. Dad was a gambler, and he turned to that, too, for solace. He did the dogs, the horses and the pools. He was hooked on the adrenaline that comes with gambling.

Inevitably, his love of the horses and the dogs also became a major part of my life. On one occasion Dad had some leave planned and he sent me off to school with a letter for my teacher. He had written something like, "My annual holiday is coming up and I would very much like to take Marco away for a week." I was excused from Fir Tree Primary and when I returned after the break, my teacher asked if I'd had a nice holiday.

I said, "Very nice, thank you very much, miss."

"Where did you go, Marco?"

"York Races for a week, miss."

Like many gamblers, my dad let superstition play a major role in his life. An early-morning sighting of a robin redbreast, for instance, would bring him good luck for the rest of that day. So on Saturday mornings our semi-detached house was filled with the wonderful smell of sizzling bacon. Dad wasn't doing a fry-up for his sons—he cooked the meat to entice the robins. The fried bacon went onto a plate, which then went out to the back garden. Dad would gaze out of the window, hoping a hungry robin would fly by 22 Lingfield Mount and swoop down for the meat. The size of the bets depended on the sighting of a bird.

Our back garden was not only a canteen for robins but also a home to Dad's cherished trio of greyhounds, which he raced on nearby tracks. Greyhounds were his true passion and each of the three dogs had a kennel in the garden. Two nights a week Dad's mate Stan Roberts would pull up in his Morris Minor (Dad didn't drive) and we'd head off to the racetrack. There'd be four of us in the car: Dad and Stan sat in the front while I shared the backseat with a greyhound.

At the track I would hover outside the bar while inside Dad enjoyed a drink with his friends. The door would open and a bottle of a pop and packet of crisps would be passed out to me. I'd sneak a glance into the brightly lit room (dimmer switches had yet to come along) with a haze of smoke lingering like a white cloud above the gamblers' heads (air-conditioning was unheard of). Coming home at eleven P.M., I'd fall asleep on the backseat. The greyhound was my pillow.

Dad was out one day when there was a knock on the door. A bloke was standing there and he asked me, "Do you sell greyhounds?"

We didn't but I told him, "Yes." I took him through the house and into the back garden to inspect the dogs.

"How much is that one?" he said, pointing at one of the animals.

"Fifty pence." It was my first business deal. (I have done better ones since then.)

The bloke handed over the money and left with the dog. I treated a mate, David Johnson, to goodies from the sweetshop and then we headed off to play in the woods. When Dad found out what I had done, he went ballistic and sent me up to my room without any tea. That was his traditional form of punishment: "Off to bed. No tea for you."

For Dad, greyhound racing was all about rigging the price and he had various tricks that he used. From time to time I assisted in this dastardly business. If you've got a dog that has won a couple of races in a row, then the odds of it winning the forthcoming race are going to be short. So with a dog that was, let's say, black with a white patch on its paw, Dad would paint out the patch and enter it into the race under a new name, thereby achieving a good price at the bookies.

Another devious trick went like this: The day before the greyhound was due to race, it wasn't fed. But then, last thing at night, it was given a bone to chew on, which would keep the dog awake. The next morning I would take the dog for a brisk four-mile walk and later on, when it came to race, it would look pristine and might be a favorite but was too knackered to win. So now the next time it raced, it would get long odds because of its previous form but this time round it would be in tip-top shape. I think I'm right in saying that one of Dad's dogs, the Governor, set track records at Halifax, Keighley and Doncaster.

When I wasn't tagging along after my father, I would play by myself in the woods or down by the river, rediscovering the side of nature that I had been introduced to during those holidays with my mother in Italy. Out of school, I was a bit of a loner, I'd say. In school, I was doomed. I was not only damaged by the death of my mother but also suffered from dyslexia. In those days "word blindness" was considered a sign of stupidity rather than a condition that calls for a special-needs teacher. One or two teachers were sympathetic but others humiliated me. For a very long time I assumed I was an idiot. What's more, I felt like a freak. Every pupil—except me—had a mother. Every other pupil—except me and a lad called Quentin, whose parents had divorced—was the product of an apparently happy home environment.

To cap it all, I had this strange name, Marco (my middle name, Pierre, remained a well-kept secret until I was in my twenties). I could only dream of what life might have been like had I been a John, a Peter, a Paul or a Timothy. I just wanted to be like everyone else.

CRAIG, THE BABY of the family, was just thirteen days old when our mother died, and for Dad, the prospect of leaving work to look after the family must have seemed an impossible one. Perhaps Dad was advised by friends; maybe he made the decision while sitting alone searching for inspiration from Shirley Bassey's lyrics. Whatever the case, he had concluded within weeks of my mother's death that he was in a horrific, no-win situation, and he could not see how he could bring up Craig as well as Graham, Clive and me. Craig, however, would not be going to the children's home.

It took a couple of months for Craig's adoption papers to be arranged and during that time he lived with temporary foster parents in York Road, not far from us. I remember him coming home to 22 Lingfield Mount for a short spell. Then for the second time in three months, another member of my family was taken away, yet this time round I can't remember witnessing the departure. Craig did not disappear forever. He was not going to become one of those poor souls who spends a decade of his adult life trying to trace his birth parents.

Craig was adopted by my mother's brother, my uncle Gianfranco, and his wife, Paola. Aunt Paola had previously been told that she would never conceive, so my mother's death provided the couple with a child. It was like a blessing from God. My father's loss was their gain. Craig was collected by Uncle Gianfranco and off he went to live with the couple in Genoa.

He underwent two name changes: White had to go (understandably) to make way for Gallina, and his first name was too much of a mouthful for his new countrymen. His middle name was Simon and so Craig became Simon, as in *Seemon*. My dad had handed him over and I don't think he ever saw him again.

There was little contact with the Italian in-laws. They would send us Christmas presents and then Graham, Clive and I would be instructed by Dad to sit at the dining room table and write thank-you letters. My father did not have many kind words to say about that side of the family and I think they were equally unimpressed by him.

When I was ten years old, I visited my uncle and aunt for the last time. I flew from Manchester to Milan. I was to go for a couple of weeks or so to enjoy the Italian countryside to which my mother had introduced me. But things were strange from the moment I arrived. I felt out of place amid all this regular family life. Simon, now four years old, didn't understand a word I was saying and I couldn't understand him. He didn't even know that I was his brother.

Then there was the food problem. Back in Yorkshire, I was used to haddock or cod that was deep-fried in batter and served with chips, all of it drenched in malt vinegar and salt and then wrapped up in newspaper. Good old British fish 'n' chips, in other words, which we'd get from the high street "chippies" as a fortnightly treat. It's unhealthy, but washed down with a mug of tea, it's divine comfort food. In Italy, my aunt cheerfully presented me with a plate of sea bass that had been sautéed in a little olive oil. I was aghast. The skin was visible. The head was still on. There was no crunchy coating of deep-fried batter to disguise the fact that this was a fish in front of me. It was extremely healthy, granted, and probably quite tasty. But for a young palate accustomed to fish with ketchup, it was utterly disgusting. "Yuk," I said, and pushed the plate away. I couldn't even manage a mouthful.

To her credit, my aunt didn't take this as a national insult (in the way I would come to expect from the proud Italian cooks I'd work with later on). There was no screaming, no broken crockery. But still, she was not pleased. Between the fish and my sulking and homesickness, my uncle and aunt were getting fed up with me. A few days before my fortnight-long holiday was due to end, my bags were packed and I was driven to the airport and put on a plane home.

Of my two older brothers, I had more of a bond with Graham, who was often fishing, shooting pigeons, hunting rabbits and ferreting. In fact, on the day my mother went into the hospital, his love of fishing had spared him the sight of her being taken away in the ambulance because at the time he was sitting on the banks of Adel Beck.

Clive, on the other hand, preferred motorbikes. For a while I shared a bedroom with the pair of them but they most likely didn't want to spend too much time with a little nipper like me and I never felt a great sense of camaraderie. When Graham was fifteen years old, and I was seven or eight, he left school and went to work in the kitchens of the Griffin Hotel, where my dad had started out. A couple of years later, Clive followed a similar path. He finished school and became a chef at the Metropole Hotel.

*   *   *

IF DAD WAS looking for confirmation that he was the world's unluckiest man, it came in 1972. "Your father is going to be home late from work tonight," my teacher told me. "You are to wait in the playground for him to collect you." I sat in the playground, the ten-year-old loner, waiting for Dad to arrive and eventually he pulled up outside. He was with David Hince, his work colleague, in Mr. Hince's car, a Hillman. We drove the half mile back to the house and once inside Dad sat in his armchair. He had some dreadful news.

"I've been to see the doctor today," he said. His delivery was emotionless and to the point. "The doctor told me that I have lung cancer." For a second or two I tried to absorb the statement. What did this mean? What would this mean? And then the sledgehammer statement: "He has given me five months. The doctor says I've got five months to live."

From then on, a crushing fear preoccupied me every night as I lay in my bed. It was a fear that come morning I would wake up and discover my father had died. Insomnia got me, and I couldn't shake it off. I had to learn to live on little sleep, which would later serve me well as a chef.

Weeks after Dad had broken the terrible news, I saw him in the bathroom one morning, coughing up blood into the sink. The doctor was right, I reckoned. Dad was definitely on his way out.

FOUR

I Delivered (the Milk)

THERE'S SOMETHING TO be said for requesting a second opinion. Dad's doctor may have been right to diagnose lung cancer, but he was way off when he predicted my father, then aged forty-five, would be dead in five months. Five months later the old man was still there. Five *years* later he was still there. He would live through his fifties, into his sixties and wouldn't reach the finishing post until he was in his seventies. He'd be around to see his children grow up and his grandchildren be born.

But in the meantime, family life continued in the belief that he would soon be dead. He jacked in his job on the grounds that he was terminally ill and we discovered quickly that his greyhounds could not be expected to bring in an income. He dabbled in "antiques dealing," and though we had never been wealthy, we now plummeted into poverty, which brought new fears that my existence was simply an extra cost for my father. I prayed that Dad wouldn't notice my shoes had holes in the soles because I reckoned he couldn't afford to buy me a new pair.

He lost weight quickly, dropping from fifteen stone to about eight. On doctor's orders he stopped smoking and kicked the bottle, then he reevaluated the situation with his gambler's mind and concluded that, as he was at death's door, he had absolutely nothing to lose by returning to the fags and booze, so that's what he did.

To compensate, he went on a health kick of sorts, eating vegetables and fruits he'd grown in the garden. I was dragged into the kitchen action, to peel potatoes and chop tomatoes and mushrooms with Dad breathing down my neck—I was frightened that I'd slice off too much of the vegetable. I was sent out to pick blackberries for jam and to pick apples, which we'd store in between layers of newspaper. My chef's training began at an early age. Sure enough, Dad regained the weight he had previously shed, but he would never be 100 percent and just climbing the stairs left him breathless.

Although he was apparently at death's door, it did little to mellow his mood. One day I was four doors down at my friend Barry Wells's house, play-wrestling in his garden. It got out of hand when Barry hit me and I hit him back. Barry's hefty father must have spotted the scrap from the house and suddenly came bounding into the garden, picked me up by the ears and started swinging me around in the air. I felt like I was preparing for takeoff.

"I'll tell me dad," I screamed, my ears burning with pain.

"Tell 'im," shouted Mr. Wells. "And tell 'im if he wants some to come round here and I'll chin 'im."

I scampered home, in through the door and into the front room, where my dad was sitting. "Dad," I screamed, "Barry Wells's dad just hit me and he said he's gonna chin you as well." I'd hardly finished the sentence when Dad leapt from his chair and set off, sprinting down the road faster than one of his treasured greyhounds. When he returned a few minutes later, he looked victorious. "We won't hear any more from him," said Dad, and we didn't.

Of Dad's various life-enhancing cautions, he had two that concerned the subject of punch-ups. The first came shortly after my mother's death, when he sat me down to give me some fatherly advice about fighting. "It doesn't matter if they beat you," he said. "As long as you hurt them more than they hurt you, they'll never come back for more." The second piece of advice was simpler: "Don't argue, just hit 'em."

He practiced what he preached. One day I was walking into town with him when we saw two men taunting a tramp. Dad told me to wait for him while he went up to the two yobs. I thought he was going to tell them to stop teasing the poor homeless vagrant. Instead, he simply punched each man in the face and strolled back to me and then we continued our walk to the shops as if nothing untoward had happened. As one of Dad's mates had said of him, "Frank was the only man I know who could start a fight in an empty room."

The old man must have reached a stage where he acknowledged the cancer was dormant but still he worried how I would fend for myself if he died. So when I was about twelve or thirteen years old, I took on a few jobs. In fact, I became obsessed with work and did quite nicely out of it too. In the mornings before school I had a milk round, delivering the pints with a milkman called Stephen Sharpe, who was also kind enough to take me rabbiting. I loved doing the round, even though in the winter months my fingers would freeze and stick to the bottles as I picked them up. Stephen would stop the milk truck and then we would race against each other to see who would be the first to pick up the empties and get them back to the truck. It made me terribly competitive. Sometimes Stephen would take me to school in time for my first class. You've heard of rich kids being dropped off by the chauffeur in a Rolls; I was delivered by Stephen on a milk truck.

After school I did a newspaper round, which brought in thirty bob a week. On Saturdays I was a caddy at Moor Allerton golf course or at Alwoodley, charging golfers £1.50 a round. I was skilled at finding golf balls that had been lost on the course—for which I earned a tenner per hundred, as well as the nickname Hawk Eye. The great Leeds United FC manager Don Revie was one of my "clients." When I first caddied for him, he hit a ball that disappeared into the trees. "Don't worry, Mr. Revie, I'll find it," I said, and went scurrying off to retrieve the ball. I did indeed find it, and when I picked it up, I noticed it had the words "Don Revie" imprinted on its dimples. Class act that he was, Don had personalized golf balls. I put the ball in my pocket and ran back to tell him it was lost, then I sold the ball for a pound at school, a marked improvement on the fifty pence I'd charged for Dad's greyhound. I handed most of my income to my father, supposedly for safekeeping. "I'll give it back to you, Marco, when we go on holiday," he'd say, though when we trundled off to Bridlington I don't recall receiving the cash in its entirety.

When I wasn't working, I used my spare time to enjoy the countryside. I was happiest when I was outdoors with my whippet, Pip. I fell in love with fishing, hunting, shooting and poaching. When there was a teachers' strike in the seventies, we finished school at midday and my brother Graham took me fishing for the first time. He sat me down by the side of a bridge and cast for me while he and his mates went and fished the best spots. I caught a trout of about a pound—the first fish I ever caught—and from that day on I was hooked, so to speak.

Graham also introduced me to poaching. My early poaching days involved chucking logs at the pheasants when they were roosting. The birds would fly down from the trees and land on the ground, and then I'd have to run after them and catch them by hand. I remember Graham taking me to Eccup, part of the Harewood estate, to shoot for the first time, but he was mean about sharing the air rifle. Graham shot four heavy hares and made me carry them across the plowed fields, rain pouring down on us. I was his chief gofer. In some ways, my childhood was idyllic because I spent my time lost in the woods or the fields, or on the riverbanks catching trout and crayfish with my hands. That is where my passion for food began. As I will doubtless mention a dozen times, great chefs respect nature, and as a child I fell in love with nature, which, in turn, would enable me to fall in love with food.

I have a vivid memory of sneaking into the bedroom I shared with Graham and Clive and rummaging around for Graham's .22 pellets. Suddenly I heard his footsteps and quickly dove under his bed to hide. Graham came into the room, undid his belt, dropped his trousers and then lay on the mattress, while I quietly waited underneath. His masturbation was interrupted by the sound of my dad coming up the stairs shouting for me. As Graham struggled to pull up his trousers, my dad came into the room. "Have you seen Marco?" he asked.

Graham, flustered, replied, "No, Dad, I've not."

If I could find the time, my mate Briggsy and I would take the bus to Otley to fish a trout stretch. We would roll up our trousers and walk into the river with a maggot bag containing a loaf of bread for bait. We used to catch sixty or seventy trout in one day; we'd keep a lot of them, kill them, and on the way back to the bus we would knock on doors and sell them for ten pence each. This was my first experience of being paid for pleasure.

In between my jobs and the life of a young adventurer outdoors, I managed to find time for school. Life at Allerton High followed a similar pattern to my stint at Fir Tree Primary, in that I distinguished myself as perfectly unacademic. In my first week at Allerton I upset the PE teacher, who was known (though not to his face) as either Smooth Head because of his baldness or Toby because, I imagine, he was as handsome as a Toby jug.

During our first lesson I was mucking around and Toby told me to lean over a bench. He then hit me very hard, several times, on the arse with a sneaker. It was a deeply disturbing experience. Dad had given me a slap in the past, but I had never had a beating like the one administered by Toby.

After the thrashing, I was sent off with the rest of the class on a cross-country race, and as we were running, I kept pulling down my shorts and asking my mate Mark Taylor to examine my swollen flesh. "Christ, Marco," he kept saying as he studied the skin while trampling over the mud, "it's bloody terrible."

The minute I got home, I found a mirror and examined my backside. The skin was mostly maroon, purple in places. I showed my bottom to my brother Clive and then, during dinner, Dad noticed that I was distressed. "What's wrong?" he asked.

Before I could respond, Clive chipped in, "He got whacked at school. You should see his . . ." Dad made me pull down my trousers and was horrified by the sight of my maroon arse. The next day a prefect came into the classroom and said that I had to go to the deputy head's office. I knocked on the door, entered, and there was the deputy head, Mr. Richardson, with another man who had his back to me. Then I saw the trilby on the table. It was my dad. "Show Mr. Richardson your backside," he said. Once again I had to suffer the indignity of pulling down my trousers. Mr. Richardson was horrified. For the next three years Toby didn't lay a finger on me.

Despite my fraught relationship with Toby, I excelled at cross-country, but not because I was desperate to win. The thing is, I was determined to be the first person back to the changing rooms because I was terrified my hairy classmates would see that I didn't have any pubic hair. I set cross-country records purely so that I would be showered, dried and back in my school uniform long before the rest of the breath-less bunch had finished the run.

In those days you were allowed to leave school without taking your final exams and so that's what I did. I left Allerton High on Friday, March 17, 1978, and as the other pupils went off to see *Star Wars* and enjoy the Easter holidays, I was gearing up for my first job. My final lesson on my last day was Games with Toby. Everyone else changed into their shorts and T-shirts but I was having none of it. The teacher said, "Where's your kit, White?"

I turned surly. "I didn't bring it. I don't want to do Games."

He went into his office and emerged with a spare kit, which I promptly told him I would not wear. My intention was to remind him that he could not intimidate me. Dad had always said to me, "Never forget what people do *for* you or *to* you."

Toby gave me some paper and told me to copy out of a textbook while the Games class continued, but when they returned from the field, I hadn't written down a single word. Minutes later I would be out of school, never to return. "White," he couldn't stop himself from say-ing through gritted teeth, "you'll be nothing, lad."

DAD WAS NOT fussed about me leaving school before sitting my ex-ams. Getting out there and finding a job fitted in nicely with his pro-gramming and, after all, Graham and Clive had done the same before me. "Become a chef," Dad had told me. "People will always need feeding."

He instructed me to go and search for work in Harrogate because it was less than ten miles away and crammed with hotels. The final stage of the programming was drawing near. One morning he made me sandwiches, gave me the bus fare and sent me off. I arrived in Harrogate, went to the Hotel St. George and knocked on the kitchen door.

"I'm looking for a job as a kitchen apprentice," I said to the head chef, just as my dad had told me to say. That was it. He gave me a date to join the brigade—Monday, March 20, 1978, the week leading up to Easter—and I took the bus home to deliver the good news to Dad. I didn't have any interest in food at this stage. Cheffing was a job, or at least that's how it started.

In order to work at the George, I would have to give up all my other jobs. And on the day before I began my cheffing career, I caddied for Mr. Bradley, a nice old boy who would always drop me home in his Bentley. We were walking up the eighteenth fairway when he said, "You've caddied for me for three years. You've been good to me, never let me down. Today is the last day you'll caddy for me. What are you going to do with your life, Marco?"

What was I going to do with my life? I was too embarrassed to tell him that come the following morning I would be a chef. I didn't think he would approve. So I replied, "I don't know."

"Do you want some advice from an older man?"

"Please tell me, Mr. Bradley."

He stopped walking and turned to look at me soberly. "You're not a bad-looking lad," said Mr. Bradley. "Go to Miami, Marco, and be a gigolo."

FIVE

The George

YOU LITTLE CUNT," yelled Stephan Wilkinson, the head chef of the
Hotel St. George. Welcome to the world of gastronomy. I had been
on the job for a week and I had cocked up something or other. Burned
some toast, maybe. Or had I overscrambled the eggs?

There was a ferocious glare from this dwarf of a man, in his tall
white hat and apron that touched his shoes, and then another boom
came out of his vulgar mouth. It was a drill sergeant scream that rose
above the bubbling of sauces, the sizzle of frying meat, the clatter of
copper pans against iron stove, the sharpening of knives: "What are
you, White? What—are—*you*!"

This tornado of furious abuse engulfed me. "A little cunt, Chef,"
I replied. "I'm a little cunt." Forgive the language, please, but in the
kitchens I've worked in, the most popular four-letter words have got to
be "cunt" and "salt." To the outside world, "cunt" is considered highly
offensive; but in the heat of professional kitchens, cooks frequently
call one another "cunt." You just need to work out whether it is being
said in a nasty way—"Do that again, cunt, and you won't have a job
tomorrow"—or a friendly way—"See you tomorrow, cunt." Sometimes
it's an adjective: "Who nicked my cunting knife?" Sometimes it's an
adverb: "Stop cunting talking and get on with the job." When Stephan
called me a "little cunt," it was the word "little" that seemed odd, since
I was the one looking down on him.

And so I took my first step along the long, bully-laden, work-obsessed, sleep-deprived, nicotine- and caffeine-fueled, passionate, hot and winding road that would end with three Michelin stars.

It's a bit shabby today, but in the spring of 1978 the Hotel St. George was still an imposing Edwardian building on Ripon Road in the heart of the delightful Yorkshire spa town of Harrogate. Today the St. George is a different entity; it is the Swallow St. George Hotel, part of the Swallow chain. Swallow St. George doesn't have the same ring, does it? But in the late seventies it had yet to be bought out and was still a grand and exceptionally busy hotel, privately owned by a man called Mr. John Bernard Kent Abel, and the food reflected its stature.

My life may well have been very different if I had started out two or three years later, but as it was, I stepped into the dying days of the golden age of gastronomy. At the George, I saw standards and style that, like so many other hotel kitchens, had been inspired by Escoffier, whose philosophy was "Good food is the basis of true happiness."

I don't think the St. George was where I discovered a passion for food, but the romance of that golden age did not pass me by. For instance, boiled ham at the George wasn't just boiled ham. The meat was cooked and then coated in a chaud-froid sauce—a béchamel or velouté sauce made with clarified butter and flour, turned into a roux and then moistened with milk, cream or onion stock, with gelatine (originally calf's foot jelly) added to it. The sauce was layered onto the ham, with the first layer allowed to set before another layer was added, and then another layer, and so on, until the ham was totally white. The ham was then meticulously studded with chopped truffles to form a design, then that was covered in an aspic jelly and the finished product was placed on a huge silver platter and carved in the dining room. It was a magnificent sight and one that we are unlikely to see again now that the restaurant business is governed by percentages and portion control.

There were probably fourteen staff in the kitchen, serving the hotel's two restaurants, the French Room and the more informal Lamplighter, and we were busy but I didn't mind. My father's programming was paying off. Hard work was a necessity of life and it did not cross my mind to pack it in and find another career. I was the son of a chef and the grandson of a chef, my brothers were chefs. Cheffing was in my blood.

First, however, I would have to pass an initiation ceremony, which all the new chefs underwent at the George. On my first day I arrived at seven thirty in the morning, changed into my brand-new chef's whites, and was given my first job. "Here's a big pot of stock," said Stephan, and he pointed toward a vat of jellied beef stock. "And here's a sieve." He told me to transfer the stock, via the sieve, from the pot into another big pot. I spooned dollop after dollop into the sieve and then pushed it through the tiny holes with a little ladle. The stock splashed all over my whites and then, once the job was done and my arm muscles were aching badly, the stockpot was taken from me and put onto the gas, where it quickly turned into liquid. I stood and watched, thinking, why didn't they just bring it to the boil and then pass it through the sieve in the first place? I didn't quite realize that they were taking the piss out me.

My next job on that day was to blanch, peel and de-seed five boxes of tomatoes. Halfway through the laborious process, my arms—already tired out by the stock-sieving chore—could take no more and they seized up. I was standing there with my arms bent and locked; I looked like a crab. I had worked seven hours straight, without a break and without a meal, and that's when I lost it. I freaked and burst into tears.

Stephan took pity. He got me a ham sandwich and I sat in his office, "the glass room," munching away and feeling that I had failed. That evening I was told to clean the walk-in fridge, but by now it was nine thirty, and as I'd only had a ham sandwich all day, I was starving. There was a massive bowl of something that looked chocolatey and sweet. I dipped my finger in and tasted the mixture. Quite nice, I thought. So nice, in fact, that I ate the whole bowl of mixture. When the pastry chef asked if anyone had seen his bavarois, I looked at him blankly and shook my head. It was only a year or so later that I learned what a chocolate bavarois was and it dawned on me that I had eaten what he had been searching for.

In time, and with experience, I became a bit more cocky. When Chef gave me thirteen sacks of peas to shell, I asked, "Chef, what does thirteen sacks of peas look like when they've been shelled?" He replied, "I don't know." So I threw away six sacks and shelled the remaining seven. When I was asked to prepare ten boxes of spinach, I chucked away four boxes and prepared the remaining six. Unaware that I was ditching a lot of the produce, Stephan couldn't believe how fast I was at sorting out the veg. On top of that, I endeared myself to other cooks who were challenging each other to drink a pint of malt vinegar. I stepped forward and downed the pint in one gulp. I felt thoroughly wretched afterward but I won the game, and after that they started to treat me like one of the fellows.

I'd do breakfasts twice a week, and when Sacha Distel, the French crooner, stayed at the hotel, he became the first famous person I cooked for. I made him bacon and eggs. It was carried up to his room and then I sneaked away from the kitchen and up to his door, bent down and peered through the keyhole. There he was, Monsieur Distel, eating my English breakfast.

In the mornings I'd work in the larder, doing the Lamplighter buffet, and one of my duties was to make the salads—Waldorf, bagatelle (with mushrooms), à la grecque, niçoise and coleslaw. I found that I could be a little bit creative with the salads and no one would make a fuss, and eventually I found that I could experiment with artistic presentation on whatever I liked. So if I was given a sirloin of beef, I might slice it very thinly and then arrange it around the joint in a fan shape. I wasn't doing anything new—I had watched the other chefs make these dishes—but now I could create my own pictures. We might do a honey-glazed ham, which I'd decorate with cloves, studding them so they made the shape of a harlequin. Or I would do a chaud-froid of ham, using the studs of truffle to create a vase of flowers, perhaps.

The back door would open and wonderful ingredients would be carried into the kitchen. Each season brought different ingredients and the menu would change accordingly—strawberries, asparagus, game . . . I stood in awe, watching as enormous wild salmon—there was no such thing as farmed salmon then—arrived to be poached, left to cool and then covered in scales of thinly sliced cucumber. In those times, meat did not arrive precut into equal-sized portions, ready for the pan. Whole lambs would be brought in and chopped up in the kitchen. The beef was brought in as sirloin and rump attached in one enormous joint. The leg of veal came as a rump, the whole loin attached to it. Milk would arrive in giant churns, rather than in plastic bottles or cartons. This was yesterday's world, when fish-and-chip shops served food wrapped up in newspaper—a popular custom that was banned because of concerns that the newsprint contained toxins.

Looking back, I realize that it was my love of nature which gave me the understanding of natural ingredients. Mother Nature is the true artist, and the chef is merely the technician. Every single day I was turned on by nature. But what would keep me going, the thing that would keep me in this career, was the desire to be recognized. The better I was at the job, the better I felt I could cope with my insecurities. I would become first and foremost addicted to the adrenaline of cooking, rather than the passion for great food.

Standards at the George were high. If you made sandwiches, you had to trim the edges of the bread to perfection and serve them on a silver platter. Customers dined on dishes like beef Stroganoff and steak Diane. Nothing went to waste. If boiled ham was served hot, the remaining meat would be used later for sandwiches. Roast lamb might be served with petit pois à la Française and pommes dauphinoise, and the leftover lamb would be served cold in the following day's buffet. Once in a while we'd serve a spectacular baron of beef, which is the two sirloins and the ribs—the better part of an entire cow. The baron was too big for the ordinary kitchen ovens, so it would be hung in the bakers' oven and roasted pink. Once it was cooked, it was put on a sort of stretcher and two chefs would carry it into the dining room for carving.

I did a bit of everything: I spent time with the kitchen's butcher, worked hours on the larder section and sometimes would help the pastry chef by making lemon syllabubs or piping cream onto the trifles. I admired everything I saw. Some weeks I would work fifteen or sixteen hours a day, bumping up my basic wage of £15 a week to £60 with all the overtime I did. As an apprentice I received a salary raise of a pound a week on my birthday.

When I turned seventeen on December 11, 1978, I had a day off, but I still went into work. Was I already hooked on the security of the kitchen? I had seen on the menu that they were doing Châteaubriand sauce béarnaise for a private party and I wanted to learn how to make béarnaise, a derivative of hollandaise, so I asked if I could come in to watch it being made.

At the George we might have a party for 350 people and I'd have to do pommes de terre château, where the potato is "turned" so that it is perfectly olive-shaped. With 5 little potatoes for each plate, that's 1,750 pieces of potato. Compare that with working in a restaurant, where you might do six portions of pommes de terre château a night, and in one evening at a hotel I had acquired experience it would have taken me nearly sixty nights to get in a restaurant. So I picked up the disciplines of cooking speedily, organization and one other thing: how to discipline my hands, almost program them, so I became really fast with a knife.

It didn't matter how fast or hard I worked, bollockings were still part of the job. Bollockings from Chef. Bollockings from the older chefs, who included a bloke from Lancashire whose accent was so deep that I could not understand a single word that came out of his mouth. I would just respond with a simple "yes" to every remark he made. Then one day he muttered something unintelligible and when I said, "Yes," he screamed, "What the fuck do you mean, 'yes,' boy? Didn't you hear what I fucking said?" That was the only time I understood him.

I was indeed the apprentice, the whipping boy, but I could take the bollockings because I had been toughened up by my childhood. It was as easy as stepping from one male-dominated, bullying world into another. Being bollocked was no big deal. Most of the time I found it rather entertaining, even enjoyable. I savored Stephan's rage.

There was something else that would make my life a little easier at the George. Stephan, like my dad, enjoyed a bet, and something happened that helped to mellow him a little. A few weeks after I joined the brigade, Stephan let off one of his drill sergeant yells: "Marco! Your dad's on the office phone."

I went into the office and took the call. The excitement in Dad's voice said it all. "Marco," he started, "I've just had Johnny Seagrove on the phone and he says there's a horse racing in the three ten at Ripon. It's a good one. Do a pound each way." He told me the horse's name, I repeated it and then said good-bye. Stephan, who had been within earshot, was curious. "What was that all about?" he asked.

"That was my dad. He's mates with lots of trainers and jockeys and he's had a tip." Stephan's eyes widened with delight. He was more than a little impressed; he was agog. Now he saw me in a different light. This teenage lad standing in front of him, young Marco White, had connections.

Dad's tip proved to be a winner, and after that news of my connections rapidly spread through the hotel. Within days my popularity had soared. Chefs and waiters, barmen and chambermaids would track me down to say sweetly, "Hello, Marco. Spoken to your dad?" If I nodded, they'd put a pound or two in my hand and ask me to back the horse for them. "Off you go," Stephan would say, pointing toward the door, and I would sprint to the bookie's in my chef's whites to place the bets. I wonder now whether I spent more time in the bookie's than in the kitchen.

Through this I devised an ingenious way of getting the brigade back for bullying me. I used to announce to them, "My dad's calling with a tip tomorrow," and they would rush toward me, handing over their cash. Then I'd go to the betting shop and put all their money on a horse of my choice. If it won, I took the profit and then gave them their money back, saying, "There was no tip from Dad." If the horse lost, I'd give them their betting slips to show I'd put the money on. It meant that on a good week I was earning more than Stephan. I felt like an entrepreneur.

The George also taught me that chefs and waiters hate each other. There's a variety of reasons but usually it boils down to nationality. At the George, the chefs were British while most waiters were French or Italian. The George's restaurants must have had a charming ambience, but in the kitchen there were battles between the front-of-house regiment and the back-of-house brigade. Usually it was just bickering, but I remember a scuffle between drill sergeant Stephan and Giovanni, the restaurant manager.

Giovanni was in the kitchen when Stephan taunted him and it could have gotten quite nasty, but Giovanni was carrying two buckets of ice, which he dropped on the floor. As the two men attempted to hit one another, the ice beneath them formed a mini ice rink and in the end they fell to the ground, arms wrapped around each other Laurel and Hardy–style.

Despite all this I liked Giovanni, and because of our Italian roots, we bonded. He was the staff playboy and drove a 1000cc Harley-Davidson. He was the coolest man in the hotel. In fact, he was the coolest man in Harrogate, and must have been the only one with a Harley. He had the best room in the hotel and would spend his days off lying in bed with his girlfriend, Joanna. Sometimes I'd chat with Giovanni and he would go all Marlon Brando on me, saying, "One day I will leave the hotel, Marco, and when I do, I will leave you two things: my room and my girlfriend."

Eventually that day came. Giovanni climbed onto his Harley, like Gary Cooper mounting his horse, and rode off into the Yorkshire sunset. I did indeed end up with his luxurious room, which meant I could move out of home. However, Joanna was heartbroken at losing her lover and I didn't have the courage to tell her Giovanni had promised her to me.

I was not good with the opposite sex. There was a posh university undergraduate whose name I forget and who had taken a holiday job as a chambermaid at the George. She seemed quite interested in me and I mustered up the courage to invite her to dinner in Harrogate. It was my first date and I took her to Vanni's, an Italian restaurant in Parliament Drive, but the evening did not go well. As I was trying to make her laugh with a funny story, I waved an arm and accidentally knocked a glass of red wine onto her white blouse. A waiter sprang into action, trying to wipe away the wine with a napkin, and I sat there dying. She said, "Don't worry," and I paid the bill and we went back to my hotel room, the room where Giovanni had been so lucky in love. She removed her sodden blouse and I gazed at her black bra before she put on one of my white shirts. Then she removed her trousers, revealing black knickers, and lay on the bed.

Uncomfortably, I lay next to her and stroked her bristly thighs. Christ, her legs are hairier than mine, I thought. Who's the man on this bed?

I wanted to explore, to experiment, but she said, "You're too nice, Marco. You're too young. I can't do this to you."

The kitchen porter—he had to wash up and keep the place clean—disliked me intensely. He was a big slob of a man, six foot four, with horrible greasy hair. When he walked past me in the kitchen, a reflex action compelled him to give me a sharp poke in the kidneys with his thumb. Probably I deserved the pokes but I had to get him back. I devised a plan.

"Chef, can I clean the walk-in fridge?" I asked.

Chef looked over at me. "Of course you can."

The walk-in fridge was enormous. I removed hundreds of bowls and containers, one by one, and put the food into clean containers. It was a laborious job for me, but it meant that the porter was left with a mountain of bowls and containers to wash up and in those days everything was washed by hand. I turned this into a regular fridge-clearing exercise, which drove him mad. "It's your turn for a beating," he'd say, his hands like prunes, and then we'd go in circles around the stove as he tried to get me.

I made friends with another chef, Michael Truelove, and together we would think up ways to annoy the porter. I would phone the kitchen pretending to be Mr. Abel, the hotel's owner, and Michael would answer the phone. He'd then tell the lackey, "Mr. Abel's on the phone. He wants to speak to you." When the porter came on the line, I would do my impression of the owner and say to him, "There are some boxes in my office for the chef. Can you come and get them, please?" Big and scruffy, the porter would waddle into Mr. Abel's office saying, "I've come for the boxes," and an irritated Mr. Abel would ask, "What on earth do you mean? What are you talking about, man?" Then the penny would drop and he'd return to the kitchen raging. "You're in for a beating," he'd say.

Michael and I were the kitchen's practical jokers. One night he helped me climb into the chest freezer, and when Mary, a waitress, came into the kitchen and asked Michael where to put the unused table butter, he said, "In the freezer, love." She opened the door, saw a chilled body inside, threw the butter into the air and bolted out of the kitchen. A few minutes later the hotel manager, Barry Sterling, came into the kitchen. "There's a body in your freezer," he told Stephan. Chef went through the freezer, chucking out the frozen vegetables while shaking his head and saying, "There's no body in here."

In the afternoons I used to go and see Bill and Ken, the hotel's porters. I'd have a cup of tea with them and help polish the guests' shoes. One day I walked into their room and, in order to sit on my favorite chair, had to remove a book that was on the seat. I glanced at it as I picked it up. It was the *Egon Ronay 1976 Guide to Restaurants and Hotels*. I sat down and flicked through the pages and realized for the first time in my life that there were restaurants out there that were awarded stars.

I stopped on a page that mentioned a restaurant called the Box Tree. The guide said it was the best restaurant in Britain. I was fascinated by the photograph of the Box Tree, which looked like one of those three-hundred-year-old inns and had nice cars parked outside. Later I asked around in the kitchen to see if anyone had heard of it. They had, but said it was impossible to get a job there; Box Tree staff were apparently blissfully content and rarely left, so there was hardly any chance of vacancies arising.

At some point in 1979 I picked up the phone and called the Box Tree to see if there were any jobs going. Luck was on my side. Some one had just handed in their notice and I was invited for an interview with Malcolm Reid and Colin Long, highly regarded as a success story in the industry and who were also known for their campness. Their sexuality provided an opportunity for ridicule in the macho world of cooking, and when I told people I had been invited for an interview, they joked that I would be going for "a Long Reid in bed."

I went shopping for an interview outfit and bought myself a smart jacket, a shirt and tie. The only shoes I could find to match the clothes were half a size too small but I got them anyway. I took the bus to Ilkley, arrived early and sat on a park bench at the top of Church Street. My feet were killing me, so I took off my new shoes to let the blood flow. When I tried to put the shoes back on, though, my feet had swollen. I managed to squeeze myself into them but only with extreme discomfort. I minced across the road to the Box Tree, walking like a man in women's stilettos. I'm sure I got the job the minute they saw my mincing walk.

Messrs. Reid and Long kept me there for two and a half hours and showed me the food. The pain in my feet subsided as I gazed at a magnificent duck terrine. I was looking at perfection. When they offered me the job, I accepted immediately and hobbled back to the George to hand in my notice. I was about to discover my passion for cooking. My world was turning from black and white into color.

IT WOULD HAVE been the most natural thing in the world to call my father and tell him of my good luck, but by then, he wasn't a part of my life. It was my silly fault, really. I had lost touch. During my first couple of months at the George I had lived at home. And after moving into the hotel, I had made weekly trips back to 22 Lingfield Mount to join him for Sunday lunch.

Then one day, shortly after I had moved into the George, he got married. Dad had met a woman called Hazel—he might have known her years, for all I know—and very quietly they tied the knot at a register office. I have to be honest, I couldn't deal with it. Of course he was right to remarry—after all, my mother had died ten years earlier—and Hazel wasn't a bad woman; she stayed with him until the end. And Christ, who am I to judge?

But back then, as a teenager, I was too immature to appreciate that the show must go on, the world keeps moving, and life continues. I don't recall talking to Dad about the marriage, but one Sunday I didn't go home for lunch with the old man and his new wife. The following Sunday I missed lunch again. Then perhaps after missing five or six lunches, that was it. A week turned into two weeks, which turned into eight weeks, which turned into years. Thirteen years would pass before I picked up the phone, called him and reestablished a relationship with the man who had raised me. I never dealt with it because I didn't have the courage. I bottled it every time.

The bond was broken. He would write to me but I wouldn't write back, and eventually, he didn't know where I was, which kitchen I was working in, or where I was living. For years I had lived by his rules— he controlled me—but now I had discovered freedom.

SIX

Black and White into Color

STEPPING INTO THE Box Tree was like stepping into a massive jewelry box. All the emotions that come with romance were fired up within me. I was seventeen years old and for the first time I felt acknowledged, an important part of a great team.

It was more than that, though. Messed-up teenager that I was, the staff and owners virtually adopted me. They became my new family, and for the next eighteen months of my life I was given responsibility, and with that came confidence—kitchen confidence. This is where I discovered my obsession with food and this is where I formed my food philosophies.

The Box Tree was the creation of the two men who had interviewed me, Malcolm Reid and Colin Long. We called them "the Boys," though they were both in their forties. Malcolm—with his handsome, sharp, distinguished features and always well-groomed in a smart suit—was the serious one, seemingly pushing the business forward. Colin—blond, blue-eyed and usually wrapped up in a big woolly jumper—was the joker. Colin would see me whisking a hollandaise sauce and say something camp like, "Oh, that's lovely wrist action you've got there. Fancy coming into the larder with me and earning yourself five woodbines?"

At some point in the fifties, the Boys had bought Box Tree House—originally an eighteenth-century farmhouse that had box trees in its front garden—and opened it as an antiques shop and tearoom.

Tourists heading to and from the Yorkshire Dales would stop off for scones and jam. Trade was good, so Malcolm and Colin expanded the business by serving lunches. That worked, too, so they opened up for dinner. They were doing so well they decided to rethink the whole setup. In 1962 they did away with cream teas and with lunch and simply opened for dinner—and what a dinner it was.

The Boys were exceptionally clever. In fact, they were the greatest restaurateurs I have ever met. Every now and again they would head off to Paris on a Saturday night and return on the following Tuesday morning, having dined out every day from midday to midnight in the French capital. Their mission in France was to eat the finest food, cooked by the greatest chefs, and then replicate it for their customers back in little old Ilkley. Malcolm and Colin would return to the Box Tree, sit down with their head chef, Michael Lawson, and recount the dishes they had eaten.

With meticulous detail, they would go through each dish, describing the presentation, the flavors, the tastes: a particular coconut ice cream; a fricassée of lobster with finely diced vegetables and a Noilly Prat sauce. Michael would listen intently, nodding along as he absorbed the information. He'd re-create the dish in his mind. "And that evening we went to Bon Auberge, where Malcolm had this, and on Friday we had dinner at La Sel, where Colin had that . . ."

Then it was Michael's job to copy each mouthwatering dish for the Box Tree menu. Sometimes he'd be able to reproduce it within a day or two. Other times it might take him a couple of weeks and many attempts to perfect the recipe. Malcolm and Colin would come into the kitchen to taste and see if he was close to success. Finally it would be, "That's it, Michael. You've got it." And onto the menu it went, alongside Michael's own clever dishes.

No one in Yorkshire had ever seen food like this. They didn't know such food existed. The most sophisticated food they ate at home would be a roast lunch or maybe toad in the hole, that hearty dish of pork sausages cooked in Yorkshire pudding and covered in onion gravy. If they went out for dinner, they might get lobster thermidor, beef Wellington, duck à l'orange, and peach Melba. Chefs didn't feel they could stray or experiment. What's more, there weren't the beautifully illustrated cookery books we have today, or the food magazines and cookery programs on telly. The world back then was a much smaller place.

Aside from serving classical French cuisine, the Box Tree also had the feel of a good restaurant that you might stumble across in a village in France. It was warm and cozy and kitted out with beautiful antiques and great paintings. The windows were stained glass and there was stained glass throughout the restaurant, so that everyone became a shimmering silhouette, a shape behind colored glass. Along with an extensive list of French wines, the restaurant had those classic qualities then associated with the French: style, finesse and attention to detail. The menu was written in French with English thrown in, or, if you like, English with French thrown in. So there was Roast Partridge, Pommes Garnished. When I later went on to own restaurants, I'd write my menus in the same English-French way.

By 1976 the Box Tree had won its first Michelin star. In 1977, a couple of years before I arrived, it was awarded its second. The only two-star restaurants in England at the time were the Connaught in London, Albert Roux's Le Gavroche in London, his brother Michel Roux's Waterside Inn in Bray—all with powerhouse kitchens—and little old Box Tree in the middle of nowhere with just eight kitchen staff.

I began on hors d'oeuvres, though my other duties included watering the flowers at the front of the restaurant, polishing the brass and washing the Boys' black Cadillac. Every morning when I arrived for work, my first job was to make the traditional Box Tree kick-starter for the kitchen staff: I'd put four pints of milk into a stainless steel pan, scald it and then whisk in a few tablespoons of Nescafé and a few tablespoons of sugar. In the microwave I'd heat up all the bread buns from the night before, which we'd eat with the coffee. Michael Lawson would ladle the coffee into a mug and then add another kick by throwing in a dash of calvados. He wouldn't touch another drop of alcohol all day until the end of service, at about midnight, when he'd allow himself a large whiskey on the rocks.

One of my chores was to take the vegetables round to an old Polish man who lived nearby and was paid a few quid to shell the peas and peel the sprouts. Another of my jobs was to clean the copper pans and dishes using a solution of egg white, flour, salt and malt vinegar; a cut lemon was used like a scouring pad to apply the paste, and once it had dried, it was washed off and the pan was buffed up to make it gleaming. Everyone at the Box Tree had to be multitasked. You didn't just go in and do your job; you did whatever you had to do.

Ken Lamb, for instance, was the baker during the day. He'd make the bread, puff pastry and the petits fours. Come evening, Ken would put on his dickie bow tie and—presto!—he was now the head waiter.

From the outset I was enchanted by the extraordinary system that operated within the restaurant. It had only fifty covers (or seats), but there were two sittings, one at seven thirty P.M. and one at nine thirty P.M., so we did a hundred covers but only needed a staff large enough to serve fifty. One coffee waitress could look after all of them.

Then there was the price of the meal. A three-course dinner might have been twenty quid, making it possibly England's most expensive restaurant in the late seventies. It was packed, too. Crammed with rich Yorkshire mill owners, the guys who had made money out of textiles in the fifties and sixties. In the evenings I would hear the cars pulling up outside, the car doors slamming. And not just any old cars— Bentleys lined the streets outside. As I beavered away, I would always try to keep an eye on the swing doors that led from the kitchen to the restaurant. When they swung open, I'd get a glimpse of the happy customers, impeccably dressed and looking rich, glamorous and sophisticated. The sounds of the kitchen would be momentarily muffled by laughter from the dining room, the sound of people really enjoying themselves. From the brightly lit kitchen I could see the candlelight in the restaurant.

Michael had his sous chef, Steve, and there were two Frenchmen, Michel on Meat and Pascale on Hors D'Oeuvres. There were bollockings, sure, but not with the ferocity of those I'd received at the George. In fact, one of my memories is of Steve getting a monstering after he burned me with an egg slice, something the size of a toast grill. He had put the implement onto the gas, and then when it was very hot, he put it onto my arm. I screamed in agony and Steve looked astonished—I don't think he realized how hot it would be and I am sure it was never his intention to burn me. He was just mucking around but he got a severe bollocking.

Aside from that though, the Box Tree generally had a friendly environment and Michael Lawson was a gifted mentor. I watched as he prepared, for instance, his game pie. He got a big breast of new-season grouse, a piece of fillet steak, put them into a pie dish, topped it with short-crust pastry and cooked it so the meat was pink. This was not the stuff of *Répertoire*.

Gastronomy begins with technique. If you haven't got technique, you will never master gastronomy. You should buy the best ingredients and cook them perfectly, but to do this you have to question what you are doing and why you are doing it. If you don't understand what makes a good, say, roast partridge—the hanging, the plucking, the trussing—before you've even started, then don't bother roasting it. You've got to hang the bird correctly, pluck it correctly (without piercing the skin) and truss it beautifully (bring in the legs and plump out the breast so that it cooks evenly), retaining the heart and the livers for sauce. Seal it on all sides and then cook it on the back. What's the timing of it? About ten minutes in my oven, but your oven is different from mine. A male partridge is bigger than a female partridge. A partridge shot in December is bigger than one shot in September.

Along the way there were also philosophies to be picked up. Words of wisdom that would stay with me forever. I remember Malcolm striking up a conversation by saying, "You know what I think?"

"No, Mr. Reid," I replied. "What do you think?"

"It doesn't matter what you spend as long as you get the desired effect."

That's inspiring. It's the sort of thing that made me realize the Box Tree bunch were passionate. Money—what the hell? If we're going to do this, let's do it properly. And he wasn't just referring to the dishes when he talked about the desired effect. Malcolm and Colin would spend, spend, spend in their quest to create the desired effect in the dining room. Malcolm might nip out to buy a newspaper and return with a £500 painting. As a lad from Lingfield Mount, I had never seen such extravagance, but this sort of spending taught me that creating a good restaurant requires thinking just as much about what goes on the wall as about what goes on the plate.

They never took inventory and they never did percentages, which would really alarm today's chefs, who have a knife in one hand and a calculator in the other. Malcolm and Colin would just say, "Three courses with English turbot. That'll be twenty quid." Costs were never taken into consideration.

I worked on Hors D'Oeuvres and then was put onto Veg for about three months. Then Michael got me to help doing meat and fish main courses, so that Michael and his number two, Steve, were the front line and I was the backup. I already had the speed, thanks to my spell at the George.

It was while I was at the Box Tree that I discovered a truly inspirational book, *Ma Gastronomie*, written by the great French chef Fernand Point. It was not so much the recipes but the stories about the man and his philosophy that "perfection is lots of little things done well." His words did more than simply stick in my mind; they became my philosophy.

Perfection was an important rule of the Box Tree kitchen. At the George food had been mass-produced, a bit rushed, but here I learned that you had to take your time to get everything just right. I realized that I had to stay focused on precisely what I was doing at that moment. Whatever we did, we had to do beautifully. When we made coq au vin, the chicken was marinated the day before cooking; red burgundy, the traditional wine for this dish, was replaced with claret, which is more full-bodied and therefore adds more depth to the final taste; button mushrooms, again a traditional garnish for coq au vin, were swapped for the flavorsome girolles. If an armagnac was used for the lobster sauce, or white wine used for a fish sauce, it was the best armagnac or the best white wine.

If I was cooking green beans, I'd do them in small amounts in separate pans.

If you're cooking green vegetables, you might think it's acceptable to throw the whole lot into a pan of boiling water. But you're going to create a problem. The water immediately stops boiling, and now that the water is not so hot, the green pigment, chlorophyll, is killed off and the vegetable loses its brightness. Whereas cooking a small quantity of vegetables will keep the water at a boiling point and the vegetables will end up on the plate looking vibrant—and green.

After I'd worked on Meats and Fish, Michael put me in charge of Pastry and I was given a week to learn the craft. A lot of the best chefs have done Pastry, Michel Roux of the Waterside Inn among them. Why is Pastry so important? Because it is all about science, and the knowledge of culinary science is vital. A precise measurement of that ingredient mixed with a certain amount of that ingredient produces this result. It's chemistry.

I beavered away, practicing dishes like Sorbet Poire Genet, a delicious ball of pear sorbet decorated with a little slice of fanned poached pear, a mint leaf and a drizzle of pear liqueur. It was served in a pear-shaped glass bowl, the top of which was removed by the customer to reveal the sorbet inside. The pink grapefruit sorbet was another beauty. If you make pink grapefruit sorbet, it will turn white, so we added a touch of grenadine to give it that pink tinge. The Box Tree menu would change every day and I would build the pudding menu out of about thirty dishes.

If I wanted to introduce something, it would have to be tasted by the Boys when they had their dinner at six thirty in the snug. Now that I had my own section, I really began to excel. I could express myself and create dishes. I took a tuile biscuit and added rose ice cream and glazed strawberries in their own coulis, put a sugar cage over the top of it and decorated it with crystallized primroses—very camp, very Box Tree. "Excellent," said Messrs. Reid and Long. "We'll call it Timbale de Fraises Pompadour." It became a specialty of the Box Tree, and years after my departure it was still on the menu.

I now knew that the kitchen was the best place in the world. At the George I had discovered that cooking enabled me to express myself, and at Box Tree I was acknowledged. There was "well done" and "that's good." For the first time in my life I was being recognized. One night Ken Lamb, the head waiter, confided in me that he had heard the Boys discussing me. Mr. Reid had said to Mr. Long, "Marco's the best pastry chef Box Tree's ever had." That sort of comment was a welcome confidence booster for an eighteen-year-old chef.

MICHAEL LAWSON, A lanky man with a kind face, took me under his wing. Like me, he was another damaged soul. As a young man he had arrived at the Box Tree and worked his way up to become head chef. Somewhere in the distant past he'd met a girl and asked her to marry him. She accepted his proposal and the wedding was organized, but shortly before the big day she was killed in a car accident, so the rumor went, when she was on her way to collect her wedding dress. Michael, poor man, had never recovered from the loss or found another woman. He had never wanted to. Instead, all his love and emotion had gone into the Box Tree. On our days off he would take me for a drink at the pub and I would sit there listening to him talk about food, the menus he had devised and Box Tree kitchen stories. Michael was understated; if you'd have walked into the kitchen, you wouldn't have known that he was the head chef because he didn't have a great presence, but boy was he a great chef.

It was while at the Box Tree that my romantic life, up until now barren and bleak, perked up. On Sundays I would work at a nearby pub, the Cow and Calf, where I met a part-time waitress called Fiona. She was a year or two younger than me and I was thrilled when she accepted my invitation to take her out for dinner. I took us by taxi from

Ilkley to Harrogate, where we had dinner at a very posh restaurant, Olivers, before getting another cab back. I lost my virginity to Fiona in bed at Mr. and Mrs. Fox's house, where I lodged during my time at the Box Tree. I was eighteen years old. For a few months, maybe six, we existed on a relationship called sex.

Sadly, Fiona left me for the restaurant manager at the Cow and Calf and they went on to have children together. Being ditched did nothing for my confidence, but I convinced myself that Fiona was simply turned on by power. Why else would she have deserted me for him?

In reality, relationships were a distraction and I would come to realize that much of the time I could only manage brief flings. My girlfriends, meanwhile, would be fitted in around my days and nights in the kitchen. This may seem terribly disrespectful, but I got more turned on by food. If I met a girl, I'd go round to her house when her parents weren't in, we'd have a quick shag and that was it. Bonds were broken long before the word "love" could be mentioned.

I remember meeting one young girl at a club and taking her home. As we stood by her gate, I was just moving in to kiss her when we were lit up by the headlights of an oncoming car. It was the Boys in their black Cadillac. The car stopped and Colin jumped out. "In, Marco," he ordered me. As I sat in the backseat being driven home by my bosses, Colin explained, "We had to get you away from that girl. You don't know what you might have caught."

From time to time, I would bump into Mr. Butler, my former teacher at Allerton High, who happened to live in Ilkley. We'd stop and chat and he'd ask how things were going and he always seemed pleased that I had found a job that made me passionate. Many of my contemporaries from school had drifted from one job to another, or were "on the dole"—living off state handouts.

My Box Tree days drew to a close not long after Steve, Michael Lawson's sous chef, handed in his notice and Malcolm and Colin asked if I knew of anyone who could replace him. I was too inexperienced for the job, they had quite rightly thought. The only person I could suggest was Michael Truelove, the chef who first taught me how to use a knife when I worked in the kitchen at the Hotel St. George. He had been good to me, at times protecting me from the bullying of head

chef Stephan, and I liked him. "Michael is a very good cook," I told
Malcolm and Colin. "About five years older than me and a hard
worker."

Michael was offered the job and he accepted. When he arrived,
we were the two pranksters from the George reunited. One day, the
French chef Pascale, who was in charge of Hors D'Ouevres, went into
the walk-in fridge to fetch ingredients. Michael and I closed the door
and locked him in there for half an hour. When we opened the door,
Pascale was sitting on an upturned crate and rolling a cigarette. He
said nothing. In fact, he said nothing for an entire week. He just
sulked. The French don't get angry; they sulk.

Michael Truelove's arrival would ultimately lead to my departure.
Once he'd settled in, he encouraged me to look for another job. "You
don't want to stay in the sticks, Marco," he'd say. "You want to spread
your wings."

Ridiculously immature, I decided to hand in my notice without
having a job to go to. I thought I'd be asked to work a six-week notice
period and during that time I'd find another job. Michael Lawson
turned pale when I told him I was off. "I'm not telling the bosses," he
said. The prospect of relaying bad news frightened him. "You'll have
to tell them yourself, Marco."

I mustered up the courage and broke the news to the Boys.

"Let's talk about this in the Chinese Room," said Malcolm, and we
went upstairs, where the three of us sat at a table. They offered to in-
crease my salary, which then was about £30 a week.

"It's not about the money," I said. "I've made up my mind and you
can't persuade me to stay."

It was wrong of me to assume they'd want me to work out my notice, staying on for a month or even six weeks. They were so badly hurt
by my announcement that they came back with a blow that broke my
heart.

"Go now," said Malcolm.

"There's no point in staying," added Colin. "It's best if you get your
things together and leave now."

I was numbed by what I saw as brutality. What's more, they wouldn't
give me a reference. Looking back, I can understand their reaction.

Today I don't blame them. I had rejected them, so they were rejecting me. But to have happiness snatched from me in a matter of seconds seemed cruel. Malcolm and Colin had been like my adopted family.

I had never imagined that I would leave on bad terms. If only I had been able to work my notice and leave on a high . . . I was traumatized. I had arrived at the Box Tree happy and excited, but eighteen months later I left via the same door, feeling destroyed. Love affairs often end in heartache, don't they? Yet the Box Tree would remain in my memory as the most special restaurant I have ever walked into, let alone worked in.

About twelve years later I was at the stove at Harveys, my restaurant in southwest London, by then the winner of two Michelin stars, when the kitchen phone rang. "Hello, Marco. It's Michael . . . Michael Lawson." It was lovely to hear his voice and I told him so. He said, "Would you mind if I came to dinner?" I told him to come whenever he wanted, at which point he revealed that he was phoning from the public phone box outside the restaurant. Poor Michael had felt nervous about walking into the restaurant. Stage fright or something like that. I ran through the restaurant and greeted my mentor at the door. I sat him at table nine and gave him a grand meal with wine. When service had slowed down, I went out to have a chat with him. "The meal you fed me tonight," said Michael, "was better than anything we ever did at the Box Tree." It was a compliment that went some way toward repairing what were then my tarnished memories of that wonderful little restaurant in the middle of nowhere.

SEVEN

It Was Meant to Be

I T WAS THE summer of 1981 and I was a nineteen-year-old in a rut, back in Leeds. After my abrupt departure from the Box Tree, I'd been drifting. I took a chef's job at Froggie's, the restaurant of a Leeds casino called the Continental, where the head chef, Jacques Castell, served good old-fashioned food.

I was a lodger in Moor Allerton, in a house owned by a Spanish woman called Esperanza. This put me in the peculiar and uncomfortable position of living just around the corner from Dad and the house where I had grown up. As Dad and I hadn't spoken for a few years, and I could not bring myself to resume relations, I found myself having to hide from him.

Sometimes I would spot him walking down the road and would have to turn away so he didn't catch sight of me, or scurry away in the opposite direction. I don't think he ever saw me—I don't remember cries of "Hey, Marco, what the hell are you doing here?" He had no idea that we were living within a few hundred yards of one another. I feel very sad about it now. It was a ridiculous situation.

I had to escape Leeds. I had escaped once, albeit only the short distance to Harrogate and then Ilkley, and had gone back to Leeds because I knew it, but once I was there, I saw the city in a different light. I didn't like it any longer. As a child I'd often felt I didn't fit in there; now I fitted in even less. I had caught a glimpse of life outside the city.

I applied for two jobs. The job I really wanted was at Le Gavroche, the two-star Michelin restaurant in the heart of London. Box Tree staff had talked romantically about this fine establishment in the capital. Albert Roux, Gavroche's chef patron, was hailed as an excellent cook. The press, the critics and customers loved his classical French food. It is fair to say that Albert Roux and his brother Michel—who ran the Michelin-starred Waterside Inn—were the most talked about chefs at the time. Or they were in Yorkshire, at least.

So I set my sights on Gavroche and phoned to ask for an application form. Around about the same time, however, I heard of a pastry chef vacancy at Chewton Glen, a country house hotel that sits on the edge of the New Forest in New Milton, Hampshire (today it is considered one of England's finest small hotels).

When a letter arrived from Le Gavroche, I opened it excitedly, knowing it would be the application form. But when I pulled out the form, my heart sank. Every single question was written in French and I imagined that the responses were expected to be in the same language. I thought it was the Roux way of saying that they would take chefs of any nationality, as long as they were French. I didn't speak a word of French, so I concluded, alas, that I would have to rule out Le Gavroche. I chucked the application form into the bin. I pinned my hopes on Chewton Glen and was delighted when the head chef, Christian Delteuil, invited me to the South Coast for a job interview.

On Thursday, June 18, 1981, I took the coach from Leeds to Victoria coach station in London, traveled across the capital to Waterloo station and from there caught the train to New Milton. There was nothing particularly memorable about the interview. I liked the head pastry chef, a nice old boy, but I don't recall having a great deal of respect for Delteuil and, having worked for Michael Lawson at the Box Tree, I knew respect for the boss was a necessity. Delteuil's parting words were, "Give me a call next week and I'll let you know if you've got the job."

I would have called him, of course, but the extraordinary events of the next twenty-four hours ensured I never needed to pick up the phone. It therefore remains a mystery to me whether or not I landed the pastry chef job.

Beginning my journey home from Chewton Glen to Leeds, I

arrived at New Milton station and discovered, annoyingly, that I had missed my train. When I finally got to Waterloo, I asked a man who I thought was a British Rail ticket collector how I could get to Victoria. "I'm not from British Rail. I'm with Royal Mail," he replied, but he happened to be going to Victoria, so he offered me a lift in the back of his van, and I made the journey perched on sacks of post.

At Victoria coach station I was told, "You've missed it, mate . . . The next coach back to Leeds isn't until the morning." A bed-and-breakfast was not a consideration: first, I was a nineteen-year-old lad and nineteen-year-old lads don't do B&B when they've missed the coach; second, I was broke. So I took a stroll. This was my first time in the capital and I was going to make the most of it.

I didn't know where I was heading, but I ended up wandering along a brightly lit street and then I stopped dead in my tracks.

There I was, quite by chance, standing outside Le Gavroche in Lower Sloane Street. I stood on the pavement, mesmerized. The lights were still on in this exquisite restaurant, a two-star heaven, and I pressed my nose up against the window. Inside there were a few customers, happy and well fed, finishing off their meals with midnight cups of coffee. It seemed elegant, stylish and grand, with the warm golden glow of dim lights and candlelight.

I couldn't stand there all night, though, I'd have been arrested, so I headed back to the coach station, where I met a German lad who was about my age and equally forlorn, and together we embarked on a sightseeing tour, walking to Buckingham Palace and Parliament Square. We went to Trafalgar Square to look at Nelson's Column, before my companion, who had more cash than me, bought me a cup of tea and a cheese sandwich.

When morning came and the Leeds-bound coach pulled out of Victoria, I was not on board.

Instead I returned to Le Gavroche, knocked on the back door and asked to see the head chef. A pastry chef called Baloo (as in the *Jungle Book*) told me the restaurant was closed for lunch and that no one else was around. I was about to walk away, perhaps back to Victoria, when he added, "You could always go to Roux brothers' head office. It's not far." I walked down Lower Sloane Street, crossed the Thames at

Chelsea Bridge, went straight up the Queenstown Road and took a left onto Wandsworth Road, and there, a few hundred yards along, was Roux HQ.

God knows what I looked like when I walked through the door. Actually, I know what I looked like: I looked like shit. It was about ten in the morning and I hadn't slept for more than twenty-four hours. Albert, a dapper little Frenchman in his midforties, was sitting there and I instantly recognized him from newspaper pictures. He was kind enough to make no comment about my shabby appearance.

"Mr. Roux. I'm hoping to get a job in one of your restaurants."

He said, "Where have you worked?"

I showed him my references and mentioned that I had worked at the Box Tree. "You were at the Box Tree, were you? How long were you there?"

"About eighteen months, Mr. Roux."

The magic name Box Tree worked well. "Go back to Leeds," he said, before adding, "get your belongings and then come back down on Monday. Report here on Tuesday." And that was that.

I OBEYED ALBERT'S orders, and the following Monday, when I returned to London, the company found me a little bedsit in Clapham, just around the corner from Roux HQ. On Tuesday, June 23, 1981, I became a "Roux robot"—what rivals in the industry called the mechanical chefs who worked for brothers Albert and Michel.

I did not start off in the kitchen at Le Gavroche but at Le Gamin, the Roux-owned City restaurant beside the Old Bailey. I did a couple of weeks there, under head chef Dennis Lobrey, who cooked good, proper food. What I saw for the first time in my life was a high standard of food served in a couple of hours to 130 people. The only desserts made on-site were ice creams and sorbets; the other pastries—things like Charlotte aux Poires and Truffes au Chocolat—came from the Roux head office. It was a smoothly run operation.

Shortly after I joined there was a bit of upheaval in the expanding Roux empire. Gavroche moved to Upper Brook Street, where it remains to this day, and its Lower Sloane Street site became Gavvers, which served watered-down versions of Gavroche's classical dishes. At Gavvers we'd make things like Sablé à Pêche, which was a Gavroche specialty, but rather than having two layers, you'd have one layer because it was cheaper.

Dennis's second chef, Alban, was my head chef at Gavvers, and in the autumn of 1981 I ended up at Gavroche. I made friends with Mark Bougère, who, as the chef tourner of the company, would go from one Roux restaurant to another, standing in for chefs who were ill. He was, in effect, Albert's right-hand man and would come to Gavvers to check on things. Mark was a very fine chef, an elegant cook with a great touch, and he took a real liking to me and taught me a lot.

He taught me, for instance, how to make great sorbets with a concentrated flavor and wonderful sauces. He also encouraged me to question what I was cooking. He was one of the most knowledgeable chefs I've ever come across and I still have an image of him making a mousseline of fish beautifully. It was clear to me why he was the most trusted of Albert's staff.

I am indebted to Baloo, the Gavroche pastry chef, and not just because he was the man who directed me to Roux HQ, but also because he offered me a place to stay in his flat in Queenstown Road, enabling me to move out of the bedsit. One night I was walking home when I spotted Baloo talking to someone outside our flat. It was Nico Ladenis, the Michelin-starred chef who owned Chez Nico in Queenstown Road.

Nico asked if I would like to do a bit of work for him. At this stage Gavroche did not open for lunch, so I had that part of the day available. I took the job. I would work in the mornings from Tuesday to Saturday for Nico in his tiny kitchen, picking up £50 a week on top of the £67 I was paid by Albert.

At Nico's I'd prepare the meat and fish while the sous chef did the starters and puddings like Prune Armagnac Parfait, Caramel Parfait and sorbets. The sous chef was camp, very precious and had a good sense of humor. He would take a bollocking from Nico and then duck down under the counter so his boss couldn't see and pretend to suck him off.

Nico, meanwhile, had established a reputation for being a perfectionist. He did not like customers to ask for well-done meat and he wouldn't allow salt and pepper on the table. He thought his palate was perfect, which I don't think is right—you have to accept that everyone's palate is different. Nico's may well have been perfect, but someone else might like a little more salt, it's as simple as that.

One morning I was in the kitchen and an electrician walked into the restaurant asking to speak to Chas. We all stood there, scratching our heads. "Chas? There's no one here called Chas." The electrician was insistent. "Chas Nico," he said.

I only did a short stint with Nico, but we became good friends and both won three Michelin stars on the same day, in January 1995. The last time I met him for lunch, Nico said, "What shall we talk about?" I replied, "What do you want to talk about?" And he responded, "Let's talk about all the cunts in the industry."

Meanwhile, thinking back to my early days with Albert Roux, I remember walking down Queenstown Road toward Chelsea Bridge and heading for work in a Roux kitchen when a Mini Metro pulled up beside me and a voice shouted, "Jump in." It was Albert.

All talk in the Roux empire was about whether Albert would collect three stars in the *Michelin Guide*, which was due to be published in the following January of 1982, and as I was in the company of the man himself, I thought I would raise the subject. "Albert," I said, "do you think you will get your three stars?"

Eyes firmly on the road and deadly serious, he said, "If I don't get them, I will throw myself in the Thames."

I went silent, pondering the words of a determined man. I had never heard a chef threaten to take his life if he didn't achieve such status in a guide. Do actors say the same thing in the run-up to the Oscars? Do athletes feel the same way about Olympic medals? How apt, I thought, that he should mention throwing himself into the Thames when the river was just beneath us. When January came, Albert was spared a watery grave. The *Michelin Guide* awarded Le Gavroche three stars—Albert had reached the top.

I compared the setup of the finest restaurants to something akin to the Mafia. On this basis, I decided that Albert was definitely the Godfather, the boss of bosses. He would be played by Marlon Brando . . . in an apron. He was a father figure with a very dominant presence and could philosophize in that Godfather style. While you worked for him, you felt you had his protection. You knew you were with the don.

That left four others in this mafia of Michelin winners: Pierre "the Bear" Koffmann, head of the Koffmann family; Nico "Nic the Greek" Ladenis, head of the Ladenis family; Michel Bourdin, head of the Bourdin family; and Raymond Blanc, who, with all his craziness, could only be Al Mascarpone.

EIGHT

The Boss of Bosses

STRANGE THOUGH IT may seem, there are many chefs who suffer a fear of the stove. You will find them in the world's finest kitchens. They might be great cooks, with heads crammed full of culinary knowledge, but the minute they are thrown into a busy kitchen, they wobble, lose it and need bailing out. Until they conquer that fear, they are destined never to rise through the ranks and find a place in the kitchen hierarchy.

You need confidence to shrug off your insecurities, push your way past the other chefs and take control of the stove. Step into a powerhouse kitchen like Gavroche's and you won't hear "excuse me" or "would you mind." Each man has his own dishes to create, his own job to do, and he has to have the required strength of character to barge his way past the others in order to cook.

When I finally made it into the three-Michelin-starred kitchen at Gavroche, Albert Roux was keen to let me know that I should never be frightened to push in with my pot or pan. One night at Gavroche, shortly after I had joined the brigade as an assistant on the Meat section, Albert called me into his office there—something akin to a large glass bowl—for a chat. He gave me a Benson & Hedges, which was his way of saying "at ease." "Don't be scared of the stove," he said to me, and then waved a hand toward the kitchen. "You can cook as well as any of those people. You have nothing to worry about." He had got me wrong: I wasn't scared of the stove; what I didn't want to do was get in the way of my superiors. But effectively his words were a confidence booster: he was saying I was showing the other chefs too much respect and in doing so I was suppressing my abilities.

Yet I understood precisely what Albert meant about fear of the stove. I had seen it before, just a couple of months earlier when I'd worked at Gavvers. There had been a chef there who was about my age and I remember him being extraordinarily precise in what he did, but in my view he was also a bit slow. He had been trained in one of those big kitchens in France, where there's such a massive infrastructure that chefs have the luxury of being able to take their time.

When this young lad arrived at Gavvers, he was put on Meat and I was an assistant on Fish, which is a tough section because it doesn't allow for error. We were doing more than a hundred covers a night, and to feed that number of people, you have to be really quick at the stove, but he found it hard to deal with. It doesn't matter how much knowledge you have as a cook, you can't run a section if you appear slow. So he moved from Gavvers and went to work at Le Gamin, where I think he helped Dennis Lobrey on the passe, shouting out the orders.

Perhaps I might never have seen that young man again were it not for the fact that he was Albert's son, Michel Roux Jr. Michel would go on to run Le Gavroche, taking over from his father in the nineties, and he runs it very well.

Albert may not have wanted any of his team to suffer from a fear of the stove but the Gavroche brigade was driven by fear nonetheless. We were driven by a fear of failing, a fear of fucking up, a fear of upsetting the boss.

It was easy to gauge the terror—when chefs arrived at the restaurant, they raced to change into their whites. There was no time to stop and have a cup of coffee in a café while you contemplated the day ahead. Every morning I found myself hurrying into work, petrified by the thought of arriving late. Once when I committed the sin of turning up five minutes late, I dashed in to be greeted by Albert, scowling. Would I be marched to the wall and shot?

"There's always an excuse for being an hour late," he said. "But there's no excuse for being five minutes late." After that I would virtually run off the bus to work. Even though I was in early and worked through my breaks, conscientious soul that I was, that sort of diligence was never acknowledged in Gavroche.

The hierarchy there kept everyone in their place. Gavroche had a traditional kitchen hierarchy like that found in the finest restaurants in Paris. At the top was Albert, the chef patron, or chef proprietor. Beneath him was the head chef, René, who stood at the passe shouting out the orders and making sure the dishes were perfect before being sent to the table. The head chef is the composer. Under René was the sous chef, the head chef's right-hand man, or deputy. Then there were the chefs de partie, the ones heading up the different sections. Those sections were Meat—sometimes referred to as Sauce—Fish, Pastry (which included all desserts, rather than just ones with pastry) and Larder. Some kitchens have a section for Cold Starters and another for Hot Starters. Within each section the hierarchy continues: each chef de partie has a premier commis chef, or assistant, which is where I started at Gavroche. And the premier commis is in charge of a couple of commis chefs, also called assistants. Then there's the kitchen porter, who does the washing up.

During service Albert was head chef, barking the orders from the passe and making sure everything came together. He was the sergeant major, seeing out the food, shouting, bollocking anyone in his path, and no one dared disobey him. When he was at the passe, nothing bad got past him. He saw everything that went out, and if he didn't touch the dishes with his hands—rearranging the ingredients on the plate to perfect the picture—then he touched the dishes with his eyes, and that is really important.

Out of service, Albert was the chef patron—the general—who would sit in his office composing menus and dealing with paperwork and suppliers. Occasionally he would come into the kitchen to carry out inspections. He would open a fridge and peer inside, and if something wasn't right—an overripe piece of fruit, perhaps, or a sauce that had spilled and not been cleaned up to his satisfaction—he would scream for the head chef, René, and the bollocking would kick off. "This is fucking filthy. What is going on?" René would always get it first from Albert, and the bollocking would then be passed down the hierarchy. René would bollock the chef de partie. The chef de partie

would bollock the premier commis. The premier commis would bollock the commis. During these inspections it was rare for Albert to
bollock the commis in the first place: hierarchy had to be respected.

Young chefs would do a year at Gavroche, just to have it on their
CV, and then move on. From day one they would be mentally preparing their letter of resignation, but because of Albert's awesome presence, staff were always scared to hand in their notice.

René initially took a dislike to me and gave me one bollocking after
another. I think he dreamed of having a kitchen full of French and Italian cooks. He had the French and the Italians—his favorites—but I
was just another Englishman who annoyed him. René would amuse
himself by telling me to go and get something from the main fridges,
which were at the front of the restaurant. I would sprint from the
kitchen, run round the side of the building to the fridges at the front,
collect the ingredient and then dash back. I'd have a second or two
to gather my breath and then René would shout, "Cream from the
fridge," and whoosh, off I'd go again. Run forward, run back, run forward, run back. That was my existence in the early days at Gavroche.
René, or maybe Albert, gave me the nickname "Horse," because even
before service I had run the equivalent of Aintree.

René's sous chef, Danny Crow, was half Italian, and when he discovered that I also had Italian blood, he became my friend and helped
René see me in a different light.

There were fifteen or sixteen of us in the Gavroche kitchen and
there was no chitchat. If anyone spoke, it was only to talk about the
menu or the food. Overall, there were hours of silence, punctuated by
orders from René and barks of "Yes, Chef." We all beavered away,
sticking to each recipe—be it Poulet de Bresse en Vessie or Canette de
Peche or Omelette Rothschild—and being precise and methodical. I
could certainly see why the troops commanded by Albert and Michel
were known, outside the organization, as the Roux robots. Later on,
when I went on to run my own kitchens, I too would insist on silence.
At Gavroche I discovered that there is something beautiful about the
sounds—chopping, clattering, sizzling—of a working kitchen.

The chef de partie on the Meat section was a Belgian called Claude.
He was the Roux robot prototype: organized, consistent and perfect

for Gavroche, Claude did not play around with the recipes that came from Albert's office; he stuck to the original and never veered. Another lad, Stephen Yare, was about my age and, like me, was an assistant, and a few years later we would work together under Raymond Blanc at Le Manoir aux Quat'Saisons. There were also a couple of Japanese guys who were also good, mechanical Roux robots.

We were doing big numbers—eighty covers—in a fast and hard, aggressive service, so it was essential that we all had three attributes: knowledge, touch and organization. I thrived on the pressure and stress of the workload. If I wasn't already an adrenaline addict, I was fast turning into one. I found gears within myself that enabled me to step up a level as the kitchen pressure increased. You cannot let the pressure get to you, though very few chefs can do big volumes and maintain a consistently high standard.

There was one guy who really stood out, and not only because of his distinctive white clogs. Roland Lahore had knowledge, speed and a sensational flair. Roland moved quickly, worked quickly and cooked elegantly. I can still see him now, doing a scallop of salmon, cooking the fish beautifully and adding a handful of sorrel to the sauce. Roland would make terrines that, when sliced, were like glorious mosaics on the plate: he had visualized the finished terrine before assembling the ingredients. I watched him finish off a sauce by throwing in a segment of pink grapefruit and breaking it up with a whisk so the fruit infused the sauce with a perfect balance of acidity (always finish a fish sauce with citrus or vinegar).

But Roland was a soloist, a Maradona. He was playing his own game and his wild streak must have rubbed off on me. If you're working in a big kitchen team, you have to be synchronized. Imagine you have two chefs, one is on Meat and the other is on Fish, and they are each cooking two dishes for the same table. If the chefs are good, they will work together, so the four dishes make it to the passe at the same time. One of the chefs will shout out, "Ready in three minutes," and the other chef will work to that.

But Roland lived in his own world, and inevitably that meant he wasn't synchronized. He was in charge of the Fish section but he might be behind or ahead of the man on Meat. So if a table of six ordered three meat and three fish dishes—the fish would be on the passe but the meat wouldn't be ready, or vice versa. Roland tended to forget about the rest of the kitchen. He worked only with his unit of two assistants, who were whipped along and kept in line by him.

He had done his time at Troisgros in France and then worked for Michel Bourdin at the Connaught in London. He left the latter because they couldn't control him, and at the Waterside Inn, Roland was deemed equally unmanageable. But though others may have found him difficult, I had the utmost respect for him, and Roland liked me too. Maybe he related to me on a mental level—perhaps he could spot the similarities. Who knows? I was not yet a soloist but it wouldn't take long. Like me, Roland worked through his breaks—if he didn't, he knew he'd be in trouble during service—and he never once sent a bad plate to the passe.

THOUGH I WOULD go on to become good friends with Albert, our relationship at Gavroche was strictly business. If you finished your job, he would find you another. If it was six thirty in the evening and the first customer wasn't due in until seven, giving you half an hour to kill, Albert would fill the gap by finding you something else to do. He was that disciplined. One night Albert gave me a severe bollocking because my timing was disjointed during service: there was a delay between two dishes. An hour or so afterward he called me into his office and produced a Benson & Hedges, signifying I should be at ease. I was convinced that I was about to get the sack but I was wrong. "I'm sorry," he said. "I overreacted."

It struck me at the time that while it was good of him to apologize, it was wrong of him to do so in private. If he wanted to bollock me in front of everybody, that was fine. But if he wanted to be correct about it, he should have apologized in public too. When I eventually came to run my own kitchens, I promised myself that if an apology was due, I would make it in front of the rest of the staff.

Despite instilling fear, Albert also instilled confidence. In one of those B&H moments in his office he told me that I did the work of two or three men. And he said, "I know which plates are yours on the passe, even when you don't deliver them. I can tell they are yours just by the way you dress them. I know it's your hands that have dressed those plates—no one does it like you. You have more natural talent than anyone else in this kitchen." What had I done to earn such compliments? I can't remember. But I had seen talent in other chefs—it's just the touch, the way the food falls, the way the sauce pours, the way the garnish is put on the plate. If you watch a great chef, he moves elegantly as he cooks. Someone can tell you how to do a picture. They can give you a paintbrush and paper and then give you instructions— paint a circle, paint a square, put a brushstroke here and another there. But the paintbrush is in your hand, so it all comes down to your artistic talent. Can you paint the perfect circle? Can you paint the perfect square? Are the brushstrokes too heavy or too light? Are the colors right?

ON DAYS OFF, I would walk down Queenstown Road, cross the Thames at Chelsea Bridge and head up to the King's Road. The King's Road was a honeypot. Young people swarmed there. Punk was born here. The place was magical. This stretch of road running from Sloane Square to Parsons Green was one long, crowded parade of ultratrendy clothes shops, cafés, bars and pubs. If you were broke, it didn't matter because you could still enjoy yourself by strolling and watching, observing the confident young rebels on show. It was the early eighties but there were still a few die-hard punks around, with pierced nostrils, swastika tattoos on their foreheads, spiky hair dyed pink, purple and lime green—and those were just the girls.

I would go to Pucci's, which to me and other King's Road wanderers seemed like the coolest café in the world, to sit and drink coffee and smoke. Queues of people would hover outside waiting for a table and Pucci himself (no one knew his first name) was nicely grumpy. If the queue was too long, he'd dash over to the people at the end of it, yelling, "Go away! Go away!" Customers who annoyed him got a blast of his pidgin English, "Shard up!"

I went to Pucci's so many times that eventually I became a familiar face. I struck up conversation with other regulars, an assortment of

New Romantics and youthful aristocrats. I was a lowly cook, but I was welcomed into the Chelsea set; it was a slow process because confidence was a requisite factor for membership, and I didn't have much of that. I was fascinated by these people, their creativity and their energy. I'd sit there making a single beer last me the whole night. I had Pils because it was all part of the image, but I didn't like the taste of beer and lager, and in the eyes of my new friends it would have looked odd to order a glass of wine. I positioned myself close to the social whirlpool, though, and slowly I was sucked in.

Just as Gavroche had a hierarchy, so did the Chelsea set. At the top was Robert Pereno, who, I think I'm right in saying, was the man behind the one-night clubs that eventually became raves. To me, Robert was the king of the King's Road, and the role of queen played by his girlfriend, Lowri-Ann Richards, a singer and actress. Then there was James Holdsworth—Little James—who helped Robert instigate the one-night clubs. And there were others on the scene and doing clubs: Rusty Egan, who was in Visage, and Steve Strange. They might hire Crazy Larry's for the night, and when I finished work, I'd head off there.

The Chelsea set also included some wild young aristocrats and children of upper-class parents. The kids tended to have been at Eton before bailing out of education and life as we know it. They wanted to lose themselves in the mayhem of the King's Road. Chelsea was a magnet for junkies, be that drug takers or adrenaline-addict chefs. Nowadays, young aristos want to have good careers rather than spend their days on the King's Road, but there was a period of a few years— a window in time, I suppose—when rich kids managed to escape responsibility and parental pressures, and the King's Road is where they went. I'd grown up thinking aristos were snobs who looked down their noses at the working classes, but the ones I met then didn't give a damn that I was a cook with a state-school education who earned in a year what they got in weekly handouts from their folks.

Often they spent their money on drugs, heroin being the drug du jour. There was dear Charlie Tennant, the son of Lord Glenconner, who was polite and gentle natured but also heavily into smack. His parents tried to help him by booking him into the Lister Hospital, just off the King's Road. They could have picked a different location.

Charlie would break out of the Lister and only had to walk a few hundred yards to get a fix. Chronically afflicted by the effects of the drug, he used to bounce up and down. The last time I saw him was in Fulham Broadway, where he had a house. He invited me in for a coffee and did one of those obsessive-compulsive shuffles a hundred times before putting his key in the front door. Sadly, Charlie has since died, and inevitably there were one or two others who had drug-related deaths, though I'm pleased to say there were many members of the set who managed to avoid the temptation of drugs.

Among the girls there was Victoria Lockwood, who went on to marry Princess Diana's brother, Charles Spencer, and Sophie Ward, daughter of the actor Simon Ward, who became a well-known actress and then left her husband for a lesbian lover. Then there was Willy Harcourt-Cooze, a Pucci's regular. He'd sit at one of end of the bar while I sat at the other, and for months we didn't introduce ourselves, but when we finally got chatting, Willy told me how his father had died when he was a child and I told him about my mother's death. A bond was formed, and years later when I opened Harveys, Willy became a regular customer and remains to this day one of my closest friends. One of Willy's girlfriends, by the way, and another Pucci's regular, was a young Rachel Weisz, who went on to become a great actress and win an Oscar for her role in *The Constant Gardener*.

I talked to my new friends about food with such passion that they all thought I'd lost the plot. They were amused by my obsession. In terms of their usual topics of conversation, eating came after drinking, clubbing, hair and clothes. A day in the life of the Chelsea set member would go like this: Coffee outside Dino's, then off to Oriel at Sloane Square to sit outside and bird—by which I mean women—watch, back up to Pucci's for a drink in the evening and then on to Crazy Larry's. In between, there were clothes to be bought. Dressing up was a big thing. In their colorful waistcoats and frilly pirate shirts, people looked like something out of Adam and the Ants. One of my favorite garments was a black T-shirt with the words "Bobo Kaminsky" stamped on it. I bought it from Jones and paid a fortune for it. Don't ask me who Bobo was. At times it seemed as if I was the only one with a job. When they were getting up, I was already into my sixth hour in the kitchen.

My Yorkshire accent disappeared and I started to sound a little posh. If you're in your late teens or early twenties and go off to the States or Oz, there's a good chance you'll end up sounding like an American or Australian. My journey from Leeds to London was not that far, but I can understand why, as a young, impressionable lad, I ditched the accent in an attempt to fit in. I thought, I'm just a boy from a Leeds council estate, but I've been accepted by all these toffs. Three years earlier I'd used my spare time to fish or poach, and now I was in this melting pot of rock 'n' roll people. The contrast seemed extreme. They did what they wanted, when they wanted, and that attitude was infectious.

In the kitchen I absorbed the knowledge that made me a chef, while on the King's Road I absorbed a confident attitude, passion for life, wildness and pace. If a rock star was born, then it must have been on the King's Road.

It was also on the King's Road that I met the man who would become my publicist, the rock star's PR, if you like. Alan Crompton-Batt was the manager of a brasserie called Kennedy's, and when I was in there one day, sitting at the bar having a coffee, he got chatting. He had been an *Egon Ronay Guide* inspector, he said. "You must know the Box Tree," I said. And he did. He had eaten in its dining room when I had worked in its kitchen.

You may never have heard of Alan but there is every chance you've heard of Jamie Oliver, Gary Rhodes, Gordon Ramsay and Heston Blumenthal. Would you have heard of the chefs, I wonder, if it weren't for Alan? He was the creator of the modern-day phenomenon that is the celebrity chef. He was the Dr. Frankenstein who saw the public relations potential of the monsters skulking in the kitchen. His clients did not include Jamie, Gary, Gordon and Heston, but Alan was the man who set the ball rolling back in the eighties, after he'd left Kennedy's. He and his wonderful wife, Elizabeth, had their own PR business that specialized in promoting the cooks as well as the food. Before then, chefs weren't really discussed in editorial conference.

Alan knew the restaurant business well and had a great palate. He was the master of the long lunch. I have never known anyone go into battle like Alan. You could have a conversation with him in an empty

restaurant at two o'clock in the morning when he was virtually coma-
tose but he'd still manage to come up with ideas as his eyelids flick-
ered. And the next morning he would be at his desk at nine, putting
those ideas into action. He was on the ball.

A few years ago I had an extremely long lunch with Anthony Ellis,
chief executive of Carlton Food Network. Anthony and I had enjoyed
four bottles of Tiagnello, a powerful Tuscan red, when Alan arrived at
the restaurant and bounded up to our table, full of energy. "That's not
fair," he said after asking how much we'd had to drink. "You two are
well ahead of me." He was determined to catch up and catch up
quickly, so he ordered two bottles of Tiagnello and a burgundy glass,
which holds an entire bottle. He poured a whole bottle into the glass
and downed it in one. Then he got the next bottle, filled up the burgundy glass and demolished that as well. It was an amazing sight.
Alan looked at his astonished companions and said, "I am now on
your level." Though having drunk the wine so quickly he only managed to utter those six words, then he was totally fucked, off the walls.

One day I got a phone call from the Lanesborough Hotel, in Hyde
Park Corner. Alan had spent a long afternoon there and staff had had
to help him out of the building. On the hotel steps he had clasped on
to the railings and wouldn't loosen his grip. Something inside him
was saying the evening was not yet over. Staff tugged at him but he
hung on like a man dangling from the cliff top, the sea lashing the
rocks below.

He was a tortured soul, but he was also immensely clever; in his
youth he had been accepted at Oxford but turned down the place. He
could be drunk but still profound and would come out with highly intelligent comments and witty remarks. His memory was faultless and
he could recite meals he had eaten decades earlier.

Looking back to those early days when I was a regular at Kennedy's,
Alan was always kind enough to give me free drinks, and we would talk
food and restaurants, and one day he said to me, "You're going to be
the first British chef to win three Michelin stars."

NINE

Dining with the Bear

MY DAYS AT Gavroche came to a hasty, unexpected end in September 1982, when Albert picked up a soup ladle and began waving it in front of my face in the middle of his three-star kitchen.

I was feeling grouchy anyway. For a week or so I'd been suffering from a stomach problem—the beginning of my ulcer, maybe—but I still turned up at the kitchen every day and worked late into the night. I was a sleep-deprived, mop-haired wreck with a stabbing pain in my belly, and when head chef René rounded on me with a thunderous verbal assault, I answered back. I can't even remember what started him off; I have no recollection of what I was supposed to have done wrong. But Roux robots were not supposed to answer back—it showed a fault in the programming—and my attempts to defend myself only increased the volume of René's rant.

The sound of the commotion must have penetrated the glass walls of Albert's office and he emerged at a galloping pace, swooping up a ladle from a kitchen surface. He was the knight embracing his lance, and he was heading toward me. Was he going to dispose of me with a long-handled, copper kitchen implement? Was I about to be ladled? Adrenaline pumped through my twenty-year-old body, but with my stomachache and exhaustion, I didn't have the patience to stand there and take a bollocking from the boss. Albert stopped his charge when he was a foot in front of me and raised the upended ladle into the air, moving it in a pecking motion in front of my face.

The spoon part of the ladle came toward the bridge of my nose, then, before it could touch me, it was swiftly retracted. Forward, back, forward, back in pendulum fashion, though metal and skin never connected. Albert stared at me and, swinging his ladle, he uttered the words, "Now [peck] . . . you [peck] . . . listen [peck] . . . to [peck] . . . me [peck] . . . my [peck] . . . little [peck] . . . bunny [peck]."

"My little bunny"—now that was patronizing. By all means give me a bollocking and shout at me, I thought, but please don't patronize me. I grabbed the spoon. "That's it," I said to him, as the rest of the robots carried on mechanically with their chores. "I don't like being patronized. I don't need this shit." Then I marched. I marched out of the kitchen, changed out of my whites and buggered off. I don't think Albert tried to stop me leaving, and anyway, I scarpered pronto. The magic chef's little bunny vanished.

I found work at a small restaurant on the other side of the river, in Battersea Park Road. We only did about thirty covers a night, but boy did those customers eat well, because I was cooking them Gavroche style food at a fraction of the price. The kitchen was run by a man called Alan Bennett—no, not the playwright. We got on well and I would later work for him at the restaurant he owned, Lampwick's, in nearby Queenstown Road. When I look back on it now, I can see that Alan was a very gentle man, soft and kind, and perhaps I needed reminding that the world was full of such people. In the kitchens where I had worked, there wasn't much gentleness, no softness or kindness, and my social life was nonexistent: I didn't have a girlfriend to give me affection.

It was in December that I bumped into Albert, and he was extremely apologetic about the way it had all ended at Gavroche. "Why don't you come back?" he asked, and I didn't need much time to think about it. In the interim period of a couple of months I had reflected on the soup-ladle incident, and now I could appreciate the comedy behind my departure. My decision to leave had been irrational, I told myself, so I accepted Albert's offer and pitched up to start my second stretch at Gavroche.

It didn't last long. The magic wasn't there anymore. In that short period of time, from September to December, my friends Roland Lahore,

Danny Crow and Stephen Yare had gone, moved on. I saw the restaurant in a different light. What had previously seemed grand, exquisite and stylish no longer had the same effect upon me. I wasn't blinded by the silver anymore. At some point early in 1983 I left Gavroche once again, this time on the most amicable terms. I left the restaurant but I didn't leave the company. I took a job at the Roux brothers' spectacularly upmarket butcher shop, Boucher La Martin, in Ebury Street.

Based on the Parisian shop of the same name, Boucher La Martin was run by Mark Bougère, the highly gifted chef who had been Albert's right-hand man when I had joined the company nearly two years earlier. We not only supplied Albert's restaurants; we also provided fine meat and poultry to the well-heeled shoppers of Chelsea and Knightsbridge. Being a butcher—or rather, a Roux butcher—has to be one of the toughest jobs I have ever done.

The working day started at five thirty in the morning. My first duty was to prepare the ducks. Entering the bird's back cavity, let me tell you, requires the utmost skill. A lot of people are too heavy-handed, and when they're finished, you could drive a bus up the back cavity. At Le Boucher I had to master the skill of opening up the cavity so that it was just large enough to get my fingers in and carefully scoop out the insides without staining the bird with its blood. The liver and heart were brought out whole, as were as the lungs, which had to be removed because if cooked, they add a bitterness to the final flavors. Each morning I would prepare about twenty ducks, their sharp bones stabbing my fingers. To ease the soreness I would have to wash with cold water and a bit of bleach.

The duck process took me about four hours and then I would tend to the customers in the shop. This was not the sort of butcher's where you'd walk in and simply buy a chicken. Everything was prepared to order. If a customer wanted a poulet de Bresse for a fricassée, then I would chop it up accordingly; if it was a chicken for roasting, then the bird would be beautifully tied and trussed. I had to be disciplined with my knife and hands and I had to work quickly. In the end it shut down, but Boucher La Martin has to have been one of Britain's finest butcher shops and is another credit to the legendary Albert.

Although money had never played an important role in my life, in the fall of 1983 I spotted an opportunity to earn a fortune and that is what seduced me away from the butcher shop and the Roux brothers' empire. There was a pub called the Six Bells serving the punters who shopped in the hustle and bustle of the King's Road and I learned that the landlord was looking for a head chef. When I turned up to see him, he seemed quite impressed by my experience and offered me the job. However, he was adamant about the money. "I'll give you a staff budget of five hundred pounds a week," he said. "That's your budget. Spend it how you like." Maybe he thought I'd have to take on a staff of five and a washer-up, but I had devised a way of earning a staggering amount of money. I paid myself £400 per week, which was a fortune for a chef then, and even by today's standards would be good money for a pub chef. That left me with £100 from the budget, so I hired a sous chef who was about my age, an American lad called Mario Batali. There was no cash left for a washer-up, so Mario and I agreed to share the chore. I was quite proud of the deal—signs of my business brain were evident even back then. We did a menu of good lamb and sweet-breads and crayfish, that kind of thing.

Sturdy Mario, with his mass of red hair, was an interesting and spe-cial guy, but not half as interesting as he would later become. After get-ting a degree in Seattle, he came to London to train at Le Cordon Bleu, but he got bored with the college course and chucked it in—Cordon Bleu's loss was my gain. He used to work hard during the day and play hard during the night and then he couldn't get out of bed in the morn-ing. So he loved his sleep and he loved Joy Division (he'd incessantly hum "She's Lost Control"), but he also loved his food. He was passion-ate about cooking. What he needed was a bit of discipline, so I found myself treating him as harshly as I had been treated by my former head chefs. I used to murder Mario every day, physically, mentally and emo-tionally. I called him "Rusty Bollocks" but he was funny and intelligent.

He responded to bollockings. Even though he may have faked it, he responded to them. If he cocked up a dish, then it would go in the bin and he'd apologize and pretend to understand. I would push him along—"Move it, Rusty Bollocks, faster, faster"—and after service we'd head off clubbing in the West End, though it was almost impos-sible to pull birds with him.

One day I sent him out to get some tropical fruits and he returned with a bag of avocados. To this day, I do not know if he was taking the mickey.

From the tiny kitchen of that pub I would eventually go on to win three Michelin stars while Mario returned to the States, where he's today hailed as the king of New York's restaurants and his places include Babbo and Lupa. He's won a heap of awards and plaudits including "Man of the Year" from GQ magazine. Although we only worked together for a matter of months, he regards me as a mentor, which is nice, and in interviews he often mentions me in entirely affectionate terms. For instance, in July 2004, he said, "[Marco] was a genius, and an evil one at that. Last time we spoke he had launched a hot pan of risotto at my chest in service."

A few years after we'd worked together, Mario's parents came for dinner at my restaurant, Harveys, and introduced themselves. They were very pleasant people, but I remember looking at his mother and thinking, I can't believe something Mario's size came out of you.

I finally jacked in the job at the Six Bells in spring 1984 because I missed working in fine kitchens. The pub wage, while amazing, was outweighed by an overwhelming desire to cook in the best restaurants. There was also an incident with the barman at the Six Bells. We were having an argument one day when he said to me, "At least I've got a mother." He saw a look of anger cross my face. Then he picked up a knife, as if to warn me off, and I tried to grab it. The blade sliced the palm of my hand and the scar is still there today. Once I had the knife, I chinned him. Motherless readers will sympathize.

THE FINEST RESTAURANTS in London in the summer of 1984 were Chez Nico, Gavroche and La Tante Claire. I had worked in the first two, but still, I needed to acquire knowledge and experience, so thought I'd try my luck at La Tante Claire.

It was a small restaurant in Royal Hospital Road, Chelsea, and while it had neither the magic of the Box Tree nor the grandness of Gavroche, it was run by one of the most gifted chefs of his time. French-born Pierre Koffmann, who years earlier had worked with the Roux brothers and had picked up his second Michelin star in 1980. Known as Pierre the Bear, he was a big, bearded man somewhere in his forties and he served big, hearty food such as pavé de boeuf, pig's trotters and turbot à la grande moutarde. He also had a reputation for being hard but straight—no bullshit—and it was said that he employed only French chefs.

English and proud of it, I turned up and knocked on the door, just as I had done six years earlier at the Hotel St. George and then later at Le Gavroche. I told Pierre that I had worked at the Box Tree, but it didn't matter—there was no room at the inn, so to speak. "I'm sorry," said Pierre. "I have no vacancies, simple as that." Then he added, "Why don't you go and ask at Le Gavroche? They might have something going."

It sounds silly now, but I didn't want to tell him I had already worked at Gavroche. Perhaps I was just reluctant to get into that conversation, because when I thought of Gavroche, the first image that came into my mind was of a soup ladle pecking my nose, and Pierre had better things to do than stand there and listen to that story. "But it's here that I want to work," I insisted. "Not at Gavroche. I really want to work here at Tante Claire."

Again he came back with, "But I haven't got any vacancies."

I had no choice. "I'll tell you what I'll do," I said, "I'll work for nothing." Pierre wasn't going to turn down a freebie and he swiftly ushered me into the kitchen so I could start my new job, or rather, "pastime," because for the first month of working in his small kitchen I wasn't paid a bean.

I think that even Pierre, who was seriously passionate about food, was slightly taken aback by my enthusiasm. I worked hard through my breaks and often felt his gaze upon me as I whipped up sauces and speedily prepared dishes, absorbing the pressure of his Michelin-starred restaurant. When he asked me to do some specialties, I produced dishes mastered at Gavroche, and that's when the penny dropped. Clearly confused as he watched me rustle up dishes being served by Albert Roux's team, Pierre said, "Marco, where did you learn those things?"

I turned to my perplexed boss; it was time to come clean. "I used to work at Gavroche," I told him and then carried on whipping and speedily preparing.

Although I was thrilled to be working at Tante Claire, I saw many other chefs come and go. In fact, Pierre's kitchen had staff turnover like I've never seen. Every week the brigade went from ten chefs on a Monday to four by Friday, and this is why: At the beginning of the week a batch of six chefs would arrive from France, dispatched by one of Pierre's Parisian contacts. They would start off jolly, thrilled and privileged because they were working for the great Monsieur Koffmann. But they soon cracked.

To begin with, they couldn't take Pierre's bollockings, his insistence on perfection. Most of the time, Pierre had a big palette knife in his right hand, and chefs who fell behind would get a whack on the arse. "Is he always like this?" the French lads would whisper to me. Their lives were made even more wretched by the claustrophobic conditions. The kitchen was cramped and our work surface was a big table in the middle. Like sardines in a tin, we had to fight for space. As the week went on, they would drop out. By Tuesday, we might be one man down, then another would fail to show up on Wednesday; the remaining Frenchmen would invariably break on Thursday. Come the following Monday morning a new batch of chefs would arrive from France, like troops going over the top.

Then came Pierre's day of reckoning: his new recruits failed to make the Channel crossing, I imagine, so he made me an official member of staff. The pay was pitiful and I was glad of my savings from the Six Bells. French recruits aside, there were now four regulars working at that table in the kitchen: Pierre and his assistant, Bruno, and then the English contingent, i.e., me and the kitchen porter, Big Barry, whom Pierre adored.

Pierre was a workaholic who got through the day by having three ritualistic tea breaks. Each break lasted precisely five minutes and took place at a specific time—the first was at noon; the second at six forty-five, just before evening service; and the third at the end of evening service at ten thirty. The tea was always made by Big Barry, who, as a reward for serving it, was allowed a cuppa himself. No one else in that kitchen was entitled a tea break. It was a rule that distinguished the boss from his minions.

However, one morning just before midday, I heard the kettle go on and saw Barry reaching for the tea bags when Pierre shocked me by asking, "Would you like a cup of tea?" It is probably the most common question asked in tea-loving Britain but there, in Koffmann's kitchen, it was a question I had never heard. Positively flattered, I joined Pierre and Barry for a noon cuppa and then, at six forty-five, my self-esteem was boosted once more when Pierre asked those special words, "Would you like a cup of tea, Marco?" Again, at ten thirty, I was handed a steaming mug of Tetley. I had made it into the inner circle. Tante Claire's elite club had just increased its membership by a third. The duo had become a trio.

Pierre had finally recognized my talents and devotion to the job, and what's more, his lovely wife, Annie—who ran the show in the front of house—took a shining to me. I came to realize that if Annie liked you, then her husband would think twice about getting rid of you. However, it was not as easy to endear myself to the other members of the French staff who worked front of house. Traditionally, Pierre's wife had looked after the restaurant, but when I was there she had just had a baby, and so she only came in for a couple of hours each day. This meant the maître d' was running the show. He looked a bit like Dracula and I don't recall him being very friendly to me. I convinced myself that he saw me as the English boy, the one he and the waiters didn't like.

Every day there was a staff lunch before service and everyone would eat the meal in the restaurant, but because I always worked through my breaks, sweeping the backyard or preparing some scallops, I had never gone for lunch. One day, however, Pierre said, "Leave your work, Marco, and come through for some lunch." I couldn't say no to the boss, so I helped myself to some food from the kitchen and went through to the restaurant to join the rest of the team. The chefs and waiters were all sitting together at a large table but there was no room for me and I was reluctant to ask someone to move up. I started to walk back through to the kitchen—I would have my lunch in there—when I noticed that a smaller table had been laid. One little table with one chair, one napkin, one knife and one fork. It had been laid for me, but there was no way I was going to sit there alone. I'm not having that, I thought, I'm not going to be treated like an idiot.

Pierre spotted the problem. "Everyone move up," he yelled at the staff. "Marco, come and sit next to me." It was the only time I had been in Tante Claire's dining room and it would be a few more years before I could walk in there again, as a paying customer.

After service Pierre would sometimes offer to give me a lift somewhere and I'd ask him to drop me in the King's Road. I might go to the Up All Night, where you could, surprisingly, sit up all night drinking coffee. I met girls and they seemed to find me amusing, but relationships rarely progressed further. My success rate at pulling wasn't great because I didn't have a huge amount of courage when it came to making the first move. I was in the Up All Night with Eddie Davenport, the young clubbing entrepreneur, when he introduced me to a posh girl whom I shall call Suzie. She was a beautiful girl, but for weeks nothing happened between us. Sometimes I would stay at Suzie's flat in Chelsea, sleeping on the floor while she was in her bed. Then one night she just came and cuddled up with me and after that we started going out with each other.

I was in the kitchen one lunchtime when Pierre the Bear said, "Your old boss Albert is here." I glanced around, expecting to see my former mentor clutching a soup ladle. "No, he's in the restaurant," said Pierre. "He's come for a meal. You can make it for him." Albert ordered the Gelée de Lapin aux Champignons Sauvages, which, I must say, I went to a lot of trouble to make. I took care to ensure it was pretty and arty, then I placed the dish on the passe for Pierre's approval, but he didn't compliment me on the presentation. Instead, he raised a hand above the plate and brought it crashing down onto the food. Then, as if he were playing a piano concerto with one hand tied behind his back, he used his chunky fingers to mess up the dish. Rabbit terrine and mushrooms that had once looked glorious became a pile of roughed-up rubbish. Without saying a single word, Pierre had told me precisely what he thought of Albert Roux.

TEN

Raymond Blanc: The Oxford Don

A**LBERT ROUX AND** Pierre Koffmann may have had little time for one another, but they would have both agreed on one thing: discipline was the way to run a kitchen. The prospect of receiving a loud bollocking from either chef forced me to discipline myself: arrive on time, keep surfaces tidy, absorb the pressure and cook well. But there is a major flaw in severe discipline. It suppresses flair, imagination and talent. At Gavroche, remember, Albert was the one who came up with the menus and his brigade of Roux robots didn't dare alter the recipes.

"Do this" was the command.

"Yes, Chef" was the response.

I had never really paused to question the screaming and shouting. It seemed natural to me and I had come to accept it. "Must be prepared to take bollockings" was part of the job description. But when I was twenty-three years old, after I had done time with Roux and Koffmann, I found myself working for a chef who was soft and inquisitive. He was a man who actually asked for my opinions and who wanted to know about my passion for food. In fact, Raymond Blanc was so enthusiastic and encouraging that I discovered a sense of freedom, and that is when my confidence started to grow. It seemed as if I had done painting by numbers and now I was being given a blank (or perhaps Blanc) canvas.

It was Nico Ladenis who, in the winter of 1984, told me about a job going at Le Manoir aux Quat'Saisons, Raymond's country house hotel in Great Milton, some eight miles from Oxford. Nico had called to say that one of Raymond's chefs, Nigel Marriage, had handed in his notice, thereby creating a vacancy. Although Le Manoir had been open only for about six months, it was doing very well and was destined to win awards and become a huge success. In fact, the hotel's restaurant already had two Michelin stars to its name, as Raymond had been allowed to transfer them from his restaurant Les Quat'Saisons in Oxford.

"You've got to ring Raymond," insisted Nico. I was working for Pierre but I made the call and arranged an interview date.

My former employer Alan Bennett, by now a good friend, offered to drive me to the interview. We arrived at Le Manoir, originally Great Milton's manor house, and my first impression of Raymond was, "Christ, he's small." The look on his face said he was thinking, "Wow, he's big." I did not get the job there and then. Raymond asked me to fix a date when I could do a two-day trial period in his kitchen.

Although the interview is a blur, I have a vivid, treasured memory of the meal that followed our chat. My chauffeur Alan had been kicking his heels for about an hour while I was being grilled, so to speak, and he had developed an appetite. When I said I was ready to leave, Alan declared that he had absolutely no intention of driving home until he had lunched in the restaurant. He invited me to be his guest and I accepted.

It was probably the finest meal I had ever eaten and certainly the most expensive. The bill for the pair of us came to £134 (and I wasn't even a drinker in those days). I can see each dish now as if it were on the table in front of me. I started with Terrine of Foie Gras with Leeks, Truffle and Wild Mushrooms; then I had Salad of Offal, which was made up of calf's sweetbreads and calf's brains; as a main course I had Pigeon en Croûte de Sel with a Sauce Périgueux (a Madeira-based sauce with veal jus and chopped truffles); and I ended the feast with a fantastic Soufflé de Pommes.

It wasn't necessarily the ingredients that made the meal so magnificent. As I moved from one course to another, I studied each plate, and then it eventually dawned on me that these were the sort of dishes the best chefs in France were serving. Raymond was clearly more in touch with the development of cuisine in Paris than either Albert or Pierre. He was doing something new and exciting.

Magazines and books had kept me up to date with how the great chefs in Paris were refining the classical dishes, so while Albert was giving his customers classical cuisine—often masculine, hearty dishes like Daube de Boeuf (braised cheeks of beef in a robust sauce)—Raymond's food was more feminine. The foundations of his food were classically French, but the concept was lighter. There were no full-bodied sauces. Raymond knew that Mother Nature was the real artist.

To illustrate the point, let's compare the veal dishes served by Messrs. Roux and Blanc:

At Gavroche we did Veau à l'Ananas, which was 140 grams of veal fillet cut into small medallions, put into the pan briefly and then taken out; a touch of chicken stock was put into the same pan with a bit of curry sauce and hollandaise—you had to work it so it didn't scramble—then back in went the veal along with big batons of pineapple; it was served with toasted almonds on top and in a dish with rice on the side.

In contrast, Le Manoir served an Assiette de Veau, which was veal fillet with the spinal cord on top of it, but on the same plate were three slices of brain and three slices of sweetbread. The visual impact was improved because on top of each slice of brain was a mixture of capers, lemon and parsley cooked in butter. And then another touch to the picture: on top of each slice of sweetbread was a mixture of flaked almonds and pine kernels, which had been ground in butter. Very light.

Raymond not only used more ingredients than his rival Albert, he also invested more energy in the presentation. At Le Manoir six or seven pans were used for one dish, which meant that three main courses could involve twenty pans. Le Gavroche's Veau à l'Ananas was all done in one old-fashioned flambé pan.

"What did you think?" asked Alan as we headed down the M40. "It was visual," I said. "There was freshness and lightness but it was so visual." What I was really saying was, "I like his style. I want that job."

A few weeks later I was back at Le Manoir for my trial period. On the first day I worked with Nigel Marriage, whom, fingers crossed, I would replace. I was also reunited with Stephen Yare, my old friend from Gavroche, who now worked in Raymond's kitchen. The kitchen, incidentally, was tiny then. It was almost as if Raymond had set out to create an excellent hotel and restaurant in this old Cromwellian manor house but had given no thought to the kitchen from which to feed his guests. Its size, however, would work to my advantage. It is far better to work in a small kitchen than a large one because that way you learn more: you are always close to the action—if you're on the garnish, you can still see what's going on with the fish, or meat or hors d'oeuvres.

On day two Raymond came into the kitchen and said to me, "I would like you to cook me a meat dish for lunch." I sensed it was make-or-break time. What would I give him? Or rather, what would I *need* to give him to get the job?

A few weeks earlier I had seen a cookery book that contained dishes by a Michelin-starred French chef called Jacques Maximum. One of the dishes was a tienne of lamb that was sliced and presented on the plate in a circular fan shape. What he had done looked as interesting as pink meat on a plate can look, yet it was clearly enough to inspire me. I thought I would cook the lamb for Raymond's lunch, but I would try to improve on Maximum's idea.

I pan fried the fillet of lamb and cut it into rondelles, just as Maximum had done, arranging it so that in the center of the plate there was a single circular piece of lamb, with the other pieces fanning out around it. On the outside of the fan I created another circle: a tiny turned potato sat next to a stuffed courgette, which was next to an aubergine, then another potato, and so on, until the circle was complete. I put tomato fondant on the aubergine and maybe on the courgette.

Then I added a couple of black olives to the dish. The plate was now the round border of a symmetrical picture of Provençal-style ingredients. I suppose it was circles within circles. Over the lamb I poured the roasting juices, juices that had been enhanced with rosemary at the end of the cooking to retain the freshness, and then I split the juices with a dash of olive oil.

The plate went out to the restaurant, where Raymond was sitting. It came back clean, closely followed by the man who had eaten from it. "Delicious," said Raymond, who looked slightly shocked; I think because he had expected me to do a Gavroche-style dish. I was pleased, obviously, that he didn't mention Jacques Maximum and assumed that he thought the whole thing had come out of my head.

But I had tapped into Raymond. When you think about it, the ingredients I had given him were always going to work because we all know that lamb, rosemary and Provençal vegetables go well together. What was significant was what I had done with the ingredients. I had given him a dish that was fresh, light, and above all, visual. It had everything that he responded to in food. Surely Raymond realized then that I was on the same wavelength as him.

However, he set me another challenge, asking me to cook him a fish dish for his dinner. I could only work with the ingredients that were in the fridges and ended up doing Panaché of Red Mullet and Sea Scallops with a Bouillabaisse Sauce. I can't recall how I cooked it or how I presented it, but I don't remember a complaint from Raymond.

I completed the trial, left on a Saturday, and on Sunday I got a call from Stephen Yare. He told me that Raymond had served his customers my tienne of lamb as a specialty. I was flattered and then came the offer of the job.

It was January 1985 and my days of virtual solitude were about to change. Five of us, including Stephen and his brother, Desmond—who worked on Pastry—decided to move in together, and we went to inspect the Bridge Inn in nearby Wheatley. Set beside the river, it seemed nice enough. We did a deal with the owner, took the rooms for a year, and I nabbed the only one that had an ensuite bathroom. "We have a nightclub here on Fridays and Saturdays," said the owner as he was handing us the keys, "and there's an admission charge. But as you're living here, you won't need to pay. You can get in for nothing."

We beamed with glee. It was as if we had just been awarded lifetime membership to an exclusive club in Mayfair.

After our first night we compared notes and all agreed that the place was overrun with mice. The Bridge Inn was infested. From then on we referred to our new home as either the Mouse House or, inspired by our place of work, Maison Mouse.

After our first Friday at work we returned late at night, pretty shattered. Deafening music blared from Maison Mouse. It was Fingles, the nightclub to which we got free entry. The club was directly beneath my bedroom and the earsplitting amplifiers rattled everything in the room, including me. I talked to the other lads and together we decided to take advantage of the free admission.

Fingles was the roughest nightclub in history. The blokes were rough, the girls were rough and the doormen were rough. They were all out to get pissed, get shagged and have a fight. Fingles was a rathole in the Mouse House. It took ten minutes to get from a table to the bar, not because there was a sea of people to push through but because the floor was littered with so much chewing gum you had to stop every three paces to peel the goo from your heels, otherwise you'd be glued to the carpet. Young, drunk lunatics pogoed along to Duran Duran's "Wild Boys," and there were cheers as the DJ played tracks by an up-and-coming singer called Madonna. Every now and again a punch-up would erupt and the "dancers" would form a ring around the brawlers.

To think that just days earlier we had gratefully clutched the hand of the owner as he awarded us VIP status. Now we wanted to throttle him. On Friday and Saturday nights, I would sit in Fingles with my Coca-Cola, observing the show. The thud of the music meant that Stephen and I became expert lip-readers. And I never scored. I was still far too inept at chatting up birds, and anyway, none of the Fingles girls ever walked over to my table; perhaps the chewing-gummed floor prevented them making the journey. In Chelsea I'd seen a bit of posh, but the Fingles mob reminded me of the Leeds I'd been happy to leave behind. It seemed strange that I had done time in the King's Road, the buzziest place in Britain, and was now enduring a rather dull social life of which the highlight was a darts match in the local pub. There was one positive. During my days in Oxford I met Piers Adam one night in Brown's, a burgers-and-steaks restaurant that's still in business. Piers was standing at the bar, surrounded by beautiful girls, and introduced himself. He went on to become a highly successful nightclub impresario and we are still friends to this day and have been business partners.

The fact is, I had no real desire to socialize. If I could have been in the kitchen at two in the morning, that is where I would have been. The schedule at Le Manoir suited me perfectly. I would start off on the Meat section working a six-day week from January to the end of the year. There were no summer holidays for staff and no Easter breaks. Staff were only allowed to take holiday in the following January, when Le Manoir shut its doors to the public for a fortnight or so.

Somewhere along the way, it seemed, I had developed a reputation for being oblivious to bollockings. Stephen told me how Raymond had announced my arrival during his Christmas speech, "We have a new boy starting next month. His name is Marco White and he has worked for Albert Roux, Pierre Koffmann and Nico Ladenis. None of them could break him."

Raymond was certainly not going to be the one to break me. Though gifted in many ways, he desperately lacked the authority of his Michelin-starred rivals. He was like the headmaster who was too kind to discipline the wayward miscreants in his seventeen-strong brigade.

Stephen and I (as well as the other Roux robots who had washed up at Le Manoir) took advantage of Chef's gentle nature. The pair of us ruled the roost. Our bond, if you like, was that we had come from the same world. And at Le Manoir, we were synchronized. If I did Fish, Stephen did Meat; if I did Meat, then Stephen did Fish. That's all we ever did. We worked well together, were never disjointed, and we respected each other.

We also respected Raymond and were never foolish enough to be ill-prepared for service. But when the opportunity arose, we were like kids who had been let loose in the playground. Stuck in the middle of nowhere, we craved light relief, practical jokes and fun. I would answer the kitchen phone by pretending to be an answering machine. "Please leave a message after the tone," I'd say, before letting out a high-pitched shriek to give the caller a migraine.

It was that sort of immature humor, sometimes cruel and merciless. A catering-college student arrived one day to do a bit of work experience and the all-male brigade decided—in a typically childish way—that she was the size of a bear. The poor girl was given the chore of shelling peas for a day, and as she got on with this menial task, the boys, one by one, ambled past her putting stickers on her back. After a couple of hours her back was plastered with ridiculous messages: "Do not feed the bear," "I love Raymond," that sort of thing. Raymond wandered into the kitchen and was horrified when he saw the sticker-covered student but he didn't give us a bollocking. Gentleman that he is, he positioned himself next to the lass, saying something like, "Continue . . . I just want to see how you're getting on," while he removed the stickers, one by one, so she would never know of our wickedness. It just wouldn't have happened at Gavroche.

Raymond tolerated our wildness, but looking back I can see that it was not what he needed at the time. His marriage to his wife, Jenny, was not flourishing like the couple's business and they would later divorce. He must have been burdened by the preoccupations of his personal life, although it was a subject he never discussed with the staff.

There were weekly rows between Raymond, Jenny and the maître d'. Invariably, every Sunday the three of them would have an argument in front of the passe and the boys would bend down under the kitchen table and start banging the pans, egging Raymond to have a punch-up with the maître d'. "Chin him, Chef. Chin him," we'd shout. "Hit him. Don't take any shit."

Raymond, it might surprise you to know, was rarely in the kitchen. Unlike my former bosses, he did not stand at the passe barking out the orders during service. He preferred instead to stay front of house, schmoozing his guests. Charming and charismatic, he was the perfect host. When he did enter the kitchen, he tended to alternate between being a genius and a comedy act.

When he was at his best, he was the finest cook I have ever worked with. Note that I didn't say finest *chef* but finest *cook*, and there's a big difference. Albert Roux was a chef who could manage a kitchen and its staff. Albert could drive his troops forward, while Raymond lacked that quality. He was a three-star chef who never got his three stars.

When he wasn't being a genius cook, he was a funny, accident-prone figure—like Peter Sellers as Inspector Clouseau. He would often clumsily bang and crash into people and things before cursing at himself in his native tongue. When he came through the doors from the restaurant into the kitchen, his team could expect another installment of slapstick.

I remember him rushing into the kitchen and crashing headfirst into a waiter carrying a tray laden with glasses, sending everything soaring into the air. He also once set the grill alight when he forgot he was toasting almonds. And on another occasion he swiveled around by the kitchen stove and smashed his skull against a hanging saucepan— he had to lie down in a dark room because he was seeing stars and didn't resurface until the following morning.

Most of the time, though, he avoided the hanging saucepans, molten jam and flying glass, and that's when I really learned from him. He was masterful and magical. And what's even more remarkable is that Raymond never set out to be a chef. After leaving his home near the French-Swiss border in the early seventies, he had started out as a waiter in Britain. He found himself in Oxford, cooking at a restaurant called Les Quat'Saisons, and not only cooking but cooking well enough to win two Michelin stars. He had been canny enough to buy Great Milton's fifteenth-century manor house and had impressive plans to enlarge it. When I was at Le Manoir, it had a dozen bedrooms, but today it has thirty-two—and probably as many awards.

Although his creative influence was sporadic, it was more often than not inspired. He would get an idea for something—a vision— and then he would throw on an apron and get to work. I would watch and absorb. He showed me how to question every little part of creating a dish and taught me how to question my palate. A typical Raymond lesson would go like this, "Say you take two deciliters of chicken stock in two different pans. You reduce one down quickly, the other slowly. The taste of each stock is completely different because if you reduce something rapidly, you retain the flavor. By reducing it slowly it stews and you lose freshness and sharpness."

Or he might say, "If you're making a stock, taste it every fifteen minutes and try to understand what's happening in that pan. Try to understand how the taste is developing. You'll get to a point where it's delicious, and if you let it cook too long, it will start to die." When most people make a lamb stock, they throw in carrots, celery, onions and in the end it doesn't taste of lamb. At Manoir we'd use lamb bones roasted with caramelized onions and simply cover those two ingredients with water and a generous dollop of veal jus; it allowed the flavor of the lamb to come through in the sauce.

Preciseness was the name of the game; a crucial factor in the creation of Blanc's Michelin-standard dishes. If Raymond made a jus de pigeon, it simmered for twenty minutes exactly, rather than *about* twenty minutes.

Then there was the question of seasoning food. "Don't just chuck in some salt and think that you've seasoned it," he'd say. "Taste it, taste it, taste it. Get inside the food."

When people talk about seasoning, they usually mean adding salt and pepper. Seasoning to me is adding salt. Salt enhances the flavor of the ingredients. Pepper changes the flavor. You see chefs chucking in pepper as if it is a necessity, but they are failing to question why they are using it in the first place. They just think, Oh, seasoning. That's salt and pepper.

I very rarely season a sauce with pepper. I was taught to monter au beurre, where you use butter to emulsify the sauce at the end of cooking. The idea is to enrich it. But I stopped doing that because in my opinion, butter has a very strong flavor of its own. By putting butter into a pigeon jus or a lamb jus, you're adding another flavor and detracting from the natural flavor of the juices. So if I used anything, I would use a little bit of cream to stabilize, because cream is a neutral; it doesn't have a flavor.

EACH DAY AT Manoir I could feel my confidence growing. "Can you make me an asparagus mousse?" Raymond asked me one lunchtime.

I made the mousse and sent it through to his table in the dining room. I was smoking a Marlboro outside when Raymond suddenly came dashing through the kitchen's back doorway, full of excitement. "The mousse," he said to me, "it's spectacular. How did you make it?"

"With chicken, Chef. I made it with asparagus and chicken." He grabbed my arm and steered me back into the kitchen. "Make it again," he said and I had to reproduce the dish in front of Raymond, who studied every detail, nodding along as he made mental notes. The traditional ingredients of an asparagus mousse are asparagus, eggs, a little bit of milk and then some cream to lighten it. I had a problem with this traditional recipe because there's no texture or body. What I had done for Raymond was use chicken to give it the two features I felt were missing. On top of that, the chicken would provide flavor. I put asparagus, raw chicken and egg white into a liquidizer, then sieved it and added a little cream before cooking. That mousse—Chartreuse d'Asperges aux Truffes—became one of Le Manoir's specialties.

Raymond not only encouraged me to share my knowledge and thoughts about food; he also allowed me to get away with a little cheekiness—but there were limits. If I pushed it too far, I could seriously wind him up. I remember a Saudi prince coming for lunch one day and requesting a green salad. Raymond insisted he would make it himself and scampered into the vegetable garden, returning laden with lettuces. He dressed the vegetables beautifully, but a minute or two after the plate was sent out, it came back again. "The lettuce is gritty," explained the maître d'. Raymond had forgotten to wash it. I followed him around the kitchen, clutching the rejected plate and saying, "Chef, they've sent the salad back. Chef, they've sent the salad back." Eventually Raymond had had enough of me. I had crossed the line. "Yes," he snapped and then glared. "I know they've sent the fucking salad back."

Impressing the royals was one thing, but Raymond was never more excited than at the prospect of cooking for his rival Albert Roux. "We have had a booking from a Monsieur Roux," Raymond told the brigade late one afternoon. "Albert is coming to Le Manoir tomorrow." When we all arrived for work at eight forty-five the following morning, there was a mountain of mucky pots and pans rising from the sink to the ceiling and there was Raymond, manic and grimy, grafting away as he finished off dozens of canapés and petits fours. "This is the day Albert comes," he told us, as if we could have forgotten. I'm sorry to say that Raymond's efforts were in vain. The Roux who arrived for lunch that day was neither Albert nor a chef.

ELEVEN

White-Balled

THE WHISTLE DID not leave Raymond's mouth. He made up for his lack of control in the kitchen on the village green as he refereed our staff football match. Chef was now Ref. He bit the whistle, sucked it and every ten seconds blew hard, piercing the blissful tranquillity of Great Milton with its high-pitched rattle. On one team were Le Manoir's French waiters, and the other team was made up of the restaurant's chefs, who were mostly Brits. Raymond, as you can imagine, was doing all he could to swing the game for his fellow countrymen.

It seemed like every time the kitchen brigade got the ball, Raymond's cheeks would puff up and we'd hear the dreaded shriek of his whistle. It didn't matter whether or not we'd fouled; Raymond would stop play to award free kicks to the waiters and wave cards at the chefs with the agility of a croupier.

"This is crazy, Chef," I shouted a few minutes into the second half. "You're blowing the whistle every two seconds. You're nuts."

He flipped. For a second or two he was speechless, perhaps pondering my impudence. Then, crimson-faced, he raised an arm and pointed toward the sidelines. I thought I was about to be sent off, but instead he yelled, "You are sacked." I was astonished. The huddle of villagers who had gathered to watch the game started muttering. Great Milton had never known such drama.

I repeated the word back to Raymond, "Sacked?" It was all too comical for words, and when I started to snigger, Raymond looked puzzled.

"Why are you laughing at me, Marco?"

"Because when I get back to London I'll tell Albert that I was sacked for playing football and he's going to think you're a lunatic."

As I marched off the pitch, I heard him bark, "In my office at five thirty." I got changed and contemplated my next step in catering. It would be unfair if I lost my job, but I'd been around long enough to witness many bizarre and swift departures. I tried to reflect on the match rather than my future. Although it had been billed as the English versus the French, it was something akin to Millwall (chefs) versus Chelsea (waiters). In the kitchen we'd come up with a motto, an adage that explained our tactics: "The ball might go past but never the player." The waiters had certainly sustained a few injuries and maybe Raymond was right to be so whistle-happy.

At five thirty I went along to Raymond's office, which was next to the kitchen. It was not what the average person would describe as an office. Barely larger than a broom cupboard, it accommodated Raymond's tiny desk and chair, and he had to share the space with boxes of dried goods. "Come in, Marco. Close the door." Like a rebel in the head's office, I stood in front of Raymond's desk. I had to stand because the carton-sized room didn't allow space for a second chair. Would this be it? Was I to lose my job for calling him crazy on the pitch? Raymond, however, was remorseful and drained of rage. "Let's forget about what happened in the football game," he said and we shook hands.

I'd got my job back. In service that evening and for a few days afterward, the waiters were limping like walking wounded. Diners being greeted by black-eyed Frenchmen must have felt as though they'd stepped into the ER at Oxford General. The waiters never mentioned a rematch, though the staff at a rough hotel up the road were keen to take us on. They challenged us to a match on the village green and mistakenly assumed we were a bunch of wimps because we worked in a hotel with pink parasols in the garden. We faced each other on the pitch; they were all pristine in matching football gear while our brigade was a shambles in bits and bobs, ragged T-shirts, putrid socks and shorts. We stuck to our motto—The ball might go past but never the player—and hammered them 3–1.

Raymond and I quickly forgot the "sacking" incident. In a way, it strengthened our relationship and we became good friends. He had given up trying to break me, if indeed he had ever really intended to. "To break you," he once told me, "you need an iron bar across your back." I became the only member of the brigade to socialize with him and we'd go into Oxford to chat over coffee. He was a natural wit, deep and philosophical, and he trusted me. Not all the chefs in his brigade were given the freedom to come up with specialties, so the way he treated me was like a status symbol. I felt important. And even more so when Club des Cent, a group of one hundred gourmets, held a dinner at Le Manoir and Raymond put two of my specialties—my asparagus mousse and a pig's trotter dish—on the menu.

Gather round for a quick lesson: which tastes more of a tomato, a cooked tomato or a raw tomato? Get a tomato, cut it up and put one half under the grill. Have a bite of the raw tomato. Nice, isn't it? Now taste the grilled tomato.

So which one tastes more of tomato? Answer: the cooked one, because by cooking it you've removed the water content, and by removing the water you've removed the acidity and brought through the natural sweetness of the tomato. Cook an onion and you'll bring out more flavor for the same reason: because you're removing the acidity and water content. Whether you want to eat a raw tomato or a raw onion is irrelevant. What's got more flavor, a raisin or a grape? A raisin, because it is condensed. All that sugar is condensed. A prune or a plum? Yes, a prune. Now you've got it . . .

There was a problem with Le Manoir's style of cooking. When we did up to thirty or forty covers, it was most probably the finest restaurant in Britain. But when we had eighty or ninety covers, the system fell apart because the food was too complex. Each dish comprised so many components and different cooking techniques that it was extremely difficult to keep up. If you were doing a table of two, it was OK. But if you were doing a table of eight, then you could be stretchered.

You can afford to be frilly and artistic with cold food because it can be prepared before service. But when you're dealing with hot food, it's a different story. When we were doing big numbers at Le Manoir, there wasn't much chance of every component being cooked perfectly or presented in the way Raymond had intended; the cracks were visible. Someone might forget to put an ingredient on the plate, or customers would end up waiting a long time for their food. It goes back to my point about consistency. At forty covers the food was consistently good, but by eighty covers it had lost that consistency, and consistency is the thing that might have taken Raymond from two stars to three.

To make matters worse, Raymond would occasionally come into the kitchen to change things at the last minute. For all his elements of genius and spontaneity, he had an annoying habit of adding an ingredient, playing around with the picture on the plate, in the middle of service. "I don't like the presentation," he might say.

If Raymond asked if you were OK, the response had to be, "I'm fine, Chef." I didn't want him joining in. I kept my surfaces clean and tidy and that way Raymond thought I was all right. If there was mess all over the place, he reckoned I was in need of assistance. I was on Meat once when I sensed his presence and heard that chilling question, "Can I help you?"

"Can you do the duck please, Chef?"

"Where is it, Marco?"

"In the oven, Chef."

Raymond bent down, removed the pan from the oven and placed it on the stove. Then he took the duck from the pan, chopped up the bird, turned around without the cloth and seized the scorching pan handle with his bare hand. His palm sizzled and Raymond crouched down in agony. He had welded himself to the blisteringly hot metal. Even the customers in the restaurant must have heard his torture-chamber screams of misery. The skin on his palm rapidly tightened

and I zoomed in for an inspection of the claw. In the center of his purple palm there was a white dot, left by the hole where the handle hung
from a hook. I feel for him now, but at the time it was the sort of Raymond episode that made the brigade chortle.

Raymond came into the kitchen one day, shortly before lunch service on a Sunday, and headed toward Duncan Walker, who was on Hot
Starters and just about to slice the Terrine de Poireaux et St. Jacques.
The terrine is straightforward enough in terms of preparation—mix
it, mold it, steam it in between paper, add a bit of beurre blanc—but if
it's sliced too slowly or too quickly, the whole thing will collapse. You
have to get it just right. Duncan started to slice, with Raymond watching from just a few inches away, when, predictably, the terrine started
to cave in. Raymond must have been having a bad day and the sight of
the sinking terrine was just too much. He wrapped his fingers around
Duncan's oxlike neck and spat out the words, "You massacred my terrine. You massacred my terrine."

Duncan stood up to his full height of six feet and Raymond's fingers uncurled themselves, his grip loosening. "Bollocks," said Duncan, whipping off his apron, "and bollocks to your job." He chucked
the apron at Raymond's chest and started to motor out of the kitchen.
Raymond grabbed Duncan's arm to stop him from leaving, but the
beast was too powerful. The boss was dragged along the floor, almost
as if he were waterskiing. Raymond, defeated, turned to me. "That's
not good, Chef," I said.

Raymond, hair ruffled, said, "What's not good?"

"We've got no one on Hot Starters and nearly a hundred are
booked." So Raymond had to do Hot Starters.

Apart from the Mouse House tenants, I made another good friend
while at Le Manoir. One morning in June I was the first in the kitchen
and there was this lad, shelling peas, the sort of menial chore I had
done in my first job at the Hotel St. George in Harrogate. I was intrigued by him because it was a hot day but he was wearing a woolly
jumper.

"Who are you?" I asked.

"Heston."

"What are you doing?"

"I'm just here on work experience because I like cooking."

"Take off your jumper, Heston," I said. "I'll give you an apron."
That's how I met Heston Blumenthal. He tells the story slightly differently. In his account, he was working in the kitchen with a French chef who was trying to pick a fight with him. Apparently I said to Heston, "You don't want to work with the French. Come and join the English." He stopped what he was doing and came to work with me on my section.

He spent about a week working alongside me in the kitchen. On the second day he saw me fighting with a waiter. According to Heston, the waiter was clinging on to the work surface and I was trying to drag him out of the kitchen, but he wouldn't loosen his grasp.

Heston was trying to cook a dish one morning when Raymond wandered past, looking displeased with the way the lad was going about it. "Use your head," said Raymond. "Use your head. *Le tête*, my little baby, *le tête*." (Raymond often called his cooks "little baby"; it was patronizing but meant affectionately.) On these instructions, Heston bent down to the ramekins that were on the counter and started nudging them with his head. "What are you doing?" asked Raymond, puzzled. Heston replied, "You told me to use my head, Chef." You'd think he was being silly and ridiculing Raymond, wouldn't you? But I wouldn't be surprised if the pressure had got to Heston and all he was doing was obeying the command.

Heston seemed keen enough, but after his stint of work experience he decided cooking was not for him and went to work for his father's business.

It would be a few years before he reassessed his ambitions and we were reunited when I gave him a job in the kitchen at the Canteen. And it would be a few more years before our memorable meeting when we talked about a restaurant he was going to buy (with the help of his dad) and wondered what it should be called. "Why not call it the Fat Duck?" I suggested. "Because then its address will be the Fat Duck, Bray-on-Thames, and everyone will think it's got a view of the river. When they arrive and see that it hasn't, they'll hardly turn round and go home." He took my advice, and has since won three Michelin stars for the Fat Duck. Oh, and he's got an OBE.

During those summer months when the rest of the world was talking about that global jukebox Live Aid, at Le Manoir we were more excited about the cover coming off the swimming pool. If staff handed in their notice, they were carried past Raymond's cherished vegetable garden, through the grounds, squealing and kicking, and chucked fully clothed into the pool. Inevitably, it went too far.

I can still see the look of horror on Jenny Blanc's face as she stood at the side of the pool trying to absorb the vision before her: chefs and waiters ducking each other in the water (the English versus the French again). "What's going on?" she yelled. "We haven't even finished serving the customers."

Raymond, however, enjoyed the ritual and once led the pack toward the duck pond, suggesting it was a better place for a dunking. It was a wild scrap, with Chef pinning himself to the pond's surrounding wall so he didn't end up in the water. The soft headmaster had succumbed. There at the duck pond, Raymond Blanc was being as childish and silly as all his wild schoolboys. It would have made a lovely picture, with the fitting caption "If you can't beat 'em . . ."

TWELVE

Coming Home

DESPITE THE FUN, a year at Le Manoir was enough. Around about Christmas 1985, when my contract was coming to an end, I took stock of my life. The best chefs in Britain had trained me but I suppose I had always been intrigued by the great chefs in France, men I had never met. When I looked at a cookery book that had been produced by one of these Paris-based Michelin-starred masters, I was like a child engrossed in a fantastic fairy tale. Colin and Malcolm, the Boys who ran the Box Tree, had also filled my head with their stories of French restaurants. Places like Maxim's and Le Tour d'Argent seemed to me the epitome of grandness and elegance. Paris was the magical kingdom. I thought I should go there. Acquiring knowledge of cooking was far more important than staying in a job simply to rise through the ranks.

So I devised a plan that, on reflection, was not particularly well thought-out. The plan in twelve words: *Go to Paris, knock on kitchen doors and ask for a job*. My knocking knuckles had got me into this profession and my knocking knuckles had got me into Gavroche and into Tante Claire.

I phoned my Battersea-based friend Alan Bennett, who now lived above his restaurant, Lampwick's. Would he mind if I stayed at his place for a week before heading down to Dover for the cross-Channel ferry? My journey, however, contained a surprise destination. What happened next has echoes of the way in which I got my job at Gavroche after missing the coach back to Leeds. If I had not stopped off to stay with Alan, then I would never have ended up with Harveys, the restaurant that launched my career, changed my life and transformed me into the so-called rock star chef.

Stephen Yare was also moving on, but before we left Manoir, Stephen and I cooked up a diabolical farewell gift for our old commander. Raymond kept a camera by the passe that he would use to photograph new dishes: the brigade would then copy the presentation from the pictures. Quite clever, really. Before leaving Le Manoir, Stephen and I thought we would use the camera to take some snaps of each other, little mementoes by which Raymond could remember us. When it was my turn to pose, I got a pig's trotter, sat on the butcher's block, unzipped my fly and positioned the trotter so it was protruding from my crotch and resting on my thigh. In terms of maturity, Stephen and I had a long way to go.

We had reckoned on Raymond getting the film developed once we had left Le Manoir, but we realized our timing had been wrong when he stormed into the kitchen clutching a set of photographs. "You two, my office," he yelled, jabbing a finger toward us. I don't think I had ever seen him so angry. The three of us crammed into his miniature office and Stephen and I studied the floor while Raymond started, "Fucking hell, boys. I took the film to the chemist's. The lady there is very sweet and we had a nice chat. And then I go to pick up the pictures and she's laughing at me."

At this point he lobbed the envelope of photographs that he'd been clutching, and as it landed on our side of the desk, the snaps spilled out. I glanced down at them. The trotter's resemblance to a gigantic human penis was astonishing. "Sorry, Chef," I said, and Stephen feigned regret as well.

"And you, Marco," said Raymond, his voice a little softer, more caring. "Now I know why you can't get a girlfriend with something that size."

I left Manoir and have never been back. It's a bit like one of those love affairs that, when it ends, you think, I don't want to see her ever again. Although I've not returned, I continue to be friends with Raymond, however. Though weirdly enough, I have just had a call—out of the blue—from Raymond. "Come for lunch at Manoir," he said, and I've accepted the invitation.

I ARRIVED IN Battersea on a chilly January day in 1986 and, following Alan's instructions, I collected the keys from the blacksmith's beside Lampwick's. Once inside the flat I realized something was wrong: all the furniture had been removed except for a TV, a three-piece suite and a desk. When Alan returned home, he made the tea, sat me down and told me the story. His marriage had collapsed, he said, and his wife had left him. She had taken the kids, along with most of the furniture. Emotionally, the man was on his knees.

Business wasn't good. Lampwick's was in Queenstown Road, about a mile from Chelsea Bridge, and in the same road there were two Michelin-starred restaurants: Nico Ladenis's Chez Nico, and L'Arlequin where the chef was Christian Delteuil, the same chef who had interviewed me for a job at Chewton Glen back in 1981. On weekends Lampwick's snatched the punters who couldn't get a table at either of Alan's impressive neighbors, but on weeknights it was quiet.

In addition, Alan was drinking heavily—restaurateurs with sorrows to drown don't have to travel far for their next drink. I felt desperately sorry for him and when he started to say, "I'm in the shit. If you fancy staying on—" I could see what was coming and jumped in with, "Well, let's see. I mean, I can work for a bit to help out."

I revised my plan. OK, I convinced myself that I had revised my plan: work for nothing at Lampwick's and do a bit of work in Nico's kitchen; then when Alan was on the mend, I would be on that ferry to Calais. I'd give it a few weeks. Six months later I was still at Lampwick's, and as I was refusing to take a wage from Alan, I had chewed my way through my savings from Le Manoir. I would have to wait more than a decade to see Paris.

I had come from Le Manoir's seventeen-strong brigade, but in the kitchen at Lampwick's there were just three chefs, which included an assistant chef called Siân and the head chef, young Martin Blunos. Highly talented, hardworking and keen to learn, Martin had worked under Alan when the latter was head chef at a restaurant in Covent

Garden. Although Alan was a chef by profession, he tended not to interfere in the kitchen at Lampwick's, remaining mostly front of house, drinking with the regulars.

Martin was cooking classical French food, and I brought in my experience and, in particular, the special Manoir touch. So I would do Terrine of Leeks and Foie Gras for starters and maybe Pigeon en Vessie (pigeon cooked in a pig's bladder) as a main course, and for dessert I might do Terrine of Fruits. Martin was spongelike, absorbing every detail of each dish as I showed him how it was created. He has since said it was as if Roux, Koffmann and Blanc were there in his kitchen, giving him a lesson.

I taught him how to do Pigeon en Croûte de Sel, which I'd first had at Le Manoir on the day of my job interview. Done well it's a superb dish. The pigeon is gutted, trimmed, stuffed with thyme, then sealed and left to get cold. Then you make a salt pastry—salt, flour, egg whites—let it rest, roll it half an inch thick and mold it around the bird, carefully creating a pigeon shape. The excess pastry is used to make a little head with a small beak, with cloves for the pigeon's eyes. The whole thing is brushed with egg white, and sea salt is sprinkled on the breast part of the pastry, so that as the salt bakes, it colors the egg. It ends up with a varnished oak appearance. At Le Manoir the dish was carved at the table. The pastry head was removed and put to the side of the plate like a garnish; then the pastry body was cut so that the herby aroma steamed out to whet the appetite.

"We haven't got the space to carve it and we haven't got the staff," said Martin.

"We must," I told him. "That's the way they do it at Le Manoir." And we did.

It's not surprising that Martin went on to become a two-star Michelin chef with his restaurant in Bath, Lettonie, and more recently he won a star for the Lygon Arms in Worcestershire. He was passionate about food at Lampwick's, but he was more fascinated by his assistant, Siân. The couple went on to marry and have a family together. Martin says his memories of working with me include the times before service when we changed into our chef's whites. Real chefs don't wear underpants because working in hot kitchens can leave you with a painful condition known in the profession as Chef's Arse, which is caused by oversweating. Anyway, Martin remembers me showing him my testicles as we got changed, and that is what first springs to his mind when the name Marco Pierre White is mentioned.

Meanwhile, Suzie—the girl I met at the Up All Night before going to Le Manoir—came back into my life. With some style, I might add. I woke up in the middle of the night and she was sitting on the end of my bed. I said, "Suzie, what are you doing here?" She had put her hand through the letterbox and opened the door. She said, "I want to go to Yorkshire with you."

"When?" I asked, rather than why.

"Now."

She didn't seem quite right but I agreed to go with her. It would be an adventure, I thought, something spontaneous. We pulled into a petrol station near Selby on the A1 and she went into the shop. I opened up the glove compartment and all these drugs fell out—cocaine, speed, and God knows what the other drugs were, but they were drugs. So when she got back in I said, "What the fuck is this?" She went ballistic and told me to hand them over. I refused. She got out of the car, so I followed and put her back in it, then we drove off. There was a nationwide police manhunt going on at the time and I think someone must have seen me pushing Suzie into the car and suspected I was a kidnapper. We were half a mile from the petrol station when police cars surrounded us. I had to stuff Suzie's haul down the front of my trousers and no arrests were made. Suzie soon disappeared from my life.

I found a new girlfriend. Lowri-Ann Richards was three or four years older than me and a card-carrying member of the Chelsea set. LA, as she was known, was also something of a starlet. As previously mentioned, I had met her a few years earlier, before I left for Le Manoir, when she was going out with Robert Pereno. When she was "resting," as they say in the acting profession, she earned a living serving customers at Joe's Brasserie in Battersea, and I had bumped into her at Joe's after a session in the Lampwick's kitchen: "Didn't you used to go out with Robert Pereno?" That's how it had started. LA and Robert had been in a band called Shock before setting up another group, Pleasure and the

Beast—LA, in her revealing outfits, was the pleasure to Robert's beast. They released a single called "Dr Sex" but chances are you've never heard it. While they couldn't crack the charts, LA and Robert were revered in the King's Road as members of the hierarchy. Pleasure and the Beast were among the New Romantics who used to play at the highly trendy Blitz club, where, incidentally, a certain George O'Dowd worked as a cloakroom attendant before going on to become Boy George. Their stage performance was raunchy, bordering on outrageous, though they abandoned an Apache dance routine after Robert accidentally broke LA's arm while trying to impress the audience by throwing her about.

LA was a confident girl. As an actress, she did stage work mostly but she had appeared (as Jane) in the 1980 movie *Breaking Glass*, which starred the singer Hazel O'Connor and was a cult classic, a sort of punk version of *A Star Is Born*. Years later LA was a Welsh Tele-tubby, I think. At the time, though, she was just what I needed. There had been a year of celibacy at Le Manoir and I was craving a bit of at-tention: it was a draining experience mothering poor Alan. Finances weren't great and I needed stability in my life. LA was a caring person and, behind the façade of Chelsea vixen, she was utterly polite and the type of girl who would charm your parents. That and the mutual phys-ical attraction held together the relationship.

LA brought fun into my life. Together we would go to parties, bars and clubs. And when she landed a part, I would be there in the audi-ence. I went to see her in a show at the Players' Theatre and when she did panto in Swindon I had a seat in the stalls.

LA invited me to move into her place, a three-bedroom flat in Bat-tersea, and I hastily packed my trunk and escaped Alan's sparsely fur-nished pad. We shared the flat with her sister, Morfudd, who was a maître d' in a West End restaurant, and our home was a five-minute stroll from Lampwick's, in the appropriately named Sisters Avenue.

It was a good time to live south of the Thames. The phrase "yup-pie" had yet to be coined, but nevertheless, young upwardly mobile professionals were settling in up-and-coming areas like Clapham, Wandsworth and Battersea. They weren't just flash City blokes in chalky pinstripe suits; they were young men and women making a bit of cash and living one big party. They worked hard and played harder, drinking and eating to excess, and then using their staff expense accounts to reclaim the cost of their exuberance. Their parents had lived the Swinging Sixties, but the kids were swinging even more than their parents. These young professionals liked Chelsea—many of them had grown up there—but the property there was too expensive, so they crossed over to the south side of the river, where they could get more for their money. They flooded in, clutching their beloved copies of *The Sloane Ranger Handbook* and chuffed that they were still so close to Peter Jones and the bustling King's Road. All of a sudden SW11 was a cool place to live and its popularity sent property prices booming. I remember one friend buying a two-bed flat in Battersea for £25,000 and selling it eighteen months later for £80,000.

It was an exciting time in my life and my food was being noticed. Fay Maschler, the *Evening Standard*'s restaurant critic, came to Lampwick's for dinner one night and gave me my first review in the London newspaper. She was quite polite about the food but I have no recollection of what I must have done for her to describe me as "the volatile but rather beautiful Marco, his intensity can glaze a crème brûlée from ten yards."

Meanwhile, that black cloud finally showed signs of shifting from its seemingly fixed position above Alan's head. Two of Lampwick's regulars, a pair of property entrepreneurs, had asked Alan to go into business with them. Nigel Platts-Martin and Richard Carr had bought a wine bar called Harvey's, which served nothing more ambitious than well-cooked burgers to a hungover crowd that craved comfort food. Harvey's was in a good location, amid a pretty parade of Victorian shops on Bellevue Road, a couple of miles from Lampwick's, and it overlooked Wandsworth Common. Nigel and Richard intended to split the business three ways, the idea being that Alan would be the head chef, or that they'd hire Martin to run the kitchen. Grasping for a chance to improve his wretched existence, Alan agreed to the deal. He closed Lampwick's in the summer of 1986, which of course meant that I had lost a job, though I was pleased for my friend. The new venture was going to bring him the fresh start he so badly needed.

I got a job at Leoni's Quo Vadis, an Italian restaurant in Soho, which paid me the extraordinarily high salary of £350 a week. Years later it would pay me considerably more than that.

The head chef at Quo Vadis was an old boy known only as Signor Zucchoni. He had been cooking the same sort of Italian trattoria-style dishes for forty years and cooking them very well. He was a traditionalist in a tall white hat, and at the beginning he viewed me as some sort of peculiar beast. There were moments when I used to catch him studying me with a look of horror in his eyes. He was thinking, "Big man with long hair, not right."

I endeared myself to Signor Zucchoni by working very hard. Then when he asked about my background—"How come you·godda name like Marco"—I explained that I was half Italian and he smiled warmly, the same sort of smile that had crossed Danny Crow's face at Gavroche when I had mentioned my Italian roots. There was another way in which I won admiration from the boss and his assistant, Pepe. They both enjoyed a drink, so each day I would ask the restaurant manager for two bottles of wine, explaining that I needed to use them for the specialty dishes. Back in the kitchen, I handed the vino to my two superiors. They used it to pick up their spirits, rather than perk up my dishes.

When Jimmy Lahoud, the owner of Quo Vadis, opened Café St. Pierre on Clerkenwell Green, he asked me to be head chef and I took the job, but it didn't last long. My life was about to change dramatically and it all started with a phone call from Nigel Platts-Martin.

"Would you be interested in doing Harvey's with us?" said Nigel. I was confused. Surely Alan Bennett was going to be the chef. Not anymore, said Nigel. He and Richard didn't think Alan was up to it. Nevertheless, I felt there was something going on behind Alan's back; was I being approached without his knowledge?

"I can't step on Alan's toes," I told Nigel. "Sort out your problem with Alan. If he says he doesn't want to get involved in Harvey's, then sure, come back to me."

He did come back to me, about a week later. Nigel said Alan was most certainly out of the picture. Martin Blunos had lost faith in Alan and had gone off to work in Covent Garden. Then Nigel reiterated that he and Richard Carr had also lost faith. "But whatever we think of him as a person is irrelevant," added Nigel. "He hasn't been able to come up with the cash to buy his share in the business, so he can't be a partner. Simple as that. Do you want to be head chef?" asked Nigel.

"My problem," I replied, "is that I can't actually afford it, Nigel. I don't know where I'd get the money to invest . . ."

It was only later that I realized Nigel and Richard were not, in fact, asking me to be a shareholder. The thought had never crossed their minds. I had wrongly assumed they wanted me to fill the position left vacant by Alan. But by now they were only after a head chef. When I told Nigel that I didn't know where I would find the cash to invest, I had inadvertently put him and Richard in a vulnerable position. I had misinterpreted what they were offering, but now they were thinking, "Christ, we're opening a restaurant in six weeks' time. We haven't got a head chef and we don't know any chefs. To keep him happy we'll have to make him a shareholder."

In the end they arranged the finance for me. Richard acted as a guarantor for a bank loan of £60,000 and all I would have to do was establish an amazing restaurant that brought in enough money to pay off the loan, leaving me with some cash for rent. At the age of twenty-four, I was a chef patron, a chef proprietor.

The dining room was horrible and nasty. It looked like an English tearoom—pinks, greens and creams were everywhere you looked. It would have to change, eventually. But first I needed to find the staff. In October 1986, I phoned Michael Truelove at the Box Tree to see if he knew of anyone and he sent down a young chef called Simon Simpson, who I called (with affection) Simple Simon. I gave a job to Mark Williams, who had cheffed for Christian Delteuil at L'Arlequin. That made three of us in the kitchen. The search for a maître d' was not exhaustive. LA's sister Morfudd Richards, with whom I shared my home, agreed to do it. She was happy working in the West End and today she reckons that had the job offer come from anyone else, she would not have accepted it because she did not really want to work south of the Thames. But she had come into Lampwick's with LA one night and seen me cook: Morfudd had faith in me.

The restaurant opened in January 1987. It had a friendly name, we all reckoned, but I didn't like the apostrophe—it was ugly—so it had to go. Harvey's became Harveys. Its days of selling fried beef patties in baps were finished.

THIRTEEN

The Christening

WITHOUT THE FOOD at Harveys there would never have been the circus.

I wasn't expecting an easy ride to the top. After all, I was taking over what had been an upmarket burger bar in Wandsworth, rather than an elegant dining room in Mayfair. The interior design was horrific, but there was no money to redecorate. The kitchen was tiny, and again there were no funds for improvement.

My business partners, Nigel and Richard, lurked around in the background; the former looking after the wine list, the latter dealing with the accounts. Understandably, they wanted to see a return from their investment, but my motivation was to serve the finest food in the world.

How could I deliver a high standard of cuisine with the restraint of limited resources? If Harveys was going to work, I would have to be smart and draw heavily from my not-insignificant experience of serving alongside the Michelin masters. I would need to use every trick I had learned on my nine-year journey from Harrogate to Wandsworth Common.

I had always admired the Box Tree's clever technique of rotating stock (ingredients, not chicken stock), because it meant they could reduce waste. Reduced waste equals increased profits. Stock rotation therefore became a rule at Harveys, and this is the way it worked: One day I might do pigeon with fresh-thyme-scented roasting juices and champagne-braised cabbage. But if the customers didn't go for it, then I would rethink the dish because I couldn't contemplate the prospect of chucking the pigeons into the bin. The next day I might put Pigeon à la Forèstiere (with wild mushrooms) on the menu and, fingers crossed, that would do the trick.

I also had to find a way to work in such a small, cramped kitchen. I had worked in a few big kitchens by now, including the Gavroche powerhouse, where there might have been four chefs on the Meat section, three on Fish, four on Pastry, two on Hot Starters and two on the Larder. At Harveys, kitchen space was a luxury, so, just like Pierre Koffmann had done at Tante Claire, I put a massive table in the middle of the kitchen. The table became the work surface and in those early days we were like a pack of wolves; three or four of us darting around, surface to stove, stove to surface, each of us doing a bit of everything.

There wasn't enough space for a separate garnish section, so to overcome this, I tried to incorporate vegetables as ingredients served on the plate with the main dish, rather than served on separate side plates. I'd serve young leeks, roast button onions and girolle mushrooms on the same plate as a guinea fowl, roasted on the bone, skin taken off, legs split, thigh bone taken out, drumstick cleaned up, the whole lot put together, breast carved and laid across the top with jus blonde. Likewise, Pigeon en Vessie was served on the same plate as a Tagliatelle of Leeks. And the Roast Pigeon de Bresse did not come with side plates of vegetables, but was garnished with potato rosti, young turnips, lentilles du pays and a single ravioli that contained mushrooms, garlic and thyme. Harveys dishes were filling and substantial.

The kitchen at Harveys was also too small for the traditional French-style chefs' hierarchy. At Gavroche hierarchical ranks were important and the system was respected by every man in the kitchen, but my Harveys brigade would only ever be as large as ten—I wouldn't have the real hierarchy until I had the Restaurant Marco Pierre White at the Hyde Park Hotel. I had two chefs on Pastry in a poky kitchen annex and the remaining eight of us were packed into the overcrowded main kitchen, not working on sections, but working together to compensate for our lack of staff. In other words, we all mucked in to do garnish, hot starters, main courses and fish. If there was a table of five, eight cooks worked on five plates, which might mean two people working together on one dish, then I'd piece it all together. Despite the unusual arrangement, consistency would have to be crucial at Harveys. At Manoir, you'll recall, in my opinion the system fell apart when the pressure increased and the number of covers went above forty. With this in mind, I wanted to ensure that each and every Harveys dish was consistently good.

So I was the head chef and every other member of the brigade was an "assistant"—there was no sous chef. I told my assistants to call me Marco, rather than Chef. I was still in my twenties and didn't consider myself old enough to be called Chef, although when I gave Kevin Broome, a cook from Manchester, a job at Harveys, he started to call me Boss, which stuck. Thereafter, I was either Marco or Boss until my retirement from the kitchen in 1999. Although I didn't go for Albert's hierarchy, I certainly adopted his high regard for discipline.

Then there was the food itself. I began questioning everything that went on the plate. Why am I doing this? Why serve this with that? Why serve that with this? Why cook this for so long? Why, why, why? I remember serving a vinaigrette with a terrine of leeks and thinking the vinegar was too harsh. It often is, isn't it? So I just cut the vinegar by diluting it with water; you still get the strength but you've taken away some of the acidity and made it palatable. I called it water vinaigrette: put oil, water and garlic in a large bowl, add salt and pepper, and then stir very gently so the vinaigrette doesn't emulsify. It looks beautiful on the plate—separate pearls of oil and water.

Other times I might pick a main ingredient—sea scallops, lamb, whatever—and then create a long list of other ingredients that I thought would go well with it. I would sit there, studying the list, allowing my imagination to go and then . . . and then I would start to see it visually. At night, when I wasn't in the kitchen, I would sit down with pen and paper and draw pictures of dishes that came out of my imagination and were intended for the following day's menu. Sometimes, in search of inspiration, I would resort to my trunk, which contained French cookery books and menus I had collected over the years from other restaurants. Then I might deface my books by drawing my own sketches of dishes straight onto the books' illustrations. Years later, at the Hyde Park, I still did my late-night sketches, then handed them in the morning to my head chef, Robert Reid, saying, "Copy these." With so many of the dishes I would start at the end, if you like, and work my way backward; the process always began with drawing that picture on the plate.

Cook's brain. It's that ability to visualize the food on the plate, as a picture in the mind, and then work backward. There's no reason why domestic cooks can't do the same thing. Cooking is easy: you've just got to think about what you are doing and why you are doing it. Too many professional chefs never think about what they are doing.

For instance, let's just think for a moment about a fried egg. It's not the most inspired dish, but then again, if you can't cook an egg, what can you cook? And actually, a perfectly cooked fried egg is quite beautiful.

Apply the cook's brain and visualize that fried egg on the plate. Do you want it to be burned around the edges? Do you want to see craters on the egg white? Should the yolk look as if you'd need a hammer to break into it? The answer to all three questions should be no. Yet the majority of people still crack an egg and drop it into searingly hot oil or fat and continue to cook it on high heat. You need to insert earplugs to reduce the horrific volume of the sizzle. And the result, once served up in a pool of oil, is an inedible destruction of that great ingredient—the egg. Maybe that's how you like it, in which case carry on serving your disgusting food.

Meanwhile, the rest of us can think about what we really want to see on the plate. We want that egg to look beautiful and appetizing, because then when we eat it, we shall all be happy. We want the white to be crater-free and unblackened around its edges. The yolk should be glistening, just a thin film that can be easily pierced by a fork to let the yellowness run out. That's the picture.

How do we create it? Slowly heat a heavy-based pan on very low heat, perhaps for five minutes, and once it is hot enough, put in some butter, letting it gently melt. Then take your egg from a basket and crack it into the pan. (I don't keep eggs in the fridge as it only lengthens the cooking process because you are dealing with a chilled ingredient.) If the heat seems too high, then remove the pan from the heat for a few seconds to let it cool down. Basically, if you can hear that egg cooking, then the heat is too high. Carefully spoon the butter over the top of the egg. After about five minutes you have your magnificent fried egg—more of an egg poached in butter—just the way you had pictured it on the plate.

If you can visualize the food on the plate before you start cooking, it means, inevitably, that you can be more precise with portions: how often have you prepared a roast dinner intended for six but ended up creating enough food for a dozen? Picture it on the plate first, and you'll not only get a better meal but save on waste as well—though do take into consideration the people who'll want second helpings.

I needed a system for making sure the brigade brought my vision to life, plate after plate. At Manoir, it had sometimes been a problem that not every chef could copy Raymond's artistic style. Quite simply, they didn't have his flair. Somehow, I had to find an easy-to-follow way of enabling my chefs to imitate my desired presentation of dishes. I devised a simple method: the plate became a clock. The top of the plate was twelve o'clock and the bottom of the plate was six o'clock; three o'clock was to the right and, of course, nine to the left. So if a chef was dressing pigeon with a petit pain of foie gras, I could shout across the kitchen, "Foie gras at twelve, confit of garlic at four . . ." You can never go wrong, as long as your cooks can tell the time.

* * *

TO ACCOMPLISH ALL this—to turn a neighborhood joint into a temple of gastronomy, perfect from the moment you opened the door to the minute you got in the cab—I was racing constantly, like one of my father's beloved greyhounds. Imagine you are running a marathon . . . at sprint speed. Now imagine what you might look like halfway through the distance and it will help you get a picture in your head of what I looked like during Harveys: gaunt, debauched and knackered.

I suppose I was trying to kill myself. But then, sacrificing your health for your career was all the rage. Harveys opened against the backdrop of Margaret Thatcher's greed culture. People talked about City types being "burnt out" by the age of thirty. Young men and women didn't stop to question the damage that can be caused by chronic obsession; we didn't pause to consider the consequences of the pace. *Wall Street* was the big movie of the year, and that was a film about greed and self-indulgence, about hunger for success. Its underlying message was that greed is destructive but the subtext was totally missed by most cinemagoers of my age. Instead everyone was reciting Michael Douglas's line—"Breakfast is for wimps"—as if it was the mantra for anyone who wanted to get to the top. (My own breakfast, by the way, has always consisted of the same three courses: a cough, a coffee and a cigarette.)

In Harveys I had found my Adrenaline Heaven. This was Pain Paradise. Customers may well have gone there to fill their stomachs but I went to feed my addiction to work, my addiction to adrenaline and to pain, and at Harveys something was always happening.

Actually, it is wrong to say that something was *always* happening. During those first couple of months after opening there was zilch happening. Things were bad and certainly not helped by the winter weather, which was particularly brutal that year. We could handle forty-four covers but most nights the restaurant was virtually empty. One evening it was completely empty, so I came out of the kitchen with Mark and Simple Simon and we stood with Morfudd and her front-of-house team of two looking out of the window at the action outside: a blizzard was raging across Wandsworth Common.

Through the snow, two scarfed-up, sludge-covered people suddenly appeared, trudging bravely in their boots and anoraks and approaching Bellevue Road as if it were the peak of Everest. It turned out to be the head jailer of Wandsworth Prison. He was bringing out his windswept wife for "a treat." When they had finished their meal, I joined them for coffee and a chat.

I was so overwhelmed by their Hannibal-esque trek to Harveys, impressed by the effort they had put into it, that I found myself telling them, "Don't worry about the bill." They wrapped themselves up again, in that cheerful sort of way that the British do before throwing themselves into a snowstorm. Stiff upper lip. Then they stepped out of the restaurant and into the blizzard and vanished.

That was the worst night. Two covers, zero takings—and I don't think Mr. and Mrs. Jailer ever came back. Life at Harveys remained quiet for the next couple of months—there wasn't a noticeable growth in popularity—but rather than worrying about the lack of cash coming in, I concentrated on getting the menu right, and the few punters who came in ate well.

Then one day in early spring, the kitchen phone rang. I got a flash back to Manoir Aux Quat' Saisons. Two years earlier, Raymond's kitchen phone had rung and I'd picked it up, as was my habit at that time, pretending to be an answering machine. "Please leave a message and we shall come back to you," I had said, before delivering an earsplitting "Bleeeeeep!" After the "tone" came a soft voice, announcing that it was Egon Ronay, the renowned critic and best-selling author of restaurant guides, and saying, "I would be most grateful if Raymond could call me when he picks up this message."

And so I was there in the kitchen at Harveys, listening to the same soft voice, totally unaware that Egon Ronay had visited my restaurant, eaten my food and was about to write a review for his column in the *Sunday Times*, and paralyzed with fear that he might recognize my voice. Instead, Egon explained that he had been in to eat at Harveys and had enjoyed his meal tremendously. He intended to write a piece for the *Sunday Times* but beforehand wanted to know a bit more about me. "I can tell from your accent that you are not Italian," he said to me. "So how did you get a name like Marco?"

"Well, that's only part of my name," I told him. "My full name is Marco Pierre White. My father was English and that's where the White comes from. My mother was Italian, hence the name Marco. My aunt Luciana, my mother's sister, came up with the name Pierre, but don't ask me why."

When Egon's review appeared, I was thrilled by his comments about the restaurant but alarmed to see that he had referred to me as Marco *Pierre* White. My middle name, for so long a well-kept secret, was not only revealed, but revealed in the pages of a broadsheet. Pierre stuck, of course.

On the Saturday night before the review we were catering for the usual small crowd. The next morning, the *Sunday Times* came out with Egon's critique, and that was it. Bang! The bookings never stopped. Egon, though short, fragile and getting on a bit, was the man with the Midas touch. For decades his guides had been telling British restaurantgoers where to eat out, and now here he was, in the spring of '87, enthusiastically advising his followers, via a *Sunday Times* column, to head for Harveys. The impact was quite extraordinary.

Before Egon's piece I had been Marco White, but from that Sunday on I became Marco Pierre White. MPW. Quite posh. Quite confusing. Some people would think I was Italian while others would say I was French. And there would be those who thought I had made up the whole lot, because, after all, who do you know with an Italian-French-English name? Egon, I suppose, had refined me.

Overnight success is a strange experience. Where there had once been virtual silence, now there was noise. Up until that point, we had all jumped when the phone rang. But after Egon's article, when the pace picked up, the ringing phone became a continuous background noise at Harveys. All you could hear was ringing, chopping, hissing, frying, ringing . . . and me shouting (which I shall come to).

The PR, of course, was picking up and my old friend Alan Crompton-Batt was out there somewhere, pouring booze down journalists' throats and encouraging them to review Harveys. Meanwhile the punters continued to flood in, coming to taste the food. They came for the Blanquette of Scallops and Langoustines with Cucumber and Ginger; the Feuillantine of Sweetbreads; the Hot Foie Gras, Lentils and Sherry Vinegar Sauce; the Noisettes of Lamb en Crepinette with Fettucine of Vegetables and a Tarragon Jus. They came for the Hot

Mango Tart, the Passion Fruit Soufflé and Lemon Tart. They came to have something different.

We live in a world of refinement, not in a world of invention. That's the way I see it. People who claim to have invented a great dish are only fooling themselves. Someone has always done it before. Customers and critics used to rave about my Harveys dish Tagliatelle of Oysters with Caviar. They thought it was a great "invention." But I'm sure I didn't invent it. Centuries before we were born, people were eating pasta with shellfish, weren't they? It was simply the concept I had created. When I was at Manoir, we used to do a dish called Tagliatelle of Crayfish, which had crayfish sitting on top of a little hill of pasta with a fish sauce poured over it and finished off with a bit of chervil. I felt that to put the pasta inside a shell with the oyster and cucumber and caviar and a little beurre de champagne was very sexy because you get all those textures in one. If it was on a plate, rather than in the shell, you might have a mouthful of pasta and no oyster. I tried to design dishes that would not turn into a mess as you were eating, and this is a good example: eating the oysters would not destroy the picture. There was more, as well: the flavor, the texture, the explosion in the mouth.

Again, the Pigeon en Vessie—pigeon in pig's bladder—might have seemed new to Harveys customers in the late eighties, but Fernand Point was serving chicken in pig's bladder in his French restaurant, La Pyramide, in the forties and fifties, and Le Gavroche did its own version of Point's classical dish.

Pig's trotter, another Harveys favorite, was inspired by a similar dish that was done by my former boss Pierre Koffmann at Tante Claire. And Pierre's pig's trotter, if you take my meaning, was his own version of the one done by the French chef Charles Barrier. So I took it from Pierre, who had taken it from Charles, who doubtless took it from someone else.

Pierre's version involved stuffing the trotter with chicken thighs and sweetbreads before dropping it into boiling water. I got rid of the chicken, which I felt had been put there to pad out the more expensive sweetbreads. The trotters have to be soaked in water for twenty-four hours, which softens them, and then you have to pull out the bones: it's like pulling tights off a woman. The trotter was then filled with the sweetbreads, morel mushrooms and onions, and bound with a chicken quenelle. Then I'd roll it up in tinfoil, gently poach the trotter in water at 85 degrees Celsius for ten minutes and then rest it before putting it onto the plate with pommes purée and truffle sauce. Pierre's technique, in contrast, was to cook the meat for double that length of time. To my palate, my method produced a more succulent taste.

From day one at Harveys I did the Pied de Cochon Pierre Koffmann, my own version of his pig's trotter dish and a tribute to him. It would stay on my menu, from one restaurant to another, for the next twelve years until I retired from the kitchen. I had not invented the pig's trotter dish, just like I hadn't invented the Tagliatelle of Oysters with Caviar. I had refined it.

They came to Harveys not only for the food but also for the Marco Pierre White show. It was a lively show, a sort of circus of tension and drama and unpredictability. It was the big top within a small restaurant. There they were, eating this sophisticated food, while some poor cook was being murdered in the kitchen. It was like hell in the back and heaven in the front. And then out came this creature—me—looking like he'd crucified himself and was ready to kick out a customer. You could come along, have a good dinner, and see the customer at the table next to you get slaughtered by the chef. I borrowed a quote from Oscar Wilde and put it at the top of the menu: "To get into the best society nowadays one has either to feed people, amuse people, or shock people—that is all."

Well, punters were fed, amused and shocked.

The media, for their part, were amused. Indeed, everyone, except for "establishment" food figures, was ready for a change and I was becoming gastronomy's symbol of Thatcherite greed, the young chef who had crossed the North-South divide when it still existed. Make way for the long-haired, gangly cook who had won the heart of Egon Ronay. Word spread and then I discovered the benefits of fame.

When you become famous, you become sexy. I might make a flirtatious remark to a woman customer and then, well, one thing would lead to another, which led to my office. The ladies' loos were also used for brief, casual intimacy, and, weather permitting, there was even action in the courtyard outside the kitchen.

I DON'T RECALL her name but we met on the staircase that took customers from the restaurant to the toilets. She was a brunette, full-bodied and somewhere in her early forties, dolled up in a low-cut black dress. She smiled at me as we passed each other on the steps. I interpreted her friendliness as willingness and so I asked, "Would you like to see my office?"

"Where is it?"

"Up there." I pointed toward the top floor to the door marked "Private," a door that led into the room where I would sit postservice, compiling menus and scribbling drawings of dishes while the rest of Wandsworth slept.

Together we galumphed up the stairs and into my office, where we fumbled and groped, unzipped and unbuttoned. The newspapers had described me as the "Jagger of the Aga." It wasn't hard living up to the reputation.

Three stories beneath my office there was a busy restaurant, where customers were eating Michelin-starred food and enjoying good company, as you hope to do when you eat out. And amid the tables, there was a table for two where a man was sitting alone. He was alone because his companion had excused herself and left the table to pop to the loo. The man had filled the first few minutes of solitude by observing his surroundings. Perhaps he had been gawking at the celebrities at a neighboring table: Is that Kylie Minogue kissing Jason Donovan?

Then there came a point—there had to come the point—when he felt concerned by his companion's absence and the questions came into his mind, "Is she okay?" "Why is she taking so long?" He was also feeling uncomfortable: he had done his gawking but was everyone now staring at him, wondering whether his date had departed? He was compelled to go and investigate the disappearance. He put his napkin on the table, stood up and started walking toward the stairs that took customers from the restaurant to the toilets.

Tinkle, tinkle. The phone rang on my desk and it continued ringing. It was the infernal internal ring tone. I answered in the grumpy, aggressive tone of a bloke who has just been interrupted in a moment of passion because I was a bloke who had just been interrupted in a moment of passion. On the other end of the line was the maître d' Jean-Christophe Slowik, a.k.a. JC, and he relayed the grim news: "The husband is on his way up."

"Do you have a husband?" I asked the lady who had been on the other end of my lips.

"He's downstairs," she replied.

"No," I said. "No, he's not."

Abort mission, abort mission. The brunette and I rocketed into reverse. Clothes on, zips up. She could hardly escape via the door marked "Private" because her husband would spot her. It was just too dangerous and risky. There was no alternative. I opened the hatch door that led from my office to the roof and quickly helped her squeeze through the space. Once on the roof she positioned herself, crouching out of sight, three stories up from the pavement but with a terrific view of the common. Just as I was readjusting my apron and lighting a Marlboro, I heard footsteps at the top of the staircase. I opened the door, assumed I was talking to the husband, and asked, "Can I help?"

"I'm terribly sorry," he said, apologizing for being out-of-bounds, "but I'm looking for my wife. Have you by any chance seen her?"

Seen her? "What does she look like?" I inquired. Brown hair, black dress. I pouted and shook my head as he gave a description. I scrunched my face, hoping to send out a signal that I was bemused. "Nope," I said. "Can't help." He turned and trotted off, back downstairs, and I opened the hatch door and tugged the shivering woman back into the warmth. She rushed back to her table, back to her mystified husband, and in time for dessert; the Soufflés of Chocolate with Chocolate Sauce, possibly, or the Crackling Pyramide, I don't know.

APART FROM THE groupies and the yuppies south of the Thames, punters crossed the bridge from Chelsea, Westminster and Mayfair to dine at Harveys. Celebrities came as well, and not just any old celebrities but the young, good-looking, sexy ones, the sort who are shadowed by the paparazzi and who would appear in newspapers alongside the caption: "XXXX pictured last night, emerging from Harveys." They all wanted to be fed by the undernourished chef who was passionate, obsessed and intense. Denice Lewis, the beautiful Texan model who featured daily in gossip columns, would turn up with her boyfriend, "Green Shield stamps heir" Tim Jefferies. Koo Stark, Prince Andrew's former girlfriend, became a regular.

Mavericks seemed to identify with me. I was at Harveys one day when I answered the phone to Oliver Reed. That's Oliver Reed, the British film star whose movie credits include *Women in Love*, *The Four Musketeers*, and, in 2000, *Gladiator*. He's never reached the heights of fame in America, but in Britain, he was well known as a scrapping hell-raiser and all-round icon who'd do TV interviews when he was drunk and slurring. Ollie introduced himself and booked for dinner, and when he arrived with his wife, Josephine, he was everything you could have hoped for—and more. He sat on the floor, and that's where he drank his aperitif before heading to the table. From that night on, he became a regular. He had to come to Harveys, he used to say, because he was barred from everywhere else.

I adored Ollie. I saw him as a kindred spirit: someone who did things his own way. Whenever I knew the Reeds were coming, I'd always try to get away from the kitchen, if for only a minute or two, to greet them at the door. One night Ollie walked into the restaurant and looked around before saying grandly, "I'd like to commend you on the décor. It is the finest." (He always spoke like a character out of a Sherlock Holmes adventure.)

I said, "But Oliver, you've been here a hundred times."

"Yes," he said, "but it's the first time I've arrived sober."

His evenings at Harveys followed a pattern. He'd drink his aperitif while sitting on the floor, then after his starter he would leave the table, sprint into the kitchen and, without saying a word, rip off his tie and throw it at me before running out. He'd return to our chaotic kitchen a dozen times each night, for a chat or to do something crazy. He must have spent as much time in the kitchen as he did at the table. In the restaurant he would summon the wine waiter, and when asked what he would like to drink, Oliver would reply, "Bring us three more bottles of what we just had." He was rarely seated when his main course arrived; instead, he'd be on the landing upstairs, arm-wrestling another customer.

The staff loved him—he was a big tipper—and the customers loved him too. He would start chatting to groups on neighboring tables, and before long the tables would be rearranged until Oliver's table had grown to four times its original size. He wasn't happy unless he had met everyone in the restaurant and kissed their hands. Harveys became a party when Oliver was in the house. He'd walk in and everything would rev up a gear—the only other person I've seen have that effect is Frankie Dettori. One night I was in a rush, dashed past Oliver, and was halfway up the stairs when I noticed he was chasing after me. I stopped, turned around to him and said, "Oliver, why are you running?"

"Where's the fight?" he said.

And among the celebrities and the politicians, supermodels, pop stars and gossip columnists . . . somewhere among that fascinating cast of customers, there must have been a Michelin inspector. The *Michelin Guide* is published every January, and in December 1987 I picked up the phone and called Derek Brown, the UK guide's head inspector. I had never met him but, like Egon Ronay, he had the power to do amazing things to my career.

I introduced myself and we had a short conversation. I said, "Mr.

Brown, I am coming to the end of my first year in business and was wondering whether I will be awarded a Michelin star."

He replied, "We never reveal information like that prior to publication of the guide." Oh well, I thought. It was just a cheeky call; I thought I'd chance my luck. I would have to wait another month before finding out if I had won a star. Or would I? Just as I was about to put down the phone, Mr. Brown added, "But I can tell you that you won't be disappointed."

I really would like to say that it was one of the happiest days of my life. But by now you know me well enough to know that it did not bring me happiness. There was no celebration, no knees-up. Somehow it didn't register as a great achievement because I wanted so much more. I wasn't used to congratulating myself and I didn't know how to reward myself. I didn't have time to attend a party, let alone organize one.

If I had managed a party, it probably would have ended up something like the Sturm und Drang affair I attended on New Year's Day 1988. A crowd of us gathered at the publisher Anthony Blond's house to toast the New Year, and Jonathan Meades was there. Previously, Jonathan—the restaurant reviewer for the *Times*—was the one critic who terrified me. He could destroy a place. But I didn't need to be scared of him: in Easter of 1987 he had booked into Harveys using the alias Hogg, and he later phoned me to say, "My name is Hogg. I was in the other night and had jelly of calves' brains. It was sensational. How did you make it?" Only when I saw the article did I realize that Hogg was Meades and vice versa. Then, in an end-of-year roundup for the *Times*, Jonathan had given the Newcomer Restaurant of the Year award to Harveys.

The gathering at Anthony's house was a few days after Jonathan had given me the Newcomer award. Apart from Jonathan, his girlfriend Frances Bentley (who worked for *Tatler* magazine) was there as well as three other chefs: Nico Ladenis, my former boss; Rowley Leigh of Kensington Place; and Simon Hopkinson, who had just opened Terence Conran's Bibendum, and whose cookery book, *Roast Chicken and Other Stories*, has more recently been voted the most useful recipe book ever written. The evening was memorable for two reasons:

First the food, or rather the simplicity of the food, considering there were four chefs in the house. It was ten P.M. and everyone was starving, but everywhere was closed and the host had not thought about catering for his guests. "My cupboards are bare," said Anthony. I volunteered to cook, partly because I found it easier to cook than socialize.

I went into the kitchen and searched around. He had a couple of onions, some pasta, a tin of tomato purée, a few rashers of bacon and a clove of garlic. I did a spaghetti sauce the way I'd been told my mother used to cook it: Sweat off the onions with the garlic without coloring them, then put in the diced bacon and sweat that off, then add generous amounts of tomato purée and sweat that all off in more olive oil. Then take the cooked pasta and put it straight into the sauce. It was very simple but Jonathan said it was one of the greatest pasta dishes he'd ever eaten. And I was too shy to say, "Well, it's not me; it's just the way my mother used to cook it when I was a boy."

The evening was also memorable for the squabble between Nico and Simon, who had a silly argument about food. If I remember rightly, the spat started when Nico criticized the "dreadful" brioche that Simon was serving at Bibendum. Nico said that when he opened his first restaurant in Dulwich, South London, he used to buy in fish soup because it was better than the fish soup he could make himself. He told Simon, "Find someone who makes brioche better than you, buy it in and serve it." I suppose Nico was saying that Simon had a duty to give his customers only the best food, but Simon was quite proud of his brioche.

"You do know," added Nico, who was angry but still eloquent, "that I'm a self-taught chef." To be self-taught is a big put-down in the premier league of chefs. In the outside world it is a bit like calling someone a cunt. And then Simon started crying. I don't know if it was the words "self-taught chef" that produced the tears; perhaps it was the strength of the criticism. I felt sorry for him being savaged and slaughtered by the great Nico, whose Chez Nico, incidentally, had won Restaurant of the Year in Jonathan's awards. I stepped in, telling Nico to forget about it. Mind you, the proof was in the pudding (and the starters and main courses): Nico went on to win three Michelin stars.

Simon, meanwhile, retired from the kitchen in the mid-nineties before he had the chance to win a star. The pressure was too much for
him. During service one day he had what he now calls a "mini-
breakdown," and to save his sanity he stepped away from the stove of
the professional kitchen.

EARLIER ON I mentioned that I hated the interior design of Harveys,
and then I said that Ollie Reed loved the décor. In between me hating
it and Ollie loving it, the restaurant was redecorated. But during that
period when I still hated it, something else happened. There was an
episode, if you like.

Morfudd came into the kitchen during service one day and told me
about a certain customer in the restaurant. He said he had played
a role in designing Harveys in its days as a burger bar, before I took
over. This man had told Morfudd that because of his contribution to
the restaurant he and his five guests should be entitled to a meal or
drinks on the house.

What he had done to the restaurant was ghastly. It was chintzy,
mediocre, charmless and lacking in imagination. It really bothered
me. Morning, noon and night I would look at Harveys' décor and
silently pray for the day when we had enough money to have the place
done up properly. So you'll understand my reaction when I learned
that this bloke was not only sitting in my restaurant but had the au-
dacity to ask for a free meal or drinks.

"No, Morfudd," I said. "No, no, no. And please go and tell him that
I am not prepared to cook for him because I dislike the way he fur-
nished the restaurant." She was reluctant at first—I can see why
now—but I was adamant, and so she went back into the dining room
to have a quiet word with the designer. "What?" he screamed as she relayed the news to him. He was outraged, furious and probably very
embarrassed in front of his friends. He stormed toward the kitchen.
From the stove, I could hear him shouting, ranting and raging. I
stopped whatever I was doing and went into the corridor that led down
to the restaurant. He was at one end while I stood at the other.

He made a mistake. The punch-up that followed was a release, in a way. For months I'd been staring at the chintz, thinking, I'd like to meet this bastard. And now he was charging toward the end of my clenched fist. Every swipe I delivered—and I delivered a few—was a blow for good taste. The kitchen brigade had to pull me off him. Ask Morfudd if you don't believe me. He staggered out of Harveys, minus a tooth or two and nursing a perforated eardrum. I had partially stripped him, as well. During the scuffle, I ripped an entire sleeve from his suit jacket, and it was left lying on the corridor floor, a casualty of battle. As his friends helped him out of the restaurant, he stepped onto Bellevue Road, looked down at his arm and wailed, "This is Gucci, for Christ's sake."

INTO ALL THIS madness stepped the intrepid Bob Carlos Clarke. I had met Bob in 1986. My girlfriend Lowri-Ann Richards was friends with him and one day she introduced us. A couple of years later, when I was offered a deal to write a cookery book, *White Heat,* I approached Bob to see if he would be interested in taking the pictures. By then he was a well-known fashion photographer. He invited me round for tea and I arrived with a pile of linen tablecloths. Bob thought I was dropping off the laundry but I explained to him how I like to draw on tablecloths and on these particular ones I had drawn pictures of the dishes that would appear in the book, as well as sketches depicting cooking in which I had tried to show the heat of the kitchen—steam pouring from pots and that kind of thing.

Bob spent about a year on and off in the restaurant, snatching snaps of the diners and of me and my brigade in the kitchen, but there was never a moment when I felt that he was intrusive. In fact I reckoned it was important, for the sake of chefs everywhere, that he showed the public what went on on our side of the passe. Bob was a good fly on the wall. There was a time when *White Heat* was considered Britain's most influential cookery book because it inspired so many young people to become chefs. It was innovative because it contained not only shots of food but also those moody black-and-white, reportage-style photos of kitchen life at Harveys. When it was published in 1990, *White Heat* became a cult classic, sending out the uplifting message that if I—the long-haired young cook from Leeds—had crossed the North-South divide to find fame in London, you too could do it. A glance at Bob's pictures gave the reader a fascinating glimpse of the haggard, exhausted cooks who produced Michelin-starred dishes and of how exhaustion equaled passion.

Alongside the photos of the brigade cooking dishes, smoking and fighting, there are quotes illustrating my outlook on life at the time. Flicking through the pages today, I'm struck by a massive quote of mine that reads, "I can't work in a domestic kitchen; it's just too confined. There's no freedom and there's no buzz. At home I'm not hit with forty covers in half an hour, so there's no real excitement." In a strange way, it may have explained why I was rarely in the kitchen at home, let alone at home.

FOURTEEN

Beautiful Doll

I MET MY first wife at the fishmonger's in the summer of 1987, some six months after the opening of Harveys. My relationship with Lowri-Ann, the onetime queen of the King's Road, hadn't worked out. I can't remember how it ended—these things fizzle out—but I had removed myself and my trunk from her place in Battersea and resettled in a flat close to Wandsworth Common. The location of my new home meant that when I wasn't sleeping in Harveys, I was at least bedding down a few hundred yards from the restaurant and my cherished kitchen.

I was living with a bloke whom I shall call Derek, who was another member of the King's Road set. Derek had been a heroin addict and I only moved into his place after he promised me he'd managed to kick the habit. He hadn't. Most nights I would return from Harveys, shattered, burned and cut, and walk into the flat to find Derek and his friends drugged up, lolling and slumping. I may as well have been living in an opium den. In the mornings I'd be awoken by a shaky hand knocking on my door. "Yes," I'd say. Then one of Derek's junkie mates would stumble into the room and ask to borrow a mirror—not to apply makeup, you understand, but to snort a line of cocaine. I got back one night to find a girl, off her face and wilting on the sofa. She asked if I could roll her a joint. "I'm sorry," I said politely. "I can't." As in, I don't know how.

"Christ," she replied, her eyeballs swiveling. "Are you that stoned?"

Derek was unperturbed by my reluctance to take drugs. As far as he was concerned, I was a dependent just like him. "You're an addict, Marco," he once told me, with a junkie's beam of confidence. "You're an addict to the warmth," by which he meant the stove, the cooking, the kitchen, the work.

It was all of those things that took me one morning to Johnny the Fish, who happened to introduce me to his secretary. Her name was Alex McArthur and she was like a beautiful doll, blond, blue-eyed and very pretty. She was, I later found out, a surgeon's daughter and was as middle class as I was working class. We chatted and established a connection, the Oxford connection. She had studied there at the same time as my friend Piers Adam, and they had known each other briefly, and I had worked at Le Manoir. We said farewell and off I went with my lobster and sea bass. But when I got back to Harveys, Alex was still on my mind. Despite all my misadventures at the restaurant, I was far from self-assured and still not good with girls, but I found the courage to call Alex and ask if she fancied dinner.

"When?" she said.

"What about tonight?"

"What time?"

"Eleven," I said, explaining, "I have to finish service first."

That night she arrived in her little Fiat Panda and I squeezed my six-foot-three-inch frame into the passenger seat. We went to Chinatown, in London's West End, for late-night noodles, and after dinner we went back to her flat in Kensington. I did not leave. Our relationship had been cemented, as they say, in less than twenty hours. One morning I had met Alex and by bedtime I was living with her.

She tolerated my addiction to work. I think—I thought—she was happy to go along with it. In fact, she would come and collect me when I was done for the night at Harveys. We were young and infatuated. I was twenty-five years old and Alex was twenty-one, and we managed to keep the relationship going for a year, long enough for me to propose. One day in June 1988 we were married in Chelsea Register Office, the place where rock stars tie the knot. We did it discreetly. My best man was Bob Carlos Clarke, the photographer. Bob's wife, Lindsay, was the other witness. That was it—just the four of us. We emerged from the register office onto the King's Road and felt a celebration was in order, so we trotted down to Dino's and the four of us sat there eating poached eggs on toast. I had a Michelin star by then but hadn't considered cooking a sumptuous feast for the occasion. When the meal was finished, I had my own speech to deliver, which went, quite simply, "I've got to get back to work." I have no recollection of the bride being bothered about her groom vanishing, but that is precisely what I did. Buggered off, back to my kitchen. A honeymoon? What do you think?

At some point during our brief marriage we did have a holiday in Yorkshire, where we stayed with Tom and Eugene McCoy, the cheffing brothers who ran the superb McCoys restaurant in Staddlebridge. Alex slipped on the landing in Tom's house, and when I got to her, she said she couldn't move her leg. At the hospital the doctors said she had a fracture and she was promptly trolleyed off to a hospital bed. Every day I would go in to visit my injured wife, taking platters of food that I had cooked in McCoy's kitchen. I used to turn up with huge lobster salads and that sort of thing, and when I heard the elderly woman in the bed opposite Alex whining about the hospital food, I got the hint. On future visits I'd take in two portions of everything—one for Alex, the other for the old lady. It transpired that the elderly woman was the grandmother of Mel Smith, the comedian-turned-businessman who cofounded the extremely successful Talkback television production company. Small world that it is, I met Mel Smith a few years ago when he asked me to do his fiftieth birthday party at my restaurant in Holland Park, the Belvedere. We had a good chat about his grandmother, a wonderful character, who by then had passed away.

When Alex gave birth on September 20, 1989, I finished my lunch service before heading off to see our new baby at the Chelsea and Westminster Hospital. We named our daughter Leticia Rosa (Rosa being my mother's middle name), which was shortened, of course, to Lettie. I was delighted at becoming a father, but emotionally I was all over the place, and mentally I wasn't prepared for fatherhood. I was so involved in my work, and Harveys had become a form of escapism.

Truth be known, I was lost within myself. How could I take on the responsibilities of fatherhood if I could barely manage to deal with myself? I couldn't really settle into the potentially blissful environment so many new parents enjoy. It was easier for me to be in the kitchen at Harveys, grafting away, sweating and toiling, and dishing out the bollockings.

Lettie's birth prompted me to get in touch with my dad. I hadn't spoken to the old man for a decade—there had been no contact with him since the late seventies, when he had remarried after I left home. On the day Lettie was born, I felt compelled to phone him. It was a brief conversation, and I cannot recall it verbatim. I said something about how he had become a grandfather for the first time; how I wanted to be the one to break the news to him and didn't want him to learn about it from the papers. And that was it. Another two years or so would pass before we came face-to-face.

THE SAME TWO questions always crop up about Harveys. First, was I really so nasty to my chefs? Second, did I really kick people out of the restaurant?

Sometimes I bump into hugely successful, talented chefs who were my protégés and they say, "You were really nasty to work for but it made life easier afterwards." And they say that without a hint of irony. I've also come across punters who tell me they came to Harveys and say, "You kicked me out, but I suppose I asked for it."

Dealing with the staff issue, first. Yes, I was a hard boss. Even without my insistence on discipline, finding staff was difficult enough. At that time the majority of young chefs aspired to work north of the Thames, rather than south. They'd rather have done Belgravia than Bellevue Road. When they accepted the job, they were in for the shock of their lives. My unmanageable desire for perfection brought out a certain tetchiness in me. I expected my chefs and waiters to match my commitment, and I let them know that. My addiction to work, my constant craving for an adrenaline fix, set the pace, both front and back of house. I was working hundred-hour weeks, but they weren't slacking either. If joining Gavroche was the culinary equivalent of signing up for the Foreign Legion, then taking a job at Harveys was like joining the SAS. We were a small unit of hard nuts.

In the early days, I allowed staff to sit down for a meal before service, but that didn't last long. Egon Ronay's glorious review a couple of months after we opened started off the nonstop bookings, which pretty much finished off the custom of staff lunches. There just wasn't time to eat. Jean-Christophe Slowik, or JC, replaced Morfudd as maître d', and one day he asked for a quiet word. JC was only in his twenties but had worked for Madame Point, widow of my hero Fernand Point, in France before doing a front-of-house stint with that genius Raymond Blanc. He was as young as the rest of us but had a wisp of premature gray hair. In his engaging, diplomatic and charming way, he explained that he had a problem. "What is it, JC?" I asked.

He said that he was having to take money from the petty cash box, nip to the deli a few doors down and buy sandwiches for his ravenous waiters. He asked, "Is it not odd that we work in a restaurant but have to buy lunch from somewhere else?" JC is good when it comes to making good points. JC was skinny enough and he added, "To lose any more weight, I will have to lose a bone." From then on I allowed staff to have a meal, a couple of times a week, before service.

I survived on a diet of espresso and Marlboros—my nutritional intake came from the morsels, nibbles and sauces I tasted during cooking. Most members of the team found that Mars and Twix were ideal for energy bursts. Then there were the plates that were returned to the kitchen from the dining room totally clean. For ages I thought the customers were so impressed with the food that they were devouring every last speck on the plate. In fact, it was the starving waiters who were responsible for the spotless dishes. As they left the dining room and walked along the corridor to the kitchen, they would polish off the customers' leftovers, guzzling the remains like famished vultures.

There was a look of horror in the eyes of JC's new waiters as they arrived for their first day at work. The sight that greeted them was one of waiters and chefs suffering chronic fatigue and hunger, all set to the soundtrack of a screaming boss. Even before service started and the first customers arrived, a new waiter would often make an excuse about getting something from his coat, only to scurry off and never return. These new waiters couldn't work a single hour, let alone an entire shift. Eventually JC accepted that many of the recruits would evaporate as fast as their enthusiasm and he worked extra hard to compensate for this problem.

In the kitchen, the first three weeks was the toughest period for the new boys. By the end of it they were usually fucked, having lost a stone in weight, gained a dazed expression and cried themselves dry. That was when the shaking started—and when many of them left. One day they were there, the next they were gone. If they could make it into the fourth week, they were doing well.

We were in the kitchen one night when Richard Neat mentioned something about feeling faint and then collapsed on the floor. He was having a panic attack between the stove and where the meat was prepared: the exhaustion had taken its toll. None of us knew what to do but one thing was for sure—the cooking continued around Richard's quivering body beneath us.

Then JC came into the kitchen carrying a tray and screamed, "Oh my God, look at Richard." JC phoned for an ambulance, which arrived within minutes, but JC was keen not to disturb the customers by letting them see the paramedics stomping through the dining room, so he directed them round to the back door. As the diners enjoyed their food, the ambulancemen tended to Richard. They had to strap him to the stretcher because he was having spasms. The next day, he was back in the trenches with the rest of us.

I MAKE NO apologies for my strict leadership methods and I have no one to blame but myself. However, I was, of course, the product of disciplinarians who included my father, Albert Roux, Pierre Koffmann and good old Stephan Wilkinson, my first chef at the George and the man who called me cunt as if it were my Christian name.

Normally only one person was allowed to speak during service, and that was me. Kitchen visitors said it was a bit like watching a surgeon in an operating theater.

Step now into my theater of cruelty:

ME: Knife. [*Knife is passed to me.*]

ME: Butter. [*Butter is passed to me*]

ME [*through gritted teeth*]: Not that fucking butter. Clarified fucking butter, you fucker.

Poor timing always upset me. If we were doing a table of six, for instance, and only four of the main courses were ready, then I was prone to flip. That's when I might send a chef to stand in the corner. "Corner," I'd say, jabbing a finger toward the corner of the room. "In [finger jab] the [jab] fucking [jab] corner." The chef would stand not with his face to the wall but facing me; that way he could pick up some knowledge while enduring his punishment. I remember one night, when I was in an intensely irritable mood, four chefs pissed me off, so each of them was sent to stand in a corner. When a fifth chef did something to annoy me, I shouted, "Corner. In the fucking corner."

"Which one, Marco?" he asked. I had run out of corners.

I went berserk if brioche wasn't toasted correctly. If it's toasted too quickly, you can't spread the foie gras on it; if it's toasted too slowly, it dries. It has to be toasted at the right distance below the grill, so it's crispy on the outside and soft on the inside. You don't scorch it and you don't dry it. Insignificant to you, maybe, but the difference between life and death to one of my cooks. If the brioche wasn't right, or if the vegetables had been chopped incorrectly, then someone was in for a nasty bollocking. "Do you really want to be the best?" I'd tell them. "If you do, that's fantastic; if you don't, then don't waste your time."

In order to achieve my dream I reckoned I needed a brigade with army-standard discipline and, as I had learned at Gavroche, discipline is borne out of fear. When you fear, you question. If you don't fear something, you don't question it in the same way. And if you have fear in the kitchen, you'll never take a shortcut. If you don't fear the boss, you'll take shortcuts, you'll turn up late. My brigade had to feel pain, push themselves to the limits, and only then would they know what they were capable of achieving. I was forcing them to make decisions. The ones who left, well, fine, at least they had decided a Michelin-starred kitchen was not for them.

Take a look at the ones who stayed, the ones who could take it and even appreciated it. Today, they are considered to be among Britain's finest chefs and they all came from that cramped kitchen at Harveys. There's Gordon Ramsay, of course. Gordon arrived in January 1988 after phoning up and asking if there was a job going. At the time he was working at a restaurant in Soho and, during a break, had read an interview with me. He thought I looked wild and crazy and a bit like Jesus, and he felt compelled to pick up the phone. I hired him, and when he came, I treated him as I would anyone else. He would eventually leave my kitchen in tears, but would go on to win three Michelin stars of his own. There are other winners too: Philip Howard has two; Eric Chavot has two; and Stephen Terry has one. Meanwhile, Tim Hughes is now executive chef of the Ivy, Le Caprice and J. Sheekey. All of the chefs who went through Harveys will say they have never worked in a more pressurized environment, but I doubt any of them will say they regret the experience. Chefs love mania.

Gordon, Stephen and Tim shared a flat in Clapham, a couple of miles from Harveys, and I used to scream at them, "Did you bunch of cunts go home last night and conspire against me? 'What stupid things can we do to wind up Marco?' Is that what you all said to each other? Did you sit down together like a bunch of plotting cunts and say, 'What can we do tomorrow that will really piss him off? What can we do to really irritate him?' Did you, Gordon? Is that what you did, Stephen? Did you conspire against me, Tim?' Because you are all being so fucking stupid today."

Other times the bollockings included physical abuse. I might severely tug a chef's apron, or grab a chef by the scruff of the neck and administer a ten-second throttle, just to focus him. One night I lifted Lee Bunting and hung him by his apron on some hooks on the wall. The cooks never knew what to expect from me—and neither did I. A film crew arrived for the series *Take Six Cooks* and happened to walk into the kitchen as I was throwing bottles of sauce and oil at an underling. The producer had to duck down to avoid being hit by flying glass. "I don't know if we can film in there," he told JC. "War zones are less dangerous."

Chefs who weren't sent to stand in the corner, throttled, or forced to duck to avoid flying sauces might even be chucked in the bin. We had a great big dustbin in the kitchen, which was filled with the usual waste produced in professional kitchens. The boys who were too slow, or simply too annoying at any particular moment, were dumped inside it. Arnold Sastry, the brother-in-law of comic actor Rowan Atkinson, was known as Onion Bhaji and he was regularly binned.

"Onion Bhaji in the bin," I might say, and the rest of the brigade would obey orders.

Why, you ask, did these poor young men continue to work for that bullying brute, Marco? Good question. And many of them not only continued to work with me, but stayed with me for years, right up until the day I retired in 1999. The thing is, a bollocking isn't personal. It's a short—sometimes not-so-short—sharp shock. It's an extremely loud wake-up call. It's smell-the-bloody-espresso time. In the heat of service, I didn't have time to say, "Arnold, would you mind speeding up a little, please?" I couldn't stop cheffing, couldn't take my mind off the game in order to say politely, "Gordon, when do you think you might finish the guinea fowl, old boy?" I had to be hard to deliver the message and the message was "Do it now and do it right." They all knew this and they all understood it. That is why, when a chef is receiving a bollocking, none of his colleagues jump in to defend him. The rest of the brigade look down and carry on with the job. Each one of them knows that sooner or later he will be the one getting a bollocking. I created fear but I don't remember anyone ever saying, "Marco, enough is enough. Pack it in." I'm convinced that a mile-wide streak of sadomasochism ran through the Harveys brigade. They were all pain junkies—they had to be. They couldn't get enough of the bollockings.

Interestingly, a number of members of the Harveys kitchen brigade were, like me, the product of a tough upbringing. They might have lost a mother or a father. They would have grown up on council estates. They were working class; from the wrong side of the tracks. Cheffing was still predominately a working-class profession then, and there was one cook who for a long time pretended he was working class just to fit in. It was a while before we discovered he was the son of rich parents and a private school boy to boot.

During the summer the tiny kitchen, with its glass-panel skylights, became blisteringly hot, and we all wore sweatbands on our foreheads and wrists. One day a chef moaned that he was too hot, so I did something that, on reflection, was rather hazardous. Carving knife in one hand, I held his jacket with the other and slashed it. Then I slashed his trousers. Both garments were still on his body at the time. "That should provide a bit of ventilation," I told him, and when he asked if he could change out of his chopped-up clothes, I said, "Yes, at the end of the service."

One evening the whole sweaty bunch got together to grumble about the heat. "Right, that's it," I said. I was annoyed and couldn't stand their moaning. I marched over to the air-conditioning machine and turned it off. "We'll all roast together," I said. From that night on they kept their complaints to themselves. If the boys couldn't stand the heat, well, that was tough because they couldn't get out of the kitchen.

When I was feeling charitable, I'd give the instruction to remove the kitchen's skylights, thus allowing some of the heat to escape. Gordon was in the kitchen one morning when the skylights were off, and he was rolling out pasta. He felt water on his head and assumed it was rain. He was wrong. A dog had wandered onto the roof terrace, cocked a leg and promptly urinated through the roof and onto Gordon and his ravioli. Gordon was enraged, if not a little embarrassed in front of his cackling colleagues. He ran outside with a knife. I don't think he was going to stab the dog; he just wanted to *look* like he was going to stab the dog. As it turned out, the beast was too fast for him.

When Gordon wasn't chasing dogs, he was usually rowing with Ronnie, his younger brother, who has spent years fighting another on-off battle, an addiction to heroin.

When I gave Ronnie a job as kitchen porter, I hadn't reckoned on the bickering it would entail. The two brothers loved each other dearly but had ferocious squabbles. I once asked where Gordon had gone, only to be told to look out the window. I glanced across the road and there was Gordon on the common, sprinting away from an angry Ronnie, who was trying to catch him and waving clenched fists.

They were hugely competitive. One day I saw Ronnie at the sink and, after examining his sparkling plates and cutlery, I told him he had the most talented hands I'd ever seen. I was winding him up, but for weeks after he boasted to Gordon that I had praised his hands, as if he was the more gifted of the Ramsay brothers.

There was another kitchen porter, Marius, and when I think of him, it makes me realize how unskilled I was at handling certain situations with my staff. Marius turned up for work one morning saying he had sore throat. I didn't send him home to bed like a sympathetic, experienced employer might have done. Instead someone or other mentioned that the best cure for Marius was Armagnac and port, so we filled a brandy glass with the concoction and told him to drink it. Half an hour later, when Marius collapsed unconscious on the kitchen floor, we carried him outside to the freezing cold, dumped him in the courtyard and forgot about him. A snowstorm came and went before someone said in a shocked way, "Marius." We rushed out to recover his trembling body. Two hours after complaining of a sore throat, Marius was suffering from alcohol poisoning and the onset of hypothermia.

Marius took some time off (to recover from the world's worst hangover) and the stand-in kitchen porter pitched up. On his first day I gave him a few hundred quid and told him to go to the bookie's and put the money on a horse that was racing that afternoon. He left with the readies, muttering the horse's name to himself so as not to forget it. We never saw him again.

Anyway, you now have a clearer picture of me as the boss. I was nasty, vicious, aggressive and blunt. I put my hands up to all of that. But, hey, don't get me wrong—along the way I had earned the respect and loyalty of the brigade. And away from the kitchen, I like to think I had my moments of compassion too. I helped out those with financial problems, and when Gordon went to work in France, I lent him the money for the trip. I was also there with the rest of them when they played football on Wandsworth Common. In fact, I was often the one who dragged them out to play when they said they were too tired to exercise.

The boys would do anything for me, and that included beating up my rivals. In the summer of 1990 I was asked to cook at a polo event and Antony Worrall Thompson, by then an established name in the restaurant world and the head chef at 190 Queensgate, kindly said he'd come along to help out.

I arrived at the Royal County of Berkshire Polo Club with my brigade and everything was going well until my boys decided Antony deserved a pummeling. Aristocrats and rich polo lovers were happily enjoying their food in the outdoor tent, but behind the scenes in the attached kitchen, Antony was being pelted with lemon tarts. He was quickly coated in sweet yellow goo. He tried to make a run for it but thought better of charging through into the tent because he looked ridiculous and it would cause too much of a scene. So Antony sprinted out of the makeshift kitchen and into a field, and that's where he was tackled by one of my boys, the wildebeest brought down by a leopard. He was then subjected to the humiliation of having a dozen eggs cracked on his head by the Harveys brigade. Antony, whom I've always liked, didn't take it very well.

Another incident that illustrates the vicious rivalry at the time, involved my boys and the ones who worked for the Roux brothers. It was during the restaurant world's annual trade fair at the Business Design Centre, in Islington, North London. The boys from Harveys were taunting the Roux brigade by calling them Roux robots and boil-in-the-bags, a reference to the line of precooked food that was produced by the Roux brothers. There was an air of tension and then, as I was onstage in the middle of demonstrating how to cook fish, a scuffle broke out in the audience between the two brigades. A couple of the lads had to be escorted from the building—which would have been fine if they had been drunk at a nightclub, but they were haute cuisine chefs at a trade fair, for heaven's sake. Newspapers got hold of the story and had a lot of fun writing about "Michelin Star Wars."

As it was, there was more than enough scrapping going on at Harveys. We had to contend with the Wandsworth yobs who thought it hilarious to wander up to the restaurant window, drop their trousers and do moonies at my customers. I'd send out chefs to deal with the bare-arsed idiots and chase them off. The Wandsworth louts might have thought they were tough, but the Harveys brigade was the toughest of the tough. One day a trio of young hooligans pushed open the front door, produced a can of Coke, shook it up, opened the lid and threw the exploding can into the restaurant. According to witnesses, it was like a gas bomb. Customers dived for cover, hoping not to be soaked by the foam as it fountained out of the missile. The yobs then legged it, stupidly unaware that their escape route was taking them right past the kitchen door at the back of the restaurant. "Get them, Gordon," I screamed.

Just as the yobs were running past the door, Gordon and a couple of other chefs greeted them in the courtyard. From my place at the stove, I could hear the biff, bang, wallop sounds of a good old scuffle. Then Gordon reappeared clutching his hand. During the fight he'd punched one of the yobs in the mouth and had somehow managed to end up with a tooth wedged in his knuckle. He extracted the gnasher, but was clearly in some pain, moaning and groaning; there was some speculation as to how long it would be before septicemia set in and killed him. "For Christ's sake," I said. "Am I the only bastard cooking?" At this point JC dashed into the kitchen, his eyes wide with terror. "They've got a hand grenade!" he screamed.

Hand grenade? Who? My maître d' spluttered something about the yobs' dads appearing on the scene for a bit of score settling and bringing with them a hand grenade. We were so exhausted and run-down that none of us thought to question JC's suggestion that our little restaurant by Wandsworth Common was about to be blown up by a hand grenade. I gave the command, "Bolt the fucking doors and get down." My SAS unit searched for cover, sheltering under pieces of furniture and in kitchen cupboards. When it was all quiet on the western front, everyone reemerged and continued with the job at hand, be it shelling peas, making pastry or trimming cheese for the evening service.

It was in the early days of Harveys that I renewed relations with my Italian relations. For some reason or other, I phoned my uncle Gianfranco, who mentioned that my younger brother, Simon—by now a man in his early twenties—was in a rut. "Send him over here," I told my uncle. "He can come and work for me." I went to Gatwick Airport and waited at the barrier to greet the brother I had not seen for almost two decades. It was a Sunday afternoon and very quiet in Arrivals. The first person to come through was a giant, a monster of a man, and I just thought, Christ, he's a big bloke. He was followed by the other passengers who had been on the flight, and when the place emptied, the giant was still standing there. He must have been six foot eight,

My mother with me and Clive on holiday in Italy in 1964;
Auntie Luciana, Nonna and Auntie Paola are behind us.

My mother enjoying life at Lake Garda, Italy, in 1952, before moving to Leeds to take up with a young cook named White.

One of my mother's favorite things: a signed photo of her admirers from her village of Bardolino.

My father and mother on their wedding day in 1954.

My father was a cook, too, a good Yorkshire bloke who loved to bet the races. When my mother died, the betting was his solace.

Fishing and the outdoors were my first great loves.
Whatever I learned about cooking, I stayed convinced
that Mother Nature is the real artist.

Me, Clive and Graham on our last vacation with our mum.

My first bird: Miss Great Britain hands me my reward for winning
two events in the Bridlington Sea Angling Festival.

Me and the genius, Raymond Blanc. He's laughing, so I must have been reminiscing about life in his kitchen. (BOB CARLOS CLARKE)

In 1987, with Lord Montgomery, receiving the Newcomer Restaurant of the Year at the Catey Awards.

When I was in the kitchen, there was no time to think of anything but what my hands were doing. (BOB CARLOS CLARKE)

Albert Roux and I savor a very private lunch at Harveys in 1989. (BOB CARLOS CLARKE)

Don't try this at home. (BOB CARLOS CLARKE)

Harveys: Step inside and enjoy the show. You can see me in the office at the top. (JEAN-CHRISTOPHE SLOWIK)

In the midst of a typically adrenaline-soaked service.
The devil in the kitchen, indeed. (BOB CARLOS CLARKE)

Alex, my first wife, put up with my obsession—for a time. (BOB CARLOS CLARKE)

Teaching a young lad called Ramsay. (BOB CARLOS CLARKE)

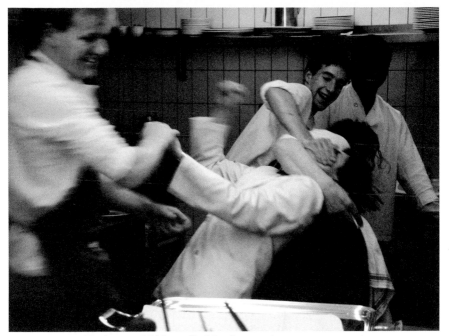

The boys and I blow off a bit of steam. (BOB CARLOS CLARKE)

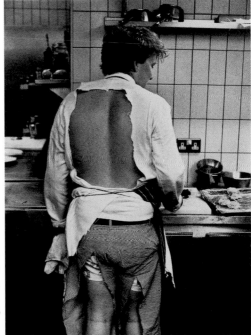

When one of my young cooks complained about the heat, I was good enough to help him cool down.
(BOB CARLOS CLARKE)

Just after being awarded my first Michelin star. Minutes later, I was back in the kitchen. (JOHN STODDART)

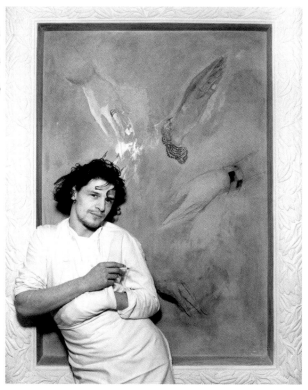

After winning my third star, I took a break for a photo with some of the lads who helped realize the dream. (TOM STOCKILL)

Mati and I finally get married.

Honeymooning in Venice (after Michael Winner finally went home).

Luciano at the beach.

Mirabelle at play.

Mirabelle, Luciano, Lettie and Marco on a day out in spring 2004.

Now that I've handed back my Michelin stars, I have time to do what I've always loved. Here I am as a young lad in Italy in 1964, and with my son Marco in Hampshire in 2003.

some five inches taller than me. He had to have been the tallest man in Italy.

We were brothers but hadn't recognized each other. We shook hands—perhaps we hugged each other, I can't recall—but apart from that, we couldn't really communicate. I didn't speak Italian and his English wasn't fantastic. After he'd said hello, he looked down at me and asked, "Do you know a shop called High and Mighty?" Nearly twenty years and that was it. Take me to High and Mighty. We swaggered out of the airport like a walking freak show: Italy's tallest man accompanied by his lanky, gaunt, hollow-cheeked older brother. At Harveys I put him on the Pastry section but it didn't work out, and after a week or so he returned home. Just like my earlier visit to Italy, his trip to Britain was cut short. At the time Simon aspired to be not a cook but a policeman and that's what he went on to become. He told one of my Italian-speaking chefs that once he was a cop, he would return to Harveys and arrest me for the way I treated my staff.

IT WAS NEVER going to last with Alex, and a couple of years after marrying, we were divorced. Two people need to have the same dream. Mine was winning three Michelin stars, and that ambition came before everything else in my life. Alex's dream . . . well, I don't quite know what her dream was. Even on paper we weren't a good match. I came from a hard, working-class world that, since my mother's death, had been dominated by men. All of a sudden there I was, married to a nice middle-class girl. I couldn't take it in. I didn't want things to be perfect. I didn't want pleasure. I was driven by my insecurities and a fear of failing, and to some extent a fear of dying before achieving my ultimate goal. The kitchen was the only place where I felt comfortable.

FIFTEEN

No Bill, No Mink

MY MANAGERESS CAME into the kitchen and she was nervous. The man on table two was complaining about the cheese, she said. I don't know what was making her nervous: his complaint about the cheese or my potential reaction to his complaint. I was curious. "What's wrong with the cheese?"

"He says he always chooses his own cheese," she replied.

"Well, tell him that's not the way we do it here," I said. "Just tell him that we do a plate that contains a selection of seven cheeses—they are all perfectly ripe—and that's how we do it. Go and tell him that." She scurried off, but returned a minute later, saying the customer was still insisting he wanted to choose his cheese rather than have the seven-cheese selection. "Can you deal with it?" she pleaded.

I walked from the kitchen to the restaurant and up to the customer. You'll have to take my word for it when I say that I was extremely polite, even though he was a particularly ugly, short-arsed redhead. I told him that we serve a selection of seven cheeses, "And that's the way we do it here, sir."

"But I don't like two of those cheeses," he said.

"Well, that means there are still five of them that you do like, sir. And each cheese is served as a substantial, generous portion."

He was having none of it. "I always choose my own cheese."

"That's not how we do it here," I repeated, not quite knowing where we were going with this one.

Slowly, with a hint of menace in his voice and a pause between each word, he said, "I always choose my own cheese." I don't know what happened in my head. I just decided that I wasn't going to tolerate it. The job's hard enough, I thought, why do I want someone like that in my restaurant? Even if there is an issue and we're wrong, there's no need to be an arsehole. And don't patronize me—and that's what he had done. He was patronizing me.

Of course I wanted to kick him out, but when you work your way up through the kitchens of Michelin-starred restaurants, they forget to teach you how to deal with rude and difficult customers. Albert was a strict boss and Pierre was notoriously hard on his staff, but I had never seen either of them give the punters what for. Raymond, of course, was charm personified, so he probably would have conceded and let the bloke choose his own bloody cheese. And what about Nico? It would infuriate him when customers booked a table and then didn't show up. So Nico would make his wife phone them to ask what had happened and then, with his hands on his hips, he would stand close by her—close enough for the person at the other end of the line to hear—and bark loudly, "Tell them to fuck off . . . We don't need their fucking money . . . Fuck them . . . Put the phone down on them."

Staring at this dwarfish, patronizing man who was slowing down the smooth-running operation of the restaurant for my valued customers, I found myself saying, "Why don't you just fuck off?" Pause. The smug smile didn't leave his face. "Forget the bill," I said. "Just fuck off." He stood up and walked out of Harveys.

THE CHOOSE-MY-OWN-CHEESE STORY is one of those anecdotes that would be used to illustrate the claims that I was an angry young man. After all, what kind of a chef kicks out a customer whose only offense is to ask if he could choose his own cheese? Yet what is fascinating about the above story is that I have since heard the customer *intended* to be kicked out. It was all premeditated. He came to the restaurant with the sole intention of getting a free meal by being obstinate. I can't think of many men who would put themselves through the humiliation of being told to eff off just so they could have a free lunch. But then, I suppose I should take it as a compliment.

Harveys had earned a terrific reputation for its food but, as I mentioned, punters also came for the show. One element of the show was provided by the celebrity clientele: star-struck customers could sit just a few feet away from them and ogle. I mean, if Ollie Reed had asked you to join his table, you'd remember it for the rest of your life, wouldn't you? Food is food, but a great restaurant is an experience. And the tension was heightened by the thought of the volatile, moody chef who was supposedly skulking in the kitchen. Customers had this image of me: the long-haired wolf lying in wait, ready to pounce on his prey, be it the customer who dared ask for salt or the one who returned his plate because the meat was undercooked.

The truth is that if customers wanted salt, they could have it. If they wanted their meat well done, let them have it that way. That's their choice. Everyone has a different palate. What bothered me was when customers started swearing and being loud, causing a scene in the restaurant and abusing the waiters, spoiling the enjoyment of neighboring tables—that's when they were asked to leave. I say *asked* to leave, though the five-step eviction process was perfected to such a degree that often not one single word was necessary. This is how it would work:

1. JC tells me about the irritating customers and I emerge to check them out before giving JC the OK.

2. JC rounds up his waiters and nods toward the table where the offending customers are seated.

3. On JC's command, the squad of waiters zooms in and clears everything—plates, glasses, cutlery, wine bottles, you name it—from the table in about fifteen seconds, so only the tablecloth remains. The customers are left sitting there, thinking the table is being cleared for the next course and marveling at the fantastic service.

4. JC swoops in, eaglelike, and snatches up the tablecloth. He disappears with it without a word, just *whoosh*. A few

minutes earlier the customers were sitting there, drunk and
imperious; now they're embarrassed. There is nothing but a
wooden table in front of them.

5. The customers get the message—they have been
humiliated—and they grab their coats and hurry out onto
Bellevue Road. And no, they did not have to pay a bill.

It was a spectacular sight. However, one night the victims—a bar-
rister, his mate and a woman—sat there for fifteen minutes, stunned
by JC's performance but puzzled as to what would happen next. Nothing happened, absolutely nothing—actions speak louder than words.
The message could not be ignored: Table number nine, your time is
up. That's the end. Please leave.

I was at the stove in Harveys one night when JC came into the
kitchen and said a customer was refusing to pay his bill. Why? Because he waited twenty minutes for his soufflé. Well, what can you
do about people like that? A soufflé has to be cooked to order because
it starts to deflate as soon as it comes out of the oven. You can't say,
"Here's one I made earlier." The customer was trying to take advantage, hoping for a free meal, but he had upset me in the middle of service. I asked JC if the customer's wife had a coat in the cloakroom and
he disappeared and returned saying, "She has a mink, Marco."

"Bring it to me," I said, "and tell the customer to come and see
me." When the man appeared in my sweatshop with his wife alongside, he was looking cocksure, as if he'd told his wife to observe how
he would handle the situation. He said, "Who is the chef?"

"I am."

"You wanted to see me."

"Please stand there," I said in my best headmaster's voice, telling
them to position themselves by a wall. "Wait until I have finished
preparing this dish." He and his wife stood silently for a minute or
two, watching me while I finished sealing or searing, then I turned to
them and inquired, "What's the problem?"

The man puffed himself up. "We waited twenty minutes for our soufflé and we're not going to pay our bill now." I said, "That's fine. No bill,

no mink." I pointed toward an underling in the corner who was holding the coat. The customers looked over. I had kidnapped their coat. I repeated the terms of the ransom. "No bill, no mink. Make your choice."

I had hardly finished the sentence when his wife perked up, "Pay the bill, darling."

I wasn't chippy, I don't think. It wasn't a case of a working-class lad having an issue with his upper-class customers. I didn't have a problem with the world I came from and I've never tried to hide from it. I was brought up on the belief that no man can choose what he's born into, but every man can choose to better himself. I tried to show customers the same amount of respect they showed my staff, although obviously there were exceptions.

JC told me the man on table twelve was being obnoxious.

I said, "What's his problem?"

"He's just obnoxious. He's not very nice."

So I stopped cheffing, went out to table twelve and said to the man sitting there, "Good evening. The maître d' tells me you've got a little problem."

The customer said, "I haven't got a problem."

"Strange," I said, "because the maître d' tells me you're being obnoxious." At that point the man sitting on the neighboring table interrupted, "I can vouch for him. He wasn't obnoxious."

I thought, What's it got to do with him? Why can't he just eat his meal and keep his nose out of it? So I said, "And you can fuck off too." Two birds with one stone.

Other customers must have found this sort of behavior extremely exciting, because a lot of the observers on neighboring tables tended to come back. So much so, in fact, that certain people actually thought I was hamming it up for effect. They reckoned my irritable nature was part of an act, designed to get more PR for Harveys. The fact is, I didn't like it when people interrupted my intensity. I was so passionate about the food and the restaurant that any criticism was destined to wind me up. A customer questioning the cheese dish was criticism. A customer saying he wouldn't pay his bill was criticism. And then there were the moments when I just happened to be in the wrong time at the wrong place.

I was at reception one evening, going through the following day's bookings, when I heard a voice and said, nose still in book, "I'll be with you in a minute, sir. Can you hang on?"

Then I heard the same voice say to me, "Are you going to insult me?"

I looked up and there, in front of me, was a mountain of a man. He was about six foot seven and broad as well. He had been in for dinner with a mate and had clearly drunk too much.

"Sir," I said, "if you're looking for insults, then you've knocked on the wrong door."

"Is that the best you can do?" he asked. He was itching for a fight.

"Look, if I decide to insult you, I'll choose my time and place to do it," I said. "And now is not the time or the place, so please enjoy your dinner, sir."

He went back to his table, and an hour or so later the big bruiser and his mate left Harveys, took a right and were walking up St. James's Drive. It was about midnight and I decided that now was the time. I told one of my chefs, Lee Bunting, and another one of the boys to fill two buckets of water. Then I sent them off to soak Man Mountain. They hurried off and returned, mission accomplished. I was having an espresso a while later when Man Mountain reappeared, perfectly dry but clutching two carrier bags full of soaked clothes. He must have gone home, changed, and then returned to the restaurant to show me the sodden garments.

"You threw a bucket of water over me," he said.

"I didn't," I replied. "I know nothing about this. Did you try chasing the people who did it?"

And his response was, "Have you ever tried running in a wet suit?" Great line, that.

Stories of my customer relations spread, but none of them deterred the restaurant guides. One day I even evicted the head inspector for the *Egon Ronay Guide*, which at that stage had awarded me two stars. He had been in for lunch and halfway through his meal came into the kitchen and, in front of all my chefs, said, "One of those oysters I had was a bit dodgy." He was only joking but I couldn't see it at the time and I flipped. "Why don't you just get out of my restaurant then?" I shouted. "As for the *Egon Ronay Guide*," I added, "why don't you just stick it up your arse?" Several months later when the guide came out, I was slightly surprised to see that I had been upgraded to three stars.

When my former boss Nico Ladenis came to Harveys, he too came into the kitchen and said, "The meal was superb." I thanked him before he added, "The veal with parsley purée was a little oversalted." I turned to Gordon Ramsay and said, "Gordon, tell him to fuck off."

Gordon obeyed. "Nico, fuck off." It was Gordon's first taste of abusing a customer.

Gordon and I were sitting in the restaurant late one night, just having a chat, when we heard a smash outside. We dashed out to the pavement and saw a man standing there. He had lobbed a brick through the window of our neighbors, an estate agency. When he ran away, Gordon chased him, and when I caught up, I saw that my underling had the brick thrower over a fence and was knocking the living daylights out of him.

Clearly, I realized, Gordon liked a scrap, and I needed him once when a fracas erupted in the restaurant. There were six customers— three men and three women on the same table—having lunch in Harveys and it was so late they were the only ones in the restaurant. I was at reception on the phone when one of the customers came up to me and said, "Can I use your phone?" I carried on having a chat when he came round and pushed me in the chest, so hard that I fell back into a chair. I still had the phone in my hand and told the person on the other end of the line that I would call them back. "I take great offense to you pushing me in the chest," I said. When he pushed me again, I hit him with all my might and he fell to the floor. JC witnessed the drama and screamed out for reinforcements, "Gordon! Gordon!" The next customer came running up to me and held a clenched fist above his head, ready to punch me. I chinned him as well, and he hit the floor. The third man who had been at the table came bounding up and he, too, went down. As the three customers scrabbled around on the floor, Gordon emerged from the kitchen, looking confused as he saw the bodies, and said, "What's up?" The customers left but, bizarrely enough, they returned a couple of hours later to shake hands and make friends.

Gordon, meanwhile, never really cracked until his final night at Harveys. I don't recall what he'd done wrong, but I yelled at him and he lost it. He crouched down on the floor in the corner of the kitchen, buried his head in his hands and started sobbing. "I don't care what you do to me," he said as he wept. "Hit me. I don't care. Sack me. I don't care." I was hardly going to sack him; he was leaving the next day. I'd gotten him a job working for Albert Roux at Gavroche.

I COULD SMELL the Michelin inspectors a mile off. The most important ones were the two at the top of Michelin UK: Derek Brown, the head inspector, and his number two, Derek Bulmer. They were the two Dereks. Or rather, the two Mr. Bs. I was not on first-name terms with the highly influential duo.

Inspectors tended to book a table for two early in the evening, let's say seven o'clock. You'd instantly smell a rat, as seven was rather early for dinner in Wandsworth. Then they would order a half bottle of wine, which, again, is suspicious, because people going for dinner to an upmarket restaurant usually order by the bottle. Then there was the fact that we knew what they looked like. After winning my first star, I had met both Mr. Bs, but when booking they would still use an alias because obviously they didn't want me to know they were coming.

They didn't arrive in disguise, wearing false beards and wigs, but although I knew they were in the restaurant, they were too clever to be outwitted. There wasn't the opportunity to make their meals more special, because they ordered dishes you couldn't change, such as a fish soup or terrine, which had been made earlier in the day.

I won my first star in 1988 and retained it the following year. Then, in the last few months of 1989, it crossed my mind that I might be up for promotion, because the Michelin men visited half a dozen times.

By now I had done several things to improve Harveys since winning my first star. During the summer of 1989 I had closed the restaurant for six weeks so that it could be totally refurbished. The provincial, unexciting décor I had inherited and despised was stripped away. I had taken on the services of interior designer David Collins, who would go on to design most of my restaurants. David made Harveys far more

stylish, elegant and chic, basing his design on New York's Waldorf-
Astoria—the walls were beautifully decorated with ornate plasterwork
and mirrors, the lighting was soft, the wallpaper was unobtrusive.

One day I saw Derek Brown in the restaurant and asked him what
he thought I could do to win two stars. "It's not for me to tell you how
to run your restaurant," replied the man I called Mr. Brown. "But if
you start serving amuse-bouches and improve your coffee, you won't
be a million miles away." That day I started serving amuse-bouches, or
amuse-gueules—little tasters to entertain the mouth. These included
grilled sea scallops with crispy calamari and a sauce made from the
squid ink; an individual oyster with watercress in champagne jelly;
and a brochette of langoustine with leeks and truffle. These amuse-
bouches had to be grand—you can't start with what I would call a little
knickknack on the plate. It was the first thing customers were going to
taste, and I had to leave them wanting more. The following week I
bought the best coffee machine and ordered a brand of delicious coffee. Harveys started serving the finest coffee in London. I could see
where Mr. Brown was coming from. Amuse-gueules provide the first
impressions of the meal while coffee provides the final mouthful.

I also asked my former boss Albert Roux what I could do to win another star, and he said, "Your menu is right; the balance is right. Just
refine the dishes and you will win two stars."

I've mentioned the refinement of classical dishes. There's
another name for it: nouvelle cuisine. The phrase probably
sends shivers down your spine if you were a restaurantgoer
in the eighties and remember the horrendous dishes involv-
ing small portions of food and crazy combinations—an assault on the palate of punters who seemed happy to pay for
the stuff. What a great shame that so few chefs—and most
restaurantgoers—do not understand the true meaning of
nouvelle cuisine. In fact, I'd say that 99 percent of chefs
haven't got a clue what it means. Nouvelle cuisine is classical cuisine with the concept lightened. It is what Fernand

Point did in France in the forties and fifties and then explained perfectly in *Ma Gastronomie*, the book I found while
working in the kitchen of the Box Tree as a teenager.

At Michel Roux's Waterside Inn, they used to do a veal
cutlet with caramelized bananas and raspberry vinegar
sauce. No, not very clever. At Albert Roux's Gavroche, they
did tournedos of beef with mangoes, oranges and lemons
with a rum sauce and served with a timbale of rice with a
fried banana on top of it. Again, it doesn't sound particularly
palatable. You'd probably describe both of these dishes as
nouvelle cuisine and you wouldn't be blamed for doing so.
But neither of them are true nouvelle cuisine because neither can be described as a classic dish that has had the concept lightened.

At Harveys, it was all about lightening. So I'd take flour
out of sauces and use natural juices. A mousselline of
scallops—a classic—is traditionally made with eggs and
cream. But if you use eggs, then you have to use the cream
to lighten the flavor, and before you know it, you've diluted
the taste of the scallops, which is what you really wanted to
eat in the first place. You don't need eggs because scallops
have their own natural protein. Simply get rid of the eggs
and there you have it—nouvelle cuisine. Classical cuisine
made new.

The Michelin men would always host a press lunch to coincide
with the annual publication of the guide, and usually the meal would
take place in a restaurant that was up for promotion. Of course,
Michelin needed to book a large table, and surreptitiously, so no one
sussed them.

Every January chefs would phone one another to see if anyone had
received an unusual booking for the day of the guide's publication
lunch. In January 1990 I didn't need to phone around. A booking had
been made for a table of twelve and the organizer was very cagey

about who was hosting the lunch. I felt confident it was a Michelin lunch, which, more than likely, meant I had won my second star.

I was in the kitchen at about twelve thirty, preparing for lunch service and awaiting the mysterious guests, whose table was booked for one P.M., when JC came in and said, "Mr. Brown from Michelin is here to see you." And there was Mr. Brown, standing right by the kitchen door. I went to shake his hand and he held up the freshly printed *Michelin Guide*. He flicked through the pages and then stopped on the entry that read, "Harveys: two stars . . ."

It was an achievement. I was twenty-eight years old, the youngest chef ever to win two stars from Michelin. It had been six years since a British restaurant had been upgraded from one star to two. I now joined a clique of two-star chefs, all of whom had been my bosses: Raymond Blanc, Nico Ladenis and Pierre Koffmann. The only three-star restaurants in England at the time were Gavroche, run by another mentor, Albert Roux, and the Waterside Inn, overseen by Albert's brother, Michel.

On top of that, Harveys was doing well, considering the slumping economy and high interest rates, which had been imposed to stop the boom. Maggie Thatcher's popularity was in decline and she wasn't doing herself any favors by introducing the poll tax. She had won her third term in office in 1987, the same year I opened Harveys, and the way business was going, my restaurant would still be open for business long after Maggie left No. 10 Downing Street.

Tears filled my eyes. I said, thank you. Yet Mr. Brown's good news did not encourage me to leave Harveys and go off and celebrate. Instead I retreated back into the kitchen and the comfort of hard work and discipline, and later that day Bob Carlos Clarke took that so-called classic shot of me smoking a cigarette and looking whacked.

Mr. Brown's guests from the press swanned into Harveys, took their seats, filled their glasses and cheerfully awaited the meal. I served them Tagliatelle of Oysters with Caviar as amuse-gueules; leeks and langoustines in jelly; pig's trotter; and then the Crackling Pyramide, a nougatine that was liquidized (the powder is then sprinkled onto a baking tray and put in the oven so that it melts, and when it is hot enough, you remove it, let it cool and then cut it into a pyramid shape and assemble it around a biscuit glace). They finished their banquet, Mr. Brown would have noted, with the most pleasant coffee money can buy.

When you win one star, the spotlight is on you. When you win two, however, the spotlight gets bigger. Approaches came in from the media but I turned down TV and said no to lots of media opportunities that would have brought me a good deal of money. As far as I was concerned, I had a duty to my paying customers. In the days when Derek Brown ran Michelin, he awarded the stars to the chef and he expected the chef to be behind his stove. These days it seems that the stars are given to the restaurant that enables the chef to spend little (or even no) time in his kitchen. I had zero obligation to the media.

When I did give a rare interview, the journalist would have to come to Harveys and stand by the stove, firing questions while I fiddled with the gas, chopped and cooked. About a year earlier we had been in the middle of lunch at Harveys when a film crew turned up to film me. Halfway through filming, I got angry for some reason or other and told them to get lost. As they headed out of the restaurant to load their equipment into their van, Keith Floyd, a brilliant chef and close friend who had been having lunch in the restaurant, left his table to come into the kitchen. "You may not like these people," he said to me. "They are, after all, television people, but it's terribly important that you are nice to them because they can help your business." I went outside and had a chat with the crew and within a few minutes they were back in Harveys, cameras rolling.

Keith says that while he still loves me, I am like a petulant child at times. But remember, I was just a young man in my twenties. I was trying to be a great chef, not a celebrity. Keith had made a conscious decision to become a television star, and at that time he reigned as king of the celebrity chefs.

If I was away from the kitchen, doing an interview or making a program, who would be in the kitchen cooking? I was chasing a Michelin dream, which had more than enough pressures attached to it. Now I was being followed by photographers and journalists who relayed my every movement and supposedly private conversation to the British public. I didn't have a team of managers like the celebrity chefs of today. Alan Crompton-Batt worked as my publicist, but unlike that of the modern-day celebrity chef, my life was not one long day of meetings with potential sponsors, TV producers, book publishers and agents. I didn't zoom from one television studio to another to sit on a sofa or stand in a mocked-up kitchen doing a Baked Alaska demonstration for the viewers at home. If you are a chef today and want to become a TV personality, then you'll have some idea of what to expect because others have gone before you. But I wasn't in a position to look around me and think, There's another young cook who's in the limelight; I'll ask him how he copes with being a celebrity. There were no other young celebrity chefs. What's more, I was a working-class lad, and the big name at the time was Keith, who was posh, highly articulate, witty, and distinctly middle class.

Away from the kitchen, it was a struggle to keep my private moments my own, and I was constantly trying to outwit the Fleet Street pack that lurked so close behind me. They were never closer than when I started going out with Nicky Barthorpe. A posh Chelsea girl and minor aristocrat, Nicky had worked with my wife Alex for Edina Ronay, the fashion designer and daughter of restaurant critic Egon Ronay. Nicky had started out as my wife's friend, and when my marriage ended, she became my girlfriend. The *Daily Mail* gossip columnist Nigel Dempster sniffed out the story that we were seeing each other and dispatched one of his reporters, Kate Sissons, to the flat in Tite Street, Chelsea, where Nicky and I had set up home. Kate rang the buzzer wanting an interview. Would Nicky and I pose for a picture? I ignored the requests. Half an hour later I looked out the window down onto the street a couple of stories below and could see Kate sitting in an open-top sports car with a photographer, another woman, at the wheel. They knew I would have to come out sooner or later and they would sit and wait all day if necessary. I was imprisoned—the only way out was through the front door and into the *Mail's* clutches—but somehow I had to escape.

I phoned the kitchen at Harveys and asked to speak to Lee, by far the most loyal of my henchmen and the one who truly appreciated my sense of mischief. I said, "Lee, listen closely. There are two people outside my flat waiting to get a picture of me. They're from the *Daily*

Mail and they're in an open-top sports car. I want you to get a couple of
the lads and give them a bucket each. Fill the buckets with flour—be
generous with the flour—then add some water and mix it to a good
paste. Once you've done that, get over to Tite Street and chuck the contents of your buckets over the two people outside my flat. Got it?"

"Yes, Marco."

I sat by the window waiting for the show to start and waved at Kate,
who waved back. Then I saw Lee and his little gang appear, their car
screeching up beside the photographer's sports car. Lee and the others
jumped out and—whoosh—three buckets of paste were thrown over
Kate, her snapper and the leather interior of the car. Goo was all over
them. They stood there, white statues on the black tarmac. On the
other side of the road was an old people's home and the elderly resi-
dents gathered and gasped. The next thing that happened was not
meant to have happened. From nowhere a red car zoomed into the
picture and four large men with guns leapt from it. "Police!" they
yelled. Lee and the other cooks were pushed up against a wall while
Special Branch put away their guns and produced batons and hand-
cuffs. A couple of squad cars arrived and my chefs were put into it and
whisked away.

It all could have gone badly wrong had I not phoned Kate and
asked her not to press charges. "Come for dinner as my guest at Harveys," I said. She saw the funny side of it, but the photographer wasn't
happy. Nigel, meanwhile, ended up with a good story and eventually
Kate got her interview. A couple of nights later I was there at the stove,
with Lee and the other miscreants by my side, cooking a Michelin-
starred dinner for the journalist we had pasted. Paying penance has
never seemed more peculiar.

SIXTEEN

Banged Up and Butchered

I WOKE FROM my sleep with a start. There was a nasty stabbing pain in my chest, which intensified, making me gasp for breath. It was as if I couldn't get any oxygen. What was happening? What the hell was going on? It was a rainy morning in the winter of 1989, and the last thing I could remember was returning home from Harveys the night before and crashing onto the bed, fully clothed, clutching my house keys. Now I looked down to my hands and couldn't see the keys. The pain in my chest wasn't easing. Had I swallowed them? Was it possible that I had swallowed my house keys? My sleep-deprived, adrenaline-fueled, thousand-meal-an-hour, workaholic existence was certainly manifesting itself in strange forms. I couldn't die now, not before I'd won my third Michelin star.

I staggered from the bed, out of the house and into the street, grabbing a spare set of keys on the way. I grabbed a spare set because it occurred to me that the keys in my gullet might remain lodged there forever, like the cowboy sheriff with the rusty bullet in his body, and I'd be unable to get back into the house.

I clutched my chest with one hand while using the other to hail a cab. "Chelsea and Westminster, please." What a wretched sight I must have looked to the medical team at the ER: a big, pallid, panting creature with wild hair. "What's the problem?" asked the doctor.

"Swallowed my house keys."

You hear those apocryphal stories of people limping into hospital because strange objects have been stuck into their orifices during kinky sex games. I could see it: the story about the wild-haired man who turned up with keys in his chest was destined to become another classic yarn in the staff canteen at the Chelsea and Westminster.

I was taken to a room and x-rayed and then the doctor stood and studied the picture in front of me. "As you can see," he said, running his finger down the X-ray, "there are no keys inside you." Reassuring news. He reckoned I'd suffered a panic attack in my sleep—there would be more of those to come. My blood pressure was an extremely dangerous 210 over 180. If I'd been an older man, I would have suffered a heart attack. I didn't ask for a second opinion and I'm glad that I didn't—I later found my house keys on my bedside table.

My God, what had I done to my poor body? I didn't really accept it at the time, but I was undoubtedly messed up, physically, mentally and emotionally. The frightening thing was, I didn't feel tired or exhausted because my craving for the next fix of adrenaline kept me going. I had this ability to drive myself beyond myself, if you get my drift. My mind was stronger than my body. My body was saying, "Give me a break," but my mind was saying, "Let's go faster." Most mornings, I would leap out of bed and dash around the house, putting on my shoes while simultaneously brushing my teeth, making coffee and reaching for a Marlboro red.

That pace continued throughout the day. I was in the restaurant from nine in the morning until two the following morning, and then back home for three or four hours sleep. It was absolutely relentless. Rumors circulated that I was a coke fiend—understandable, I suppose, when you consider the whirlwind that engulfed me. However, I couldn't have done the job or worked those hours if I'd have been on drugs. Sitting in Harveys once, aware of the gossip, I amused myself by lining my forearm with salt and sniffing it up my nostrils. Onlookers would have thought I was snorting cocaine, but I won't try that joke again. At the time I wasn't much of a drinker either; I wouldn't really take up drinking until I was thirty-eight.

I was in the kitchen one afternoon, probably jabbing an incompetent lackey, when JC poked his head through the doorway and said, "Your doctor is here." Eh? My doctor?

"How weird," I said. Wandsworth was a bit off the beaten track for her. "Has she ordered?" I asked JC.

"No, she's not eating," he replied. "She says she wants to see you." I went through to the restaurant and, sure enough, there was my doctor at a table. I was surprised by her presence but sat down and joined her. She explained that Nicky Barthorpe was very concerned about my health and had requested she come and see me. How peculiar.

I lit a Marlboro, swigged a double espresso and mumbled something about feeling fine. My doctor explained that I was an adrenaline junkie (I'm paraphrasing, of course) and that I was pushing myself too far. She said I was exhausted and depressed.

She certainly had me sussed. "You need to be sedated," said the doctor, and she gave me a prescription for some pills. "Take the pills, go to bed and stay there for three days." She made me promise to obey her orders. I took the pills, climbed into bed and had an extremely good night's sleep. But it was no use. The following morning I woke feeling refreshed, jumped out of bed and zoomed back to Harveys.

There were rarely moments of normality. Nicky Barthorpe collected me from Harveys one night and was driving us home to Chelsea when we heard a police siren behind us. We pulled over and the cops asked Nicky to step out of the car, so I got out at the same time. After accusing Nicky of taking an illegal left turn, the police asked if she'd had a drink. Nicky said she hadn't had a drop (which was true) and then she was asked if she'd been smoking drugs (again, she hadn't). Having done a tough night at the stove, I found it all a bit too demanding. It was wrong-time, wrong-place stuff again. I lurched forward when the drugs question came up, most likely looking haggard and sweat-drenched. "That's an unnecessary question," I said to the copper, "and I think you should retract it."

The cops turned from Nicky to me, the monster in the darkness. Let's be honest, I don't suppose there was the slightest possibility of the question being retracted. One of them sneered, "Come again?"

I said, "I think it's unnecessary to ask her if she's been smoking drugs, and I think you should retract the question and apologize for asking it."

They told me to get back in the car. They didn't want trouble. "No,"

I said, "not until you apologize." I think it was probably three seconds later that I found myself facedown on the warm hood of a police car, handcuffed and heading for a cell at the Battersea police station. They locked me up for seven hours, then released me and told me to be in court at ten A.M. I failed to keep the appointment. Instead I went to my solicitor and told him what had happened, and when I said I'd failed to present myself at court, he was sick with worry and angst. "You can either become a fugitive or surrender yourself," he explained.

"This is all a bit serious," I said. "I mean, all I've done is ask a policeman to say sorry to a lady." Anyway, I surrendered myself, got locked up for another couple of hours, and then made my appearance at the magistrates' court. I was bound over to keep the peace for six months. One of the three magistrates said, "We'd like you to sign the book on the way out, Mr. White." I assumed she was referring to *White Heat*, which had recently been published.

"I'm terribly sorry, Your Honor," I replied, "but I didn't bring a copy with me."

The magistrate was puzzled. She turned to the judge on her right and they whispered for a bit before turning back to me. "Not *your* book," she said impatiently, "*our* book." She pointed toward the clerk's office, where reprobates have to sign various court documents.

THE PRESS COULDN'T get enough of it. I was in the papers every day. One minute I was "the enfant terrible of haute cuisine," the next I was "the enfant terrible of British cooking," then I acquired global domination by becoming "the enfant terrible of the culinary world." I was the "anarchic Byron of the backburner," who was "almost psychopathic." Most of them saw me, unequivocally, as "London's rudest chef," which had no detrimental effect whatsoever on business.

Women who had seen my picture in the papers, or observed my mug on the telly, felt compelled to raid their drawers and send me explicit letters along with their knickers. Chefs aren't supposed to receive knickers in the post, no matter how many Michelin stars they've won. If I'd kept the contents of those Jiffy bags, I could have opened an underwear shop.

Instead I used to auction the knickers in the kitchen before service. I'd start the bidding at a pound and invariably it was the young Gordon Ramsay, emotionally battered and bruised by my bollockings, who outbid the others and ended up with these mementos—perfumed, lacy souvenirs of his life with the man he later described as his mentor.

Even after a seventeen-hour day at Harveys, I didn't particularly want to go home and sleep. I was both an early bird and night owl. Several years earlier, when I'd first come to London, I had headed to the King's Road and hooked up with the postpunk crowd. But during my Harveys days I went from socializing with the Chelsea set to mixing with the Mayfair mafia (affluent young people, rather than gangsters) and I moved into a flat in Pavilion Road, Knightsbridge.

I would go to Tramp, the renowned rock-star-crammed nightclub in Jermyn Street, just off Piccadilly, which was owned by the so-called King of Clubs, Johnny Gold. I didn't dance and I didn't drink, but I liked the place, nevertheless. Johnny was very kind to me, and although I wasn't a member, he allowed me to come and go as I pleased and always invited me to join him at his table of beautiful people.

To keep things interesting, I would flick french fries across the room at famous people, though obviously not when Johnny was sitting beside me. One night I spotted the Rolling Stones' Bill Wyman and I thought I'd chip him. He was moving in to chat up a blond, and just as he put his arm around her waist, I flicked the chip. It hit him hard on the hand. Bill snatched his hand back and ran off, probably thinking the girl had smacked him.

Tramp was the setting for an encounter with Lisa Butcher, the woman who would become my second wife. I was walking into the club one night in late 1991 when three young ladies were getting a hard time at the door. Johnny didn't like Tramp to be seen as a pickup joint—it was there for couples and friends—so single-sex groups were usually turned away. As I passed reception, I felt sorry for the girls and said, "They're with me," and as a result they were allowed in. I carried on walking down the stairs when one of them said, "Hello, Marco."

I turned round and stared at her face, but I couldn't put a name to it. In fact, I didn't recognize her at all. "Who are you?" I asked.

She said, "We met at Harveys. I'm Lisa Butcher."

Then she reminded me that she had been one of the guests at photographer Norman Parkinson's birthday party, held at Harveys in 1990. Bob Carlos Clarke, who was also at the party, had brought her into the kitchen to introduce her. I remembered the occasion then. She was an eighteen-year-old model, dressed glamorously in a sailor suit. She was a big name; people had been talking about her. While in school she had won the *Elle* Face of the Year competition, and when she arrived at Harveys, she was something of a celebrity because Parkinson had recently photographed her and publicly predicted that she was "the face of the nineties." I suppose Parky had done for her what Ronay had done for me. It had been a brief introduction at Harveys and now, on the stairs at Tramp, our conversation was equally short. I didn't see her again that night.

The next day Lisa phoned me at Harveys. She wanted to say thanks for helping her and her friends get into Tramp. She suggested coffee sometime. "I'm at Harveys all afternoon," I said. "If you want to come over, I'd love to have coffee with you." I couldn't let a beautiful girl get in the way of Harveys. That afternoon we had coffee at my restaurant, followed by a walk on Wandsworth Common. It was all quite romantic. A dinner date was fixed, and the next thing I knew, we were partners.

Lisa was undoubtedly one of the most exquisite-looking women in the world. I was enchanted by her beauty, and that was the problem.

I was a young man who was visual and found her looks intoxicating: The mere sight of her was so amazing that I completely forgot to think about her personality. But if I'd thought about it, it would have dawned on me that we weren't a good match because we had so little in common. Within three weeks of meeting her at Tramp, I had proposed with the line, "Do you fancy running off and getting married?"

What on earth was I playing at? I thought I was happy, but I was lonelier than I had ever been. If I'm honest with myself, I never had any emotions for Lisa. It wasn't her fault. Apart from having nothing in common, there was also a big age difference: she was twenty-one and I was thirty. Of course, I didn't step away from my one true love. I continued to work like a dog at Harveys while Lisa set about organizing the wedding, a Catholic number at Brompton Oratory in Knightsbridge, followed by a reception for seventy guests at the Hurlingham Club, beside the Thames in Fulham.

The night before the wedding I had a memorable meeting with a man called Rafiq Kachelo. Rafiq had been a regular at Harveys since the early days and was such a big spender that he was single-handedly responsible for keeping us going in the days before Egon Ronay's glorious review. I think I'm right in saying that he was the world's richest mango grower and he could torch money like no other person I've known. We all adored him.

He would arrive at Harveys and order a £2,000 bottle of Pétrus '55—and that was just as an aperitif. There had been weeks when Rafiq alone was accountable for 50 percent of Harveys takings. When I was married to Alex, Rafiq took us and another couple for lunch at Michel Roux's Waterside Inn. The bill for five was an astonishing £10,000. He spent big, seven days a week. He looked the part too, and was always immaculately dressed. Although he could drink huge quantities, Rafiq never appeared drunk and the waiters used to say he never left the table to go to the loo. He gave new meaning to the phrase "hollow legs."

Anyway, the night before my wedding, I was sitting with Rafiq and for some reason he asked me what sort of cuff links I would be wearing for the wedding ceremony. "Oh my God," I said. "I haven't got any cuff links." I'd never needed cuff links before. Rafiq removed the ones he was wearing and handed them to me. They were monsters: heavy, large and with fifty diamonds in each of them. They were beyond vulgarity because they were so beautifully crafted.

Before I left Rafiq that night, he said, "Are you sure you're doing the right thing?"

Of course I was doing the wrong thing, but I didn't have the courage to accept it, so I replied, "Yeah."

He was continually spouting words of wisdom, and one of his favorite sayings was "Never let an illusion turn into a delusion." Those words came back to me in the Brompton Oratory on August 14, 1992, as my bride walked down the aisle toward me and my best man, Albert Roux. It was all so showbizzy, the rock star chef marries the upmarket young model. The illusion that I could be as successful in the home as I had been in the kitchen was rapidly turning into a delusion.

I do remember thinking I shouldn't be there, but there was something inside me that said that rather than cancel the whole thing, it was better to go through with the wedding, let Lisa have her big day and then let it break down naturally afterward. It seemed like an easier blow, though I accept that many people might be appalled by my rationale.

It didn't take long for it to break down. Right from the start the signs were obvious to the outside world. A reporter had asked for my opinion of the bride's dress—a floor-length, backless white dress designed by Bruce Oldfield—and I mumbled something about how she looked like she had dressed to go down the catwalk rather than the aisle. My unkind remark spawned newspaper features along the lines of, "How would you feel if the man you were marrying hated your dress?" Even at the reception, as guests relaxed and chatted over champagne, I disappeared into the kitchen of the Hurlingham Club to check up on my brigade of boys, who were preparing the wedding breakfast. Terrine of Salmon and Langoustines in a Sauternes Jelly followed by a Fillet of Scotch Beef en Croûte with Pommes Fondants, Haricots Verts and Sauce Périgueux. Amid the heat, the smells, the noise and the pressure, I felt secure.

I don't remember blazing rows with Lisa; it just fizzled out. I was at Harveys much of the time and Lisa was working abroad a good deal. Within fifteen weeks we had separated. Let it break down naturally, I had told myself before taking my vows. And it did.

I promised to return the cuff links to Rafiq after the wedding. When that moment came, however, he refused to take them back, saying, "I meant them as a gift." Months later, when I asked Lisa to rummage through my belongings and give the cuff links back, she said they were lost.

About five years ago I was in the Pharmacy, in Notting Hill, with my wife, Mati. We were having dinner with Jane Proctor, then editor of *Tatler* magazine, and Jane's husband, Tom. A woman walked into the restaurant and all heads turned to observe the apparently striking blonde. She was with a group of friends and they walked over to a table and sat down.

Customers were transfixed by the woman, muttering, "Wow, who's

she?" and that kind of thing. I glanced at her but couldn't see it myself;
I didn't understand what all the fuss was about. Then I found myself
studying her and thinking, I know those expressions, I know those
looks; I've seen them before.

A few minutes later the woman who'd caused the commotion
walked toward our table. As she got closer, she said, "Hi, Marco." It
was only at that point that I realized it was Lisa, my ex-wife. Just like
that night on the stairs in Tramp, I had failed to recognize her. Had
she really played such an insignificant role in my life that I didn't have
a clue who she was until she spoke?

She said, "Do I get a kiss from you, Marco?" and bent down to kiss
me, but my immediate reaction was to recoil. I moved my head to
avoid her pouting lips and said, "Please don't, Lisa." My marriage to
her had been a mistake and I don't have many good memories of the
experience. Lisa didn't say another word, she just walked back to her
table and that was the end of it. A couple of minutes later, though, I
felt a thud on my chest as I was hit by a missile. Someone from Lisa's
table had chucked an ice cube at me. Mati, Jane and Tom were horrified. In the old days, the days when I did spontaneous things like marrying Lisa, I would have responded rock-star style by charging over to
the table with a bucketful of ice. But then I did nothing. Lisa—or another good shot at her table—had finally exacted her revenge.

SEVENTEEN

Not a Lot of People Know This

IWAS IN the kitchen at Harveys one day in March or April 1991 when I got a phone call from Steven Saltzman, the son of Bond movie producer Harry Saltzman. Steven had been a Harveys regular since the day he'd phoned to book a table after reading a *Sunday Times* article about the restaurant. In the article I was quoted as saying something controversial like, "Everyone who eats at Harveys is fat and ugly." So when I told Steven there were no free tables, he'd replied, "What if I tell you I'm fat and ugly?" After that amusing remark I found room for him on that evening and any subsequent evening.

On this particular spring day Steven called for a chat and, apropos of nothing, he asked what I'd been up to. I mentioned that I'd nipped over Wandsworth Bridge to look at a potential restaurant site in Chelsea Harbour and we talked for a minute or two about the area, how it was up-and-coming with luxurious, expensive apartments, a few boutiques and a couple of so-so restaurants. Princess Margaret's son, Viscount Linley, and the aristo photographer Patrick Litchfield had opened a burger bar called Deals, which seemed to be doing well and was getting heaps of publicity. There was also a nice hotel where punters could sit and have a cocktail on the terrace while admiring the yachts in the marina.

I finished the chat with Steven and ten minutes later he phoned again saying, "You're going to be getting a call from Michael Caine."

"Whatever for?" I asked.

Steven explained that following our conversation he had phoned Shakira Caine, Michael's wife, and mentioned that I was planning to open a restaurant in the harbor. Michael had been milling around in the background and overheard Shakira mention my name. His ears pricked up—though we'd never met, he'd eaten at Harveys a few times—and when she came off the phone, he asked, "What was that all about?" So Shakira told him I was going to open a restaurant on their doorstep. Michael was really interested. In his time, he'd made a bit of cash from restaurants and he saw the opportunity of making more with me. Remember, though, I wasn't going to open a restaurant in the harbor; I'd only been to look at a site, nothing more than that. My remark to Steven had been embellished wonderfully in the retelling.

As a kid I didn't watch much TV because I was too busy poaching and nosing around the Harewood estate. But I had seen two of Michael's movies, *Get Carter* and *The Italian Job*. So when he rang, the voice was instantly familiar.

"May I speak to Marco Pierre White?" he said.

Feeling mischievous I asked, "Who's speaking?"

"My-cool Caine," he replied and then swaggered straight to the point. "I hear you're opening a restaurant in Chelsea Harbour."

Fifteen minutes ago I hadn't been opening a restaurant in the harbor, but now I was. "Yes, that's correct," I replied. "What if I am?"

"I want in," said Michael—pure Harry Palmer stuff.

That was how it started. We must have had a meeting, but I don't remember it, and then we hooked up with Claudio Pulze, who'd made a few quid out of the Italian restaurants he owned in London. Claudio owned the lease to the site I'd seen that morning before speaking to Steven, so he was in, as well. This was the setup:

Michael was the man with the vision. He'd wanted to open a restaurant in the harbor because his London home was a penthouse flat overlooking the Thames in Chelsea Harbour, and he quite liked the idea of owning a restaurant that would be virtually next to his living room. He'd just been waiting for the right thing to come along and now it had. Michael had the cash and he was going to give me—yes, hand me—a stake in the business.

Claudio was the guy with the property and he knew about the catering business. He was a bellhop in Turin before coming over to England and, in 1975, opening his first restaurant, Montpeliano in Knightsbridge, which, incidentally, is still there.

I was the one passionate about food and with the reputation for being a workaholic. And Michael liked me, so there you go.

The three of us went to see the site. It was a monster. We thought, this is going to be bigger than any top restaurant London has ever seen. We were looking at a 200-seater, which meant about three thousand covers on a good week—and when it eventually opened, we reached that target. We knew the more punters we got in, the more money we would make. This place was going to revolutionize restaurants. From then on, size would matter. The phrase *gastrodome* had yet to be coined, but what we had in mind was a gastrodome, nevertheless.

There was a hitch, however, which prevented us from opening quickly. The trouble was, Britain was hobbling along in one of the worst recessions of the twentieth century. The restaurant industry was really suffering and there we were, talking about opening a huge restaurant and expecting it to be filled every night. People were broke, for Christ's sake. The yuppies had done their bollocks, as my old man would have said. John Major was the prime minister but there was an overwhelming feeling that he was on his way out, and then there would be a hung Parliament or an end to Labour's years in the wilderness. "We'll wait," said Michael. Come again? And he explained his strategy: we would wait for the outcome of the general election and take it from there. He didn't want to invest until he felt comfortable that he was onto a winner. He was asking himself the crucial question: If Labour wins, will the economy sink so low that it kills all hopes of opening our Chelsea Harbour monster? It was, then, a Major hitch.

So we waited, and during the pause Michael and I underwent a bonding process. He is a gourmet who likes good food cooked well, no fuss, and he likes to talk about restaurants. Michael invited me into his confidence, his home and the world of the glitterati. He didn't need to be so good-natured because we were, after all, simply business-partners-to-be. But as our restaurant site sat waiting for the general election outcome, Michael and I started to spend time together. The Caines would come for dinner at Harveys and I would go for lunch at their house near Wantage, in Oxfordshire.

Lunch chez Michael followed a pattern. He was the one, rather than Shakira, who would do Sunday lunch, and he was more than capable of the job. He is what I would describe as a proper cook: he did what he did—usually simple stuff, nothing too aspiring—and he did it very well. We'd sit down and have a good roast with all the trimmings. There were times, certainly at the beginning of our friendship, when I felt slightly intimidated by Michael, not only because he was a legend but also because I wasn't used to sitting down to a meal with people thirty years my senior.

When the food was finished, he'd produce a bottle of that ghastly herbal alcoholic drink Fernet-Branca. Then we'd leave the table and go for a stroll in his beautiful garden. As we ambled through the garden, Michael would recount amusing stories about the people he had met during his fascinating life, as well as a story or two about Peter Langan, the legendary restaurateur and Michael's former partner.

He'd smile nostalgically while reminiscing about Peter's custom of staggering from his restaurant to collapse on the pavement outside, his legs extended over the curb so his feet were in the gutter. Michael was at the restaurant once when Peter stumbled in and said in his Irish brogue, "I don't know why, but me feet are fookin' killin' me." Michael said to me, "I looked down at his spats to see bloody tire marks on each shoe. Some bastard had driven over his bloody feet. And Peter didn't even know it."

While we were still waiting to see what would happen in the general election, Michael invited John Major for lunch at the penthouse. "Will you cook for us?" Michael asked me, and of course I said yes. I was something of a hired gun at that time. Celebrities and anyone who was wealthy enough to have outside caterers at their home would call me in and I'd pitch up with a few of the Harveys boys. I arrived at Michael's penthouse with my mini team of cooks and got to work on the meal. I don't remember what I cooked, apart from the main course. Remember, Michael is a straightforward eater who doesn't like fuss, so there were no surprises when he asked for a roast chicken with all the trimmings.

In at least a million homes every day a chicken is put into an oven, left to sit there for a couple of hours and removed when it's brown.

That's not how to roast a chicken. This is what I would do at Harveys and in the restaurants I had afterward, and this is what I did for Michael:

I'd get the best chicken, a poulet de Bresse, and then I would sous-vide it—cook it under pressure. Sous-viding is a process by which the bird is sealed in a bag, almost vacuum-packed, and poached for ten minutes at 175 degrees Fahrenheit so that the heat gently penetrates from each side. Then it's lifted out of the water and allowed to rest. After that you cook the skin by browning the bird on each side in a pan of clarified butter, sitting it on its back and putting it in the oven for thirty minutes or so, depending on how big it is. Done— you have a golden brown chicken, cooked to perfection.

If you just put a chicken in the oven, it's cooked before it's brown. In my restaurants I had sous-viding machines, but you can do the same thing at home by wrapping the bird in plastic wrap until it's perfectly sealed and then poaching it for twenty minutes. The beautiful juices will collect in the plastic wrap and can be poured over the cooked meat before you finish the cooking process in the oven.

The sous-viding process means you don't need to stuff the bird. Stuffing is an important part of roasting fowl, and when I was a boy, it was traditional to stuff ducks and geese and then sew up the arse before roasting. Why were they

stuffed? To slow down the cooking so the bird cooked from
the outside in. If you don't stuff it, the heat gets into the cavity and the bird cooks from the inside out, so the skin isn't
cooked and the bird is very fatty.

Michael greeted his guests at the door and John and Norma Major
came in. Then Mick Jagger and Jerry Hall. And finally, Bryan Forbes
and his wife, the actress Nanette Newman. I was in the kitchen with
the boys and we were cooking and chatting—it must have been one of
those rare occasions when I allowed conversation—about *The Italian
Job*. We were talking about that classic scene in the movie when
Michael's team blow up a mini and he delivers the classic line, "You
were only supposed to blow the bloody doors off." As we were chatting, we found ourselves in our own drama. Smoke erupted from the
cooker and the air-conditioning wasn't working. So before we knew it,
we were all coughing and spluttering, engulfed in a fog of smoke, and
then the fire alarm went off. One of the choking boys opened the
kitchen doors to get a bit of oxygen, and a thick, dark cloud of smoke
poured out of the kitchen and into the living room, where Michael was
standing with the PM and a cluster of stars, no doubt telling them how
they were about to be fed by a Michelin-starred chef. Through the
smoke I could see Michael with a look of shock on his face—he knew
the fire brigade didn't have hoses long enough to reach his penthouse—
and then he became the action hero we all know and love. Michael
dashed in with the window key, yelling, "You're supposed to open the
windows, not the bloody doors."

John Major survived that lunch date and went on to beat Neil Kin-
nock and win the election in April 1992, stretching the Conservatives'
winning streak to four general elections in a row. The pollsters and
pundits were alarmed by the victory but Michael, Claudio and I were
delighted. Major might not have halted the recession, but we opened
the restaurant anyway, perhaps because Michael felt we had escaped
the worst-case scenario, which was a Labour win.

The Canteen opened in November 1992, just as Bill Clinton was about to beat George Bush Sr. in the U.S. presidential elections. It was heaving, just as we'd hoped, and was bright, spacious and busy, clocking up a few thousand meals each week. Another gastrodome was opened shortly after we appeared on the scene, Terence Conran's Quaglino's. The nation was still in recession but that couldn't stop us. We were a destination restaurant, by which I mean punters traveled to Chelsea Harbour just for a meal at the Canteen, for superb ingredients cooked to perfection.

We cooked dishes like Roast Wood Pigeon with a Perfume of Ceps and White Truffle Oil and Roast Saddle of Lamb with Juniper Jus. There was poached salmon and there was sautéed salmon, served with savoy cabbage leaves that had been cooked, liquidized to a purée and then blended with chicken stock and cream and infused with white truffle oil. The Canteen won a Michelin star and I can't think of another restaurant that size that has achieved that.

I didn't step away from Harveys. I was still there during lunch and evening service, but the rest of the day was spent at the Canteen, where I had installed former Harveys chefs Stephen Terry and Tim Hughes. It wasn't until the following year, in late 1993, that I bailed out of Harveys. I sold my stake and Mark Williams, who had been my Harveys assistant from day one, became the restaurant's head chef. Eventually, my little gem on Wandsworth Common was no more. Harveys had played such an influential role in the career of so many talented chefs, and then it was gone. Today it is still a restaurant and a good one at that. It's Chez Bruce, a Michelin-star winner where Bruce Poole is the chef. I have never been back to eat at that restaurant, though. You move on, don't you? I didn't feel sad to leave. I felt it was time to move on, time to progress.

EIGHTEEN

The Best Thing That Ever Happened to Me

Give me me a rule and I'll probably break it. As a boss I had one sacred rule, which was never to go out with a staff member. I managed to keep to it from the day I opened Harveys in January 1987 right up to the final days of 1992. Business was business, and I reckoned a fling with a waitress or manageress would be an unnecessary distraction. You can appreciate the dangers, can't you? Think of all those horror stories about the office boss who has a romance with his secretary. This is one of the reasons I haven't had too many female cooks working with me. Women chefs are very good, probably better than men at cooking because they don't take shortcuts. But from my experience, when I have employed women, they tend to end up going out with one of my boys and that can lead to a major breakdown in the discipline of the kitchen.

I resisted the urge to date attractive women on my payroll for five years, a full half decade, but when I broke the rule, I did it stylishly.

The story begins not in 1992 at the Canteen, but a year or so earlier. Antony Worrall Thompson was a mate of mine and would often phone up, asking me to go along to the Char Bar in Chelsea. "There's a beautiful Spanish bird who works there," he used to say, as if that was enough to make me charge over the river. Antony's intention was not to set me up with "the Spanish bird," but he didn't want to turn up at the bar on his own, otherwise he risked looking like a lonely bloke. Despite Antony's pleading phone calls, I don't think I ever went with him, so at the time I never met the woman in question, and I'm sure he was never so precise as to mention that her name was Mati.

Then one night I finished service at Harveys and went for a drink at Antony's trendy restaurant 190 Queensgate. At the time, 190 was like a chefs' club. We all gathered there after service just to wind down. In fact, to digress slightly, one night I was seriously wound up and there was a punch-up. I didn't drive but had taken on a driver called Trevor who had gypsy origins, which meant that he was deemed unsuitable by some of the posh clientele who drank at 190. Another customer started taking the mickey out of Trevor, and when I asked him to stop with the nasty comments, he refused to do so and then he started squaring up to me. My father's old line, "Don't argue, just hit 'em," came back to me. I broke the guy's nose and no one blamed me—he was a snob who needed bringing down to size.

Anyway, moving on. Antony's charm offensive had reaped dividends with Mati. She was no longer serving him drinks at the Char Bar, but sitting at his table having enjoyed a long dinner.

Mati wanted a packet of cigarettes but the cigarette machine was broken, so Antony said, "Don't worry. I'll ask my friend Marco." They came over and she remembers that I was a huge guy slumped forward on the table, wearing a white T-shirt and white chef's jacket, with one arm draped around a girl and the other arm draped around another girl. On the table, there was an overflowing ashtray as well as scattered packs of different brands of cigarettes. Antony said, "Marco, this is my friend Mati. Can I have a cigarette for her, please?" I said to her, "What do you smoke? Marlboros are for hard-core people, Bensons are disgusting, Silk Cuts are for wimps."

She said, "I'm afraid I'm a Silk Cut person." I didn't have that brand, so she took a Marlboro Light and that was it. No eye contact. These days she'll tell you, "He must have left some sort of impression because I remembered the encounter, but it wasn't a particularly good impression."

MATI KNEW THE Canteen's restaurant manager Torquil, and he called her to say this great new place was about to open—mentioned the fact that Michael Caine was behind it—and offered her a job as a waitress. She didn't want to do waitressing and turned down the job. Two weeks later Torquil phoned to say the bar manager had dropped out so would she prefer that position? She said yes. Amid the buzz of getting the Canteen up and running, I didn't really notice her. But in those first few weeks after opening the Canteen, I became entranced. There were scores of good-looking female punters coming in each night, dressed to the nines and being friendly to me, but I was more interested in the woman serving the drinks than the ladies drinking them.

Mati Conejero was olive-skinned and beautiful. She was born in Majorca, the daughter of Spanish parents, but she grew up here, so her accent is London rather than Palma. My initial seduction technique with Mati—my own little way of telling her I was interested—did not involve conversation. At the end of evening service I would sit at the bar, flicking matches and rolled-up pieces of paper in her direction as she took care of the customers. Feeling the gentle stab of a match in her neck really annoyed her, but I figured that at the end of the night, when she came to sweep the floor, she would be forced to think about me.

Within a month or so I must have moved on from match-flicking to conversation and we became friends. If I saw Mati going for a break, I would follow her out of the restaurant and jump out behind her. "Fancy a coffee?" She'd agree and we'd take a cab from Chelsea Harbour to Pucci's café on the King's Road.

At first, neither of us remembered that we had already met at 190 Queensgate. Then one night Antony Worrall Thompson came into the Canteen, headed up to the bar and asked Mati if she would like to join him for a glass of champagne. She said she couldn't because she was working, so he said, "Don't worry. I'll ask my mate Marco if it's OK." That's when Mati realized that I was the "huge guy" with the cigarettes at 190. And when Antony came up to me to see if I would allow Mati to have a drink, that's when it dawned on me that Mati must have been that "Spanish bird" he was always going on about.

One of the things I liked about Mati was that she came from the same humble beginnings as me. Her mother, Lali, was a seamstress (and, as I would later learn, a magnificent cook); her father, Pedro, was a waiter. I'd been out with posh girls—hell, I'd even married a couple of them—but I reckon you can only really love your own. In my opinion, if you're from the poorer side of society, you can't marry into upper-class circles because you'll never be understood.

There were two obstacles that threatened to stop us turning from friends into lovers. The first was that Mati had a boyfriend.

She had been seeing this bloke, on and off, for about two years. She told me, more recently, that her boyfriend had asked her one night, "Are you in love with Marco?" She had said that no, of course she wasn't in love with me, and told him off for asking such a ridiculous question. But I suppose it got her thinking. Shortly afterward she split from her boyfriend, moved out of his house and into her parents' home in Holland Park. She then had a row with her father about her lurcher's nonstop farting, so she and her dog moved out of her parents' house and into a friend's flat in Tower Hill.

When she told me about this, I gave her the keys to my flat in Pavilion Road, Knightsbridge, and said, "Go and stay there if you need to."

She said, "I've got a lurcher that farts."

"That's fine," I said, but she declined the offer and handed back the keys a few weeks later.

Some nights Mati would give me a lift home to my flat, and one evening I kissed her before leaping out of the car and hurrying into my flat. She didn't see me for two days afterward, and even then I didn't mention our snog—is that evidence that I was shy with girls?

So Mati was now young, free and single . . . The second obstacle was that Lisa Butcher, my estranged wife, wanted to get back together with me. Between the spring and fall of 1992 I had managed to charm Lisa, get engaged to her, marry her in Brompton Oratory and then separate. People make wedding speeches that last longer. Occasionally Lisa would pop into the Canteen for a chat, and then at some point in December, she said, "Why don't we have another go? Let's give it a try."

Looking back it seems crazy that I even considered reconciliation. I'm sure I knew by then that Lisa and I were not suited and that our marriage had been a mistake. Meanwhile, Mati and I hadn't done anything more intimate than the occasional kiss, but there was a feeling that we were growing closer. However, for some strange reason, I found myself agreeing to Lisa's suggestion.

Lisa and I spent Christmas together at the Manor House Hotel, in Wiltshire. Surrounded by a few hundred acres of parkland, the setting was romantic enough, but our attempted reunion was disastrous. It just didn't work, put it that way. I was reminded of all the reasons we'd broken up, one of the major ones being that we had nothing in common. I just didn't know her and she certainly didn't know me.

It's never going to happen between us, I thought, so I said to Lisa, "I have to get back to London." We cut short our stay and a friend of mine, Gary Bentley, came and collected us and drove us back to London. He dropped Lisa at her flat and me at mine. That's it, I thought. I've got my freedom now. I had promised to spend New Year's Eve with Lisa and it was a promise I kept, but before she turned up at the flat, I spoke to Mati on the phone.

"What are you up to tonight?" she asked.

"I'm spending the evening with Lisa," I told her.

"That's nice," said Mati sweetly. "You're going to try and make it work again, then?"

I said, "Well, I'm not in love with her. I'm in love with somebody else."

"Who?" asked Mati.

I didn't tell her and she later said she didn't think I was referring to her. I ended the conversation by telling Mati, "I'm very fond of you."

The dillydallying with Mati couldn't go on forever, though. My uncertainty, indecision and hesitation were proving too frustrating for her. Our relationship was cemented in early January 1993, when we sat alone in the Canteen in the early hours of the morning. The customers had long since paid up and gone and the staff had cleared up and headed off. It was just the two of us together in this massive restaurant at a table at the end of the bar. We were talking about this or that when Mati suddenly stood up, climbed over the table and kissed me. We spent the night together and then I gave her the keys to my flat again; this time she held on to them.

Michael Caine kept his nose out of it. I can't recall him expressing an opinion about me breaking my never-date-the-staff rule. He had never been enthusiastic about my marriage to Lisa, although he'd never said, "You're making a mistake." Michael was too polite to say something like that. But then again, when I told him I was going to marry Lisa, he hadn't said, "Great stuff, Marco," either.

When word leaked out that Mati and I were seeing each other, newspapers dispatched their hacks and hackettes to trail us. One of the most persistent reporters was Deborah Sherwood of the *Sunday Express*. She was on my case morning, noon and night and arrived with a photographer at the Canteen one evening asking if she could speak to me. Deborah was thinking to herself, It could go one of two ways: Marco might want to have a drink with us or he might tell us to get lost. When she saw me walking in her direction with a glass in my hand, she thought, he's obviously decided he wants to have a drink with us. I was not in that sort of mood. Instead, I removed the photographer's camera from his hands and smashed it into tiny bits by hammering it hard on the Canteen's tiled floor. They got the message and left the building, but not before Deborah, ever persistent, fired a few questions at me. I later paid for the camera. Like I said, she caught me in the wrong mood.

Mati became pregnant, and in December 1993 Luciano was born. A couple of months before he was born, Mati and I and a couple of friends went off for a break in Yorkshire. We were driving back down the A1 when I nodded off in the backseat. I must have had a nightmare and woke screaming, "Please stop the car. Get this car off the motorway." I came to my senses and apologized for the outburst, then about fifteen seconds later we were overtaken by a lorry that pulled into our lane; the next thing we knew, our car became lodged between the lorry's trailer and cabin. We were dragged down the road, with smoke all over the place and sparks flying, and then our car was catapulted across the road. We freed ourselves from the wreckage and wondered how the hell we'd survived, and when the police arrived at the scene, they were just as shocked that we were alive. They dropped us off at some motorway café and we called a taxi to take us back to London. When we arrived home, the house was freezing because the louvre windows had been left open. I stood on the window ledge trying to shut the window when it suddenly jolted upward and my head was crushed between the window and window frame. I was half dead. Weird that I should survive a horrific car crash then nearly kill myself trying to close a window.

NINETEEN

The Dream
Becomes Reality

M Y DREAM, OF course, was to win three stars from Michelin and I wouldn't have come by the third one had it not been for Michael Caine. He was the instigator, the one who introduced me to his friend Rocco—that's Sir Rocco—Forte, who had taken over the helm of the hotel company started by his father, the great hotelier Lord (Charles) Forte. Michael and Rocco met for lunch one day in 1993 and my name cropped up.

Rocco liked the idea of teaming up with Michelin-starred chefs. He had recently done a deal with Nico Ladenis, renting him a restaurant of the Grosvenor House Hotel, which Nico called Nico at Ninety. It went on to win three stars—so Nico had done well out of the deal. There were also benefits for Rocco, though. First, he got the glorious PR that comes with having an outstanding chef on the premises; and second, Nico's restaurant provided an alternative for guests who didn't want to use the main dining room of the hotel but didn't want to travel too far to eat. Rocco is blessed with vision, and I think he was the pioneer of this clever idea of renting hotel space to chefs. So the deal with Nico had worked very well and having sorted out the Grosvenor House, Rocco had turned his attentions to the Hyde Park. The old grill was on its last legs, perhaps because the punters were dying off. Nothing lasts forever.

Michael brought together me and Rocco for a meeting. Rocco was a real gentleman, very charming and courteous, and he asked me,

"How do you fancy taking your two stars from Harveys to the Hyde Park?" Transferring Michelin stars was possible. Others had done it, including Raymond Blanc, who had transferred his two stars from his city-center restaurant to Le Manoir. I would need approval from Michelin, but it was certainly doable. What's more, I liked the prospect because I had outgrown Harveys and Wandsworth. With its forty-four covers, Harveys had brought me two stars, but it was too small to win me another. I had started to see it as little more than a shop front with fifteen tables. The Canteen, meanwhile, was not set up to be a three-star venture. The restaurant at the Hyde Park Hotel, on the other hand, *was* the big stage. It was Forte's flagship hotel, a magnificent Victorian building that sits imposingly on that stretch from Knightsbridge to Hyde Park Corner. At the back, the hotel overlooks the park and across from the front entrance you'll find Harvey Nichols and Harrods. It was the platform that would enable me to win three stars in the *Michelin Guide*. It was the place where my dream could—and indeed would— come true.

I visited the site with Rocco, did the deal and it all came together pretty quickly. In July 1993 I left Harveys, and two months later we opened Restaurant Marco Pierre White at the Hyde Park Hotel. At Harveys there had rarely been more than eight in the brigade, but at the Hyde Park I had sixteen, sometimes eighteen cooks. My team included five chefs who had been with me in the final days of Harveys: Robbie McRae and the aptly named Donovan Cooke, both of whom had worked at Michel Roux's Waterside Inn before joining Harveys; Mikey Lambert, who had also worked at the Waterside and L'Ortolan before Harveys; Roger Pizey, who had won the Pastry Chef of the Year award while at Harveys; Lee Bunting, who had joined me at Harveys when he was a kid of sixteen or seventeen, after an unsuccessful and brief career as a waiter. Donovan and Mikey, by the way, later moved to Australia, where they have been voted the country's best chefs.

Others in the Hyde Park brigade included Robert Reid, who had just left Robuchon in Paris; Spencer Patrick, who'd come from Hambleton Hall; Richard Stewart and Robert Weston. Thierry Busset had worked at Gavroche and came in to join Roger on Pastry, while Charlie Rushton, who'd done time at Harveys, was brought back into the fold.

The average age of the chefs was twenty-five. They weren't kids. They were strong people whose heads were full of experience and culinary knowledge and whose bodies could stand the pace and physical demands of working sixteen or seventeen hours a day in a kitchen. I also introduced the sort of classical hierarchy I'd seen at Gavroche. There was me, my head chef, four or five sous chefs, three on Fish, three on Meat, three on Pastry and four on Larder. There were the chefs de partie, the premier commis chefs and the commis chefs. Each of them was a head chef in his own right.

This kitchen was big. The one at Harveys was so small that we had to store the vegetables in a shed in the courtyard. The size of the kitchen at Wandsworth prevented me from winning three stars because I was unable to show off different cooking techniques. You need to have the right number of staff and the right amount of space to do that, and as the kitchen was so cramped, I couldn't fit in the staff or the techniques. At the Hyde Park, however, we had braised dishes, confit dishes, dishes en cocotte, dishes en vessie—an array of dishes that we couldn't have done at Harveys. At Harveys there had been just a few dishes on the main course, but now, on the Fish section alone, we'd have six or seven dishes and the entire menu might contain fifteen main courses.

The food stemmed from classical French but veered toward simplicity. Pigeon with Foie Gras, wrapped in cabbage and served with pommes purée and black pepper, was a favorite. Lobster was grilled and served with a little truffle butter, pig's trotter was served with sweetbreads and sauce périgueux, while the menu also included a French fillet of steak with horseradish, and guinea fowl with risotto of white truffle.

On the top of the menu I used a Salvador Dalí quote: "At six I wanted to be a chef, at seven Napoleon and my ambition has been growing steadily ever since." The pudding menu contained the quote from the eighteenth-century food writer Brillat-Savarin: "To know how to eat well, one must first know how to wait." That was a message to all those customers who kicked up a fuss when their food took time to prepare.

(Later, when I had an investment in a restaurant called Sugar Reef,

I put on the menu "Be blonde," and attributed the remark to General Custer. It was made up, of course, and was really a tribute of sorts to the captain of the *Titanic*, who apparently shouted, "Be British," as his ship was sinking. On the pudding menu at the same restaurant, we used the quote "Yes," and attributed it to the man from Del Monte— orders for desserts have never been better.)

To start with, we struggled. The trouble was we weren't used to doing big numbers at lunchtime. At Harveys we'd been busy every night, but because we were in the middle of nowhere, we only did fifteen or twenty covers for lunch on a good day. At the Hyde Park we were doing three times that amount, maybe fifty or sixty for lunch. Then just as we were recovering from that service, we had to do up to a hundred covers for dinner. Cooks who had been strong enough for Harveys were now not so strong. They couldn't grow. They couldn't move on and up their game. I suppose it's like a football team that goes from second to first division. If they don't up their game, then they're not going to stay in the premiership.

Consistency remained a priority. Derek Brown, head inspector of Michelin UK, had visited the Canteen one day and I'd chatted to him. I had asked him why Gavroche had been demoted, going from three stars to two. "Well," he had replied, "three of the four meals I had that year were not up to a three-star standard." Mr. Brown did not like compromise. His remark underlined my belief that every dish heading from the kitchen to the table would have to be of a three-star standard. I said to him, "I have always dreamed of winning three stars and what I do is look at the only three-star restaurant in London, Tante Claire. If I can beat them on all levels, you cannot deny me three stars."

"Very clever," Mr. Brown replied.

I would visit Tante Claire and study the dishes as they appeared on the table in front of me. As far as I was concerned, if we put our mind to it, we could beat Pierre on amuse-gueules, hors d'oeuvres, fish, meat, cheese, pastry, puddings and petits fours. The one area where Tante Claire exceeded was with its bread. He served the best bread in the country and that's because it was one of his true passions; and to have a passion for something means that you have to seek great understanding of its creation, which, in turn, gives you a very good chance of perfecting it. It wasn't just the recipe or the environment or the flour—which he imported from God-knows-where—it was the passion that put him ahead of me. You have to have the right pair of hands making the stuff.

For a while I worried about how Pierre's customers were being served better bread than my customers at the Hyde Park. Then I remembered what Nico Ladenis had always said: if you can find someone who makes it better than you, give it to them to make it. I had no desire to learn about bread, it just didn't turn me on, so I found a bakery that could do the job for me and they worked from our bread recipe.

Yet even before I started to tackle the cooking side, I became obsessed with what I call the illusion of grandness. The plates and silverware had to be the finest, and the tablecloths had to be beautiful. The walls of the restaurant were lined with wonderful paintings—I treated the Hyde Park as an art gallery. Not one of these things makes the food taste any better, of course, but all of them frame the food and help to make the customer feel that he or she is sitting in a magnificent restaurant. I also wanted to take the show from the kitchen into the dining room, so that there would a lot of carving in the room. I would do dishes for two, like gigot of milk-fed lamb, and roast pineapple with vanilla, which were carried into the dining room on silver trays. The impact was greater than at Tante Claire. For instance, rather than saving cash by putting five halves of scallops on a plate—as would have been customary in those days—I'd put five medium-sized scallops on a plate, so the dish had height and presence. You smelled three stars when you walked into the room. I had put Michelin in a position where they could not deny me my third star.

The pace was relentless. We worked six days a week and had little time for life outside the kitchen. I was living in Pont Street, a ten-minute walk away, and would leave home every morning at eight forty-five. In the kitchen I might do a bit of butchery, perhaps the mise en place, and then talk to the chefs de partie about dishes that were coming up. I'd talk through dish ideas with my head chef, Robert Reid. At eleven forty-five A.M. Mati would come in with Luciano and our new baby, Marco, and she would sit them on the passe while she had a cup of coffee. I was on one side of the passe and my family was on the other. Fifteen minutes later lunch service would start and we'd finish about two thirty P.M. Then I would do whatever paperwork was required, or perhaps meet with suppliers. People came to me; I would never leave the restaurant. In the late afternoon, Mati might come back and we'd have a coffee while the boys sat on the passe, then after dinner service I'd talk through the evening with my brigade before heading home. My head would hit the pillow at about one in the morning, so it was a fifteen- or sixteen-hour day Monday to Friday. Other members of the kitchen staff would start at seven thirty or eight in the morning. On Saturday I would go in at two o'clock in the afternoon and work until midnight, then on Sundays I slept.

In terms of standard, the front-of-house team matched the kitchen brigade. I had joint managers, Pierre Bordelli and Nicolas Munier, both in their early thirties, good looking and amazingly diplomatic; they knew how to handle the customers. Then I brought in the veteran Jean Cotat. He had worked for years with the Roux brothers and was known throughout London, rightly or wrongly, as the finest maître d' who'd ever worked at Le Gavroche. Then Jean had a job at Tante Claire, which ended in strange circumstances. A lady customer had asked where the toilets were and he had walked her to the door and then, as she went into the ladies', he'd said, "Making room for the next course, madame?" Lord knows what had encouraged him to say such a thing, but the long and short of it is that Nic Munier knew Jean's son, Simon, who, in turn, phoned to find a job for Jean. I was delighted to have him on board and he would work the last ten years of his career with me.

The exhausting routine made me tetchy when food wasn't up to the right standard. One evening a chef presented a bowl of soup on the passe, awaiting my inspection. I would always dip my little finger into the soup to test its temperature and on this occasion the chef had delivered a fish soup that was lukewarm rather than piping hot. I called him over. "What is this?" I said.

"Soupe de Poisson, boss."

"Cold Soupe de Poisson," I told him and then I pulled his bib apron away from his chest and emptied the contents of the bowl down his front. I picked up the croutons and chucked them in. Next, I put the bowl in between his apron and chef's whites. Then I sent him back to the stove. Everyone in the kitchen found this incident very amusing, except for the young chef who was a walking bowl of fish soup. Yet he knew that five minutes later he'd be sniggering when one of his colleagues got a bollocking.

Customers were also prone to get on my wick. They would arrive in the restaurant and, in a flashy way in front of their friends, tell the maître d'hotel, "Get Marco to cook it." This annoyed me. One day a man came in and ordered a bowl of chips, or french fries, adding, "Get Marco to do them." He thought he was being funny by ordering fries in a posh restaurant when such a dish was not on the menu. I thought, fine, you can have chips, it's not a problem, but if you are asking me to cook them, then you will have to pay accordingly. So I charged him £25, which made him look like an idiot. When he got the bill, he was astounded and summoned the maître d' to complain. I sent the waiter back to tell the customer, "Marco cut the potatoes, Marco blanched them and cooked them. Marco put them on a silver dish and then personally put the garnish of tomato ketchup on the side just as you requested. His hourly rate is higher than the other chefs." I suppose that customer has been dining out on the story ever since, so he's had his £25's worth.

Nicolas Munier, one of the restaurant managers, came into the kitchen one day to tell me there was a problem in the restaurant. A fight was about to erupt in my beloved dining room, he said. Two very camp men had been sitting in the restaurant when a trio had arrived and been seated at the table beside them. The trio consisted of a wide boy—a sort of flashy geezer, a rough 'n' ready type—and two blonde women. They were too crude and ostentatious for the camp couple, who started to loudly make rude comments about the women. The wide boy didn't like it and by the time I walked into the dining room he was holding the two men by their ties as they knelt on the floor in front of him. "If you don't apologize to the ladies, I'm going to do the pair of you," he was saying. He was pulling their ties so hard that they were being throttled and were incapable of speech, so there's no way they could have said sorry even they'd wanted to. "Please, sir, let me

deal with this," I said to him, and when he let go, I helped the two men
to their feet and took them outside.

"I'm terribly sorry," I told them. "The problem is, when someone
books a table, we never quite know what sort of person they are. His
behavior was atrocious and I cannot apologize enough, but the table
may have been booked by his p.a. or someone else. What I can tell you
is I certainly won't allow him into this restaurant again." I waived their
bill and they departed into the night, shaken by the experience of being roughed up and strangled, but placated nevertheless.

Then I returned to the dining room and went to the table where the
geezer was sitting with his birds. "I am terribly sorry, sir," I said to him.
"The problem is, when someone books a table, we never quite know
who's going to come, and on this particular occasion it was those two
dreadful men, wasn't it? What I can tell you is I certainly won't allow
them into this restaurant again and your meal is on the house."

I was not so charming when a French couple arrived for dinner.
They were in their early fifties and well-dressed and they told my manager, the impeccably mannered young Pierre Bordelli, that over the
years they had dined in the finest French restaurants—Joel Robuchon,
Guy Savoie—and that they were at the Hyde Park because they had
heard of my reputation and were keen to taste my food. They asked
Pierre to choose for them from the menu, which he agreed to do. For
starters we gave them crab, which was served with tomatoes, and a
mosaic of chicken, leeks and foie gras. When Pierre asked if they had
enjoyed it, they said that they were "disappointed." For their main
course, they had pigeon wrapped in cabbage and served with foie gras,
and cod cooked with a green herb crust. Again, Pierre asked them
what they thought of the food, and they said it was equally unimpres-
sive. He relayed their remarks to me. "Ask them to leave," I said.
Pierre approached their table and said, "I am sorry, but Mr. White
does not want you in the restaurant. In fact, he would like you to leave
now and please don't worry about the bill. Your meal is on the house."
He pulled the table toward him slightly, a gesture designed to tell
them that their time was up. The couple sat there, astonished. "For the
past thirty years I have been dining in the finest restaurants in the
world and I have never been asked to leave," the man said.

Pierre tugged the table a little closer to him and said with utter charm, "There is always a first time for everything, sir."

I tried to be as calm as possible when I ventured front of house. Although at about seven one evening I was strolling through the dining room, on my way to look at the reservations book, when I walked past a table of six Americans who were having an early dinner. They were chatting away happily, and as I got closer to them, I heard one man say, "The chef here is crazy. I mean, he is kerrrr-razy." I carried on walking, but as I looked at the book, his words came back to me. I thought, hang on a second, he was talking about *me*. When I walked back through the dining room, I stopped at the table and said to the customer, "I might be many things but I am not crazy, do you understand?" He sat there petrified, not knowing what to say. I had to fill the silence. "So now you can do one of two things," I continued. "Stay here and have a nice dinner, or leave now." He shuffled uncomfortably and then asked meekly, "Would you mind if we stayed and had our dinner?" The following day I got a graceful letter from him, apologizing for his comments and saying that he had enjoyed the best meal of his life.

There was one man, however, who didn't have the best meal of his life. Tom Jaine, editor of the *Good Food Guide*, came into the restaurant looking so scruffy that one of the other customers commented on his appearance. He also brought his bicycle clips to the table, which I must say was a first. When I asked him to leave, he looked shocked. Then he stood to his feet and marched out of the dining room, waving his bike clips above his head and in my direction, yelling, "May curses rain down on this man!" This was nicely offset by Nicholas Soames, the politician and grandson of Winston Churchill, who had been having lunch with the food critic A. A. Gill. When Nicholas finished his meal, he walked from the table to the cloakroom, stopping in the middle of the dining room and shouting, "This is the benchmark to all restaurants!"

MENTALLY, I WAS all over the place in January 1995. The *Michelin Guide* was due out on Monday, and by the Thursday before, the waiting game to find out whether I had won three stars was intolerable. In fact, I was so preoccupied that one day I couldn't cope with the pressure any longer and had to go off fishing with a couple of friends, Tim Steel, my oldest mate, whom I have known since childhood, and Edgar Barman. At about eleven A.M. I got a call to say that Mr. Brown and Mr. Bulmer had dropped into the Hyde Park to see me. They said they would nip back at two thirty P.M.

I hurriedly packed away my fishing gear, loaded it in the car and we drove back into town. By then I had sussed that I'd won three stars. Why else would they want to see me? But I would have to wait a little longer to find out for sure. Bang at two thirty they arrived back at the Hyde Park. "Have you got anywhere private?" asked Mr. Brown. We went into my office, where some coffee arrived, and then Mr. Brown said, "In the 1995 *Michelin Guide*, Restaurant Marco Pierre White will have three stars." Three stars. Two words that established me in the history of British gastronomy as the first British chef to win three stars. At the age of thirty-three, I had become the youngest ever chef to achieve such an award (a record I still hold, incidentally). My old friend Nico Ladenis also won three stars that year. This meant that Rocco had a pair of three-star chefs in his hotels.

I can't really tell you what went through my mind. I was confident that I had done enough to win them, but it was still a bit of a shock. I felt as though I'd finished my race. Boxers win Heavyweight Champion of the World and lose the hunger, so to speak. Why should chefs be any different? I can understand why chefs get to the top and then go off and do other things. The simple reason is probably that they become bored in the kitchen.

Shortly before Mr. Brown retired from Michelin UK, I got a call from Derek Bulmer, who would be his successor. He said, "I am taking Mr. Brown for a farewell meal and have asked him where he would like to go. He wants to eat at the Hyde Park." I was touched that Mr. Brown had chosen my restaurant for his last supper. It confirmed my feelings that we had won the award for all the right reasons. After dinner I walked Mr. Brown from his table down the hotel steps. I wanted to say good-bye and thank you. It was late at night, and as we stood on the pavement, a doorman hailed a taxi. The Michelin man shook my hand and said, "Never forget what made you great." *Great* might be an overstatement, but the theme of his remark was that my success was down to the time I'd spent in the kitchen and what I put on the plate. His message: stay behind the stove.

THINGS WENT WRONG at the Canteen in the summer of 1995. There was a disagreement of sorts and Michael and I decided to go our separate ways. A legal battle erupted and the consequences resulted in a settlement that prevents me discussing the reasons behind our fallout. What I can tell you is that Michael and I did not have an argument— there was no screaming match—and the end of the partnership had nothing to do with Michael wanting to put fish and chips on the menu, as is widely believed.

Michael and I have only seen each other once since then. It was a few years ago when I was invited to Liz Taylor's birthday party at the Café Royal. I walked into the room and saw Michael sitting at a table with Harvey Weinstein, the man behind Miramax. I thought, this is ridiculous; I've got to say hello. So I went over to the pair of them and said, "Good evening, gentlemen."

Harvey shook my hand and, clearly unaware of the difficulties Michael and I had been through, pointed at Michael and said to me, "This guy here is the toughest guy you'll ever meet."

Michael looked at his moviemaking friend and said, "Harvey, if you think I'm tough, try dealing with him."

I'd had Michael as a business partner, but Rocco had big plans. We did a deal to buy the Criterion, a massive restaurant in Piccadilly Circus. It was to be a joint venture between the two of us, but before the paperwork was to be signed, Forte became the victim of a hostile takeover by Granada. Forte's business ground to a halt because of it. Once a hostile takeover begins, everything stops. I felt desperately sad for Rocco and thought it was wrong that he was about to lose the company. It was a particularly rough ride for him.

There was a clause in my unsigned contract that stated that if the management of Forte changed, I would have a right to buy its 50 percent of the Criterion, and that is how I thought things would end up.

When Granada took over, I was called in to see the company's chief executive, Charles Allen. Not so much called in, actually, as we had dinner at Le Gavroche. During the meal I said to Charles, "Well, you know I've got my contract and it's not signed. But the Criterion is open now and it is certainly implied in the contract that I have an option to buy you out."

Charles said, "We don't want to sell. We want to do more with you." Oh.

I then had to go see Granada's chairman, Gerry Robinson. He was charming and polite, and when the tea was carried into his office, he looked at me and said, "Shall I be mother?" The night before the meeting I had asked myself, why does Gerry want to see me? I reckoned he wanted to suss out my relationship with Rocco. Granada was a PLC, and the last thing they wanted was a loose cannon like Marco Pierre White running around saying all the wrong things. About eight minutes into our cup of tea, Gerry said, "What do you think of Rocco Forte?"

"Sir Rocco Forte," I replied, "is the only man who ever gave me everything he promised." Despite my words of support for Rocco, my relationship with Granada continued. The deal was that I would have the lease to the restaurants in their major hotels—the Meridien, the Piccadilly, the Capitol, the Regent Palace and the Waldorf. The deal also included the Queens Hotel in Leeds, the hotel where my father had worked as young chef. Around about 1999 I traveled up to Leeds with a Granada executive and we were greeted in the foyer by a manager who said he wanted to show us around.

How interesting, I was thinking, to be in the hotel where my old man had toiled with his friend Paul La Barbe, the cook who had trained in France and was the subject of so many of my father's stories. I tried to visualize the grandeur of the hotel when it was in its prime, and as we walked into the bar, the manager said, "What you're about to see is the biggest minibar in the world." The biggest minibar in the world? What on earth did he mean? The Granada executive and I stood in silence, transfixed by the gruesome sight of a Mini car suspended from the ceiling above the bar. The manager was really proud of his "Mini bar," but I can tell you that it was one of the naffest things I've ever seen, and the Granada executive wasn't impressed either.

In the end I didn't do the Queens Hotel because I wanted to concentrate on the restaurants in the London hotels. I talk about some of them in forthcoming chapters, but this is a good point at which to say that the Granada relationship ended in 2002. It was my first experience of the corporate world and I thought it was horrible. You think blue-chip companies are run perfectly, but in my opinion they are worse than private companies. Board meetings are painful. We'd have an hour-long meeting about the price of coffee, with them wanting to produce coffee for five pence a cup and spending sixty minutes talking about how every penny counts. "You can get spectacular coffee for twelve pence a cup," I'd say, and then emerge from the meeting brain dead. It was all about percentages rather than working out what's going to make the customer happy. I handed back everything, but kept the Criterion.

There were amusing moments while it lasted. I went to Charles Allen's fortieth birthday at the Meridien and the cabaret was provided by a Shirley Bassey look-alike. An executive high up in Granada leaned over to me at one point and said, "That's influence and power for you," pointing toward the stage and the prancing drag queen.

I said, "I'm sorry. What's influence and power?"

He said, "Getting Shirley Bassey to come and sing for your fortieth birthday."

TWENTY

Just Another Day

PEOPLE FOUND IT peculiar that I had won Michelin's coveted three
stars without ever setting foot on French soil. Journalists would arrive to interview me and ask me to tell them about my favorite meal in
a French restaurant. "I haven't got one," I'd tell them. "I've never been
to France." Oh, they'd say, and we'd move on to the next question. The
other big players—Albert, Michel, Raymond, Pierre—had all come
from that side of the Channel, but there I was, serving some of the
finest French food in Britain, without having visited the great Parisian
restaurants whose dishes had set me on the path to Michelin stardom.
I'd simply say, "Well, there you go. Proof that you don't need to go to
France to win three Michelin stars."

I met Jean-Christophe Novelli, or JC, back in the late eighties (he
has since run restaurants that include Auberge du lac at Brocket Hall,
Herefordshire). He says that he wanted a job in my kitchen and arrived at Harveys to introduce himself to me. There was a man mopping the floor who apparently told young Monsieur Novelli that Marco
Pierre White was not around. JC says it was only later, when Nico introduced us, that he realized that the man mopping the floor was, in
fact, me. My version is that JC came to my restaurant with his restaurant manager, Guiseppe, and then returned a short while after with
Keith Floyd. JC was embarrassed because he was wearing track suit
with trainers but I said, "Don't be so silly," and put them on table six.
That's how our great friendship started.

On October 1, 1995, Forte was sponsoring the Arc de Triomphe
race and Rocco was hosting an event at Longchamps on the final day.
He had chefs on hand in Paris and a few of my boys from the Hyde
Park brigade were going to be there as well, but Rocco wanted me to
oversee the cuisine for him and his two hundred guests.

I invited Jean-Christophe Novelli along, not to help, but because he
has been like a brother to me and I enjoy his company. I was visiting
the world's most romantic city, so I wanted Mati to be there as well. As
I have never passed a driving test—possibly because I have never
taken a driving test—the two of them agreed that they would share the
time behind the wheel. Things started to go terribly wrong when we
got to the Eurostar terminal in Dover at about two thirty in the morning, bought our tickets and were ready to drive onto the train. JC was
asked to go into an office where there were French gendarmes. He
was asked for our passports, so he came back to the car, poked his
head in and said, "Passports."

I said, "I haven't got one." JC looked totally confused. Was I joking?
Was this one of my wind-ups? But the passport did not appear. He
said, "What do you mean? If you go abroad, Marco, you need a passport." I didn't have one. I told him the last time I had traveled abroad
was as a ten-year-old when I went to visit Uncle Gianfranco and Aunt
Paola in Italy. JC was not in the mood to hear about my childhood ad-
ventures. He looked a bit nervous, went back to the office and told the
gendarmes, "My friend doesn't have a passport but he is the greatest
chef the world has ever known and I am taking him to cook a banquet
in Paris. Believe me, he is a very important person."

He was told, "I don't care if he's cooking for Monsieur Mitterand."
They were convinced that JC was trying to take me into the country as
an illegal immigrant and they even talked of arresting him. Then he
glanced back at the car and saw me waving something that looked like
a passport. He dashed back to the car, grabbed the document from my
hand and hurried back to the office. "I'm sorry," he told the gendarmes. "My friend has found his passport." But it wasn't my passport; I had given him my fishing license, which contained a mugshot
of me on its cover. They started screaming at him, "What is this!"
From the safety of the Range Rover, Mati and I could hear the word

merde being used a lot. Somehow JC managed to talk us out of being questioned, but we were turned away. It was the middle of the night and at lunchtime I was due to be cooking lunch for Rocco and his two hundred guests. JC saved the day. He happened to be well connected with the ferry companies and, don't ask me how he did it, but he drove us to the ferry port, my fishing license was produced once again and this time it did the trick.

From Calais we motored down to Paris, and when we hit the capital, JC announced that he wanted to take us on a tour of the city. We drove to the Eiffel Tower and parked illegally, and then JC dragged Mati and me out of the car and made us stand underneath the tower because "it is so romantic." Once that was done, we clambered back into the Range Rover and zipped through the streets, nearly killing the French actor Alain Delon along the way. Alain was crossing the road, clutching croissants and coffee, when all of a sudden he stopped— rabbit in the headlights—as JC applied the brakes and the car screeched to a halt. JC is a dead ringer for Alain, so for a few seconds the petrified actor stood at the tip of the hood, gripping his croissants and looking into the window of our car thinking, My double almost killed me.

We had breakfast in La Coupole, which was a lively place. There was some nasty art on the walls, but it was busy, stylish and . . . French. Then we went on to Longchamps, where there was an enormous queue to get into a car park. After queuing for what seemed like ages, I told JC to drive over the pavement and into the car park, but when he followed my instructions, police surrounded the car, screaming and yelling at JC to get the vehicle back on the road. We had to drive back over the pavement into a traffic jam of cars hooting at us and furious pedestrians dodging us and yelling, "*Merde.*"

Things didn't improve when we finally arrived at our destination. I realized that we were cooking in a tiny, cramped kitchen above a betting shop. What they hadn't told me was that this was a kitchen that didn't have an oven. There was a massive, gas-burning hot plate, which I transformed into an oven by removing all its shelves except for the lowest one, which was just above the heat. The main course was sea bass with a crust of thyme leaves and it took about forty-five minutes to cook it. Luckily, the starter (terrine of foie gras with Sauternes gelée) and pudding (jelly of red fruits) were served cold, otherwise we'd never have done it. There were no complaints. Quite the contrary. JC said that guests had told him the meal was "spectacular."

We headed home exhausted. At Calais the customs officers asked to see my passport. "I don't have one." How did you get out of England in the first place? "We drove." The irritated officer waved us through with, "*Allez! Allez!*"

At Dover we were stopped and asked to show our passports. I explained that I didn't have one and the customs officer asked if I had any form of ID. I fumbled around in the glove box and confidently produced my fishing license. The Pierre part of my name must have made him suspicious. "How did you get out of Britain in the first place?" he asked. "We drove," I said for a second time. Eventually we were waved through the barrier with the officer shouting, "And get a bloody passport."

THE KITCHENS WERE my escape zone but I was intrigued by the business side of restaurants. The likes of Michael Caine and Rocco Forte had encouraged me to be entrepreneurial and they had made me more confident. I set about building a restaurant empire. One night in the summer of 1996 I was driving around London when I found myself heading down Curzon Street and past the door of the Mirabelle. I felt an urge to nip inside, just to have a look at the place, so I asked my driver to stop.

I had been to the Mirabelle only once before, though not for a meal. It was back in the summer of 1981, when I first came to London and was working for Albert Roux. I was nineteen years old, and on my first day off I took a bus across the river and up to Hyde Park Corner, then crossed Park Lane, walked through the little streets of Mayfair and into Curzon Street. I had gazed at the Mirabelle for a few minutes. There she was, the grand old dame, once the equivalent in London society of Maxim's in Paris. I walked through the doorway and down the stairs and politely said to someone at reception, "I collect menus. Do you have an old menu I could keep?"

At home that night I studied the menu, which contained classical French dishes like Omelette Arnold Bennett, Quenelles of Pike, and Cutlets of Lamb Prince William, which is made with truffles. The menu would have been the same for years, influenced by Escoffier and that invaluable cookbook that can be found in every professional kitchen, *Le Répertoire de La Cuisine*. Mirabelle, which opened in 1936, represented romance. Marilyn Monroe, Jackie Onassis (she always sat at table one) and Maria Callas all loved the place and Princess Margaret and Grace Kelly would dine there, as would Liz Taylor. Maurice Chevalier had been a regular. Lord Lucan held his engagement party in a private room at the Mirabelle. Just think of the people who had walked through those doors, the things that had been said, the deals that had been done at those tables.

On that Saturday night in 1996 I walked in just to have a look at the restaurant that had once been so full of romance, mystique and life. It was dead. The menu was—get your head around this—a mixture of French and Japanese food, and the lack of customers told me it was only a question of time before the Mirabelle would be up for sale. I introduced myself to the restaurant manager Takanori Ishii and we had a two-hour chat. The Mirabelle was owned by a Japanese company, and Mr. Ishii was good enough to confirm my suspicions that business was not great. Still, they weren't interested in selling. Mr. Ishii was a charming, polite, soft-spoken man, and from then on I stalked him. I would find the time to pop into Mirabelle once or twice a week to let him know that if it ever came on the market, I would be interested in buying it. I felt it was only a matter of time before they'd want to sell.

In the meantime a restaurant in the same street caught my eye. Les Saveurs was owned by another Japanese company, although it served only French food and hadn't been so bold as to throw a few Japanese dishes onto the menu. There was no movement on the Mirabelle front and I was determined to have a presence in Mayfair, so when I heard a rumor that Les Sav might be up for sale, I pounced.

Then, a tragically short two months after I bought Les Sav, the Mirabelle came on the market. But there was a problem: there were others who wanted to buy it, and they were richer than me. There were four contenders. There was Anton Mosimann, the renowned chef who was regarded as an establishment figure in British gastronomy. Then there was Jeremy King and Chris Corbin, owners of Le Caprice and the Ivy, who were financially backed by the awesomely successful City figure "Black Jack" Dellal. There was the Chez Gerard group. And there was me—the small fish in a big pond. So if I wanted Mirabelle, I would have to use my wits.

I had courted Mr. Ishii, spending long nights talking food and restaurants, so that could do me no harm. And I had also done the Les Sav deal, which had taught me a bit about the way the Japanese like to do business.

I started my strategy with my knowledge of serving Japanese customers. They are discreet people, not loud and raucous in restaurants. They come for the meal, and when they order coffee, you get the bill ready because you know they're not going to spend any more. Once they order a coffee, that's it—they rarely have two.

From this I deduced that they liked quiet deals, didn't like things being on the open market, and if something fell through, they wouldn't like it to be publicized. The way I saw it, two Japanese companies had opened restaurants in Curzon Street and neither restaurant was doing well, but the companies were too embarrassed to sell. Only when the first one made a move and sold Les Sav to me did the other company feel confident enough to sell Mirabelle. Up until now, pride had prevented them from selling.

Mr. Ishii, by now my dear friend, told me to make an offer of half a million pounds less than the highest bid, which had come from Black Jack and the Caprice and Ivy boys. I took his advice, but my offer included something I felt sure would appeal to Mr. Ishii and his bosses. I told him that if the restaurant was sold to me, I would continue to employ its staff and added, "If I step in and buy the Mirabelle, Mr. Ishii, you will have a job for life."

It is an important aspect of Japanese culture that the boss looks after his employees—or rather, does all he can for the people who have worked for him. Essentially, my offer was something Black Jack's money simply couldn't buy. My intention of retaining Mirabelle's Japanese employees suggested I was a man who was not only in touch with the owners' code of conduct but also wholeheartedly supported it.

Mr. Ishii rang me and said, "I'm on your side." Then he spoke to his bosses in Japan, telling them, "I think Marco should own it because he will look after everyone who has worked here. We will still have jobs." And with that I was given the Japanese equivalent of the thumbs-up. I went to bed happily scheming up plans for my new restaurant in Mayfair.

The next morning I woke up horrified: I now owned two restaurants on the *same street*, competing with one another. I thought, fucking hell, this wasn't supposed to happen, what am I going to do? I had put myself in a ludicrous position, but luckily for me, Rocco Forte also wanted to own a restaurant in Mayfair and he phoned and asked, "Can I buy Les Saveurs?" Certainly, sir.

I wanted to take Mirabelle back to what it originally had been. I wanted to reinstate the romance.

I knocked out walls and turned the Tapestry Room, cashier's office and wine cellar into one room, which is now the Chinese Room. A space that had once seated ten people now sat forty. A cloakroom was put in, but when I saw it, I was alarmed because it took up part of the bar area, so the cloakroom was knocked down and the bar became massive. Pillars were put into the bar but they weren't right—they didn't fit in with the character of the restaurant—so they came down and were replaced. A wooden floor was laid, but a few days later I noticed it was buckling because it had been put down too tightly. The restaurant was about to open to the public, so it was too late to rip up the whole floor; instead, the builders had to come in after evening service, between two A.M. and eight A.M., and replace the wooden floorboards with tiles. It was a time-consuming, painstaking process, night after night, and took about three months to finish. In addition to all this I wanted the color of the ceiling to match the blue in a painting I'd hung on the wall. When the ceiling was painted, it didn't match, so it was painted again. It still wasn't right, so it was painted a third time—we finally got there.

The food was restored to its classical French foundations, but with a modern twist of refinement. The Parsley Truffled Soup contained bacon and chicken stock; there was Cappuccino of Mushrooms, Tarte of Endive with Sea Scallops, and Spring Lamb Provençale. The chefs included Charlie Rushton, Spencer Patrick, Lee Bunting and Curtis Stone, who today is something of a TV personality. I wanted it to win a Michelin star and it did.

The Mirabelle's romance doesn't rub on everybody, however. My manager came to see me one night, complaining that Marianne, the receptionist, was in floods of tears. A customer had walked into the restaurant, where he was meeting his wife and friends, and Marianne had asked him to wait for a minute before taking him through to the table. He didn't have time to wait. "Fuck off," he said to Marianne and stormed through to the table, his shocking treatment leaving her in tears.

I went up to the table where the man was sitting and they looked quite flattered that the boss was paying them a visit. I politely said, "Sir, do you have a problem?"

He looked up quizzically and replied, "No."

"I find that very strange."

"Why?" he asked.

"Because I have a receptionist in my office in tears because of the way you treated her."

"What did I say?"

"You told her to fuck off, sir. You humiliated and upset her and she feels terribly insulted. Either pluck up the courage to go and apologize to her or leave. I'll give you five minutes to make your decision."

I was in the bar when the rude man came up to me. He was furious and said, "You just made me look like a cunt in front of my wife and friends."

I said, "That's because you are a cunt."

He said, "We're leaving."

But before he could get his coat, I said, "You must be a cunt, because anyone with any decency would go and apologize. So fuck off."

Those last two words were important. I had treated him exactly the same way he had treated Marianne. All he had to do was say, "You're absolutely right, I'll go and say sorry." If a man comes into one of my restaurants and swears at the receptionist, he is clearly in the wrong restaurant.

What of Mr. Ishii? He left Mirabelle, but returned to work for me a couple of years later. He is my chauffeur and assistant. Sometimes his driving is as good as Jean-Christophe Novelli's. Once he fell asleep at the wheel; another time, after we'd nearly killed a pedestrian, I asked in astonishment, "Mr. Ishii how close were we to killing that woman?" and he replied, "About six inches."

He knows I like to wind him up. I've used his mobile phone to photograph my genitals before and applied the picture as the phone's "wallpaper." One day we were driving out of a hotel car park and there was this big trailer with two big blokes in boiler suits. I spotted an opportunity to amuse myself. I said, "Stop the car, Mr. Ishii." He stopped and I said to him, "Can you ask those two blokes if they're wearing suspenders?"

He wound down the window and said, "Excuse me, are you wearing suspender?"

One of the bruisers looked perplexed. "Sorry, mate?"

Mr. Ishii asked again. "Are you wearing suspender?"

"No, we're not."

"Thank you very much." Window up and off we drove.

I have a laugh at his expense, but Mr. Ishii is very dear to me. We work really well together because while I am spontaneous and cavalier, he is straightforward, extremely polite and well-balanced. When my life is veering all over the place, Mr. Ishii, with his self-control, is there to offer stability. He is the yin to my yang. Throughout our ten-year friendship we have never had a single row, and I have given him plenty of cause to pick a fight with me. In fact, I can't remember the last time I heard him raise his voice. Mr. Ishii is the perfect gentleman.

Sometimes after we've had a particularly long day, I'll apologize and he'll always reply, "Not at all, Marco. It's been a pleasure."

He is the best ambassador that I have because his unswerving loyalty suggests I must have a few good things going for me.

If there was another one out there like him, I'd hire him tomorrow. But there is only one Mr. Ishii.

People ask, why do you still call him Mr. Ishii rather than Takanori? I respect him very much, that's why.

There's another thing. I have to pay him credit for helping to launch my career as a restaurateur. Without his support I would never have got the Mirabelle, and since then I have opened a further thirty restaurants.

GORDON RAMSAY, MY protégé from Harveys, was ready to become a chef patron and in the nineties I helped him launch Aubergine, in Chelsea. I even came up with the restaurant's name. In the restaurant's first few months, his kitchen wasn't right, so my chefs at the Canteen cooked a lot of the food for Aubergine and his boys came over to collect it.

I visited Gordon one day at Aubergine to show him a copy of the *Egon Ronay Guide*, which had awarded him one star. We were standing on the pavement outside—Gordon, his then-girlfriend Ros, Mati and me—when I saw a meaty, nasty-looking skinhead walking in our direction. "Look at that," I said to Gordon.

He glanced up to see what I was talking about, and the skinhead growled at Gordon, "What are you looking at?" It turned ugly quickly. Gordon received a headbutt but came back with a powerful right hook. The two men grabbed each other and danced around a little before falling down toward the pavement, during which Gordon banged his head against a parked car. The next thing I knew, Gordon's brother Ronnie emerged from the restaurant, where he had a kitchen job, and began kicking the hell out of the skinhead. I tried to break it up and when the fight was eventually over, the skinhead picked himself up, dusted himself off and staggered away. Gordon stood to his feet, dazed and severely confused.

Gordon was not only becoming a famous chef but was also on his way to launching a TV career. He became the subject of a fly-on-the-wall documentary called *Boiling Point*, which showed the British public just what it was like to work in a manic kitchen. When the crew said they'd like to film Gordon enjoying a day off, he phoned me to say, "I've told them I always go fishing with you."

I said, "But that's rubbish, Gordon."

"I know, but I've told them, so can we go fishing?"

We headed off to Marlow weir and that's where it became clear that he didn't even know how to tackle up. I played along with his fib, whispering instructions to him so that the producer couldn't hear. Then to amuse myself I set his line at ten foot deep when the water was only eight feet deep. This meant that his line was lying on the riverbed and the best he'd catch would be a rusty tin. He nearly slipped over several times and was petrified when he walked across the weir. I caught ten fish. Gordon caught zilch. When it was time to leave, the mystified producer buttonholed me and said, "Has Gordon ever fished before?"

"Lots," I replied.

ONE DAY IN the summer of 1996, Alan Crompton-Batt told me the Prince of Wales wanted me to cook for him. Of course it's a privilege to be asked to cook for a member of the royal family, but it was to be a grand affair and Vanessa Mae would be there, playing her violin to entertain Charles's two hundred guests. The menu was not scary—it was summer, so I decided on a very English affair—but the performing-seal prospect seemed chilling. I'd have to be very clever with my timing. I'd have to arrive just in time to do the starters (Ballotine of Salmon with Herbs and Langoustines) and escape as the main course (Sorrel d'Agneau à l'Anglaise) was being picked up from the passe. It was crucial that I wasn't there to see out the dessert, Jelly of Red Fruits, otherwise I'd be dragged out to meet the Prince and his guests.

I sat with my driver in my Range Rover on the road outside Highgrove, smoking my way through Marlboros and watching the dashboard clock. I didn't want to be paraded. In the grounds, Charles would be greeting his guests, and in the kitchen adjoining the tent, my team would be waiting for me to arrive, give the orders and dish out the bollockings. And then, just when the time seemed right, we drove up to the gates and security waved us in. I got out of the car and that's when I was nabbed. One of the Prince's aides grabbed me and I was whisked off to meet Charles. This was what I didn't want. But they knew the gig, didn't they? They knew Marco always ran away after the main course so as to avoid the backslapping.

The heir to the throne gave me a confident handshake, smiled

warmly and then said, "Bonjour Monsieur White . . ." For three minutes I listened to his monologue, each and every word of it in French.
I just nodded along—it would have been rude to interrupt—then
when he finished, he handed me a little collection of books about
Highgrove, each of them inscribed to "Monsieur Pierre White."

I had to tell him. "I'm terribly sorry, sir," I said, "but I'm not
French. I grew up on a council estate in Leeds . . ."

He looked at his assistant, as if to say, You've fucking done it this
time, boy. You've made me feel like the biggest prick in history. I had
my picture taken standing beside a red-faced prince and then off I
went, into the kitchen to cook.

TWENTY-ONE

Everything I'd Worked For

I **HAD WON** three Michelin stars but my race was not yet finished. I realized that in fact the finishing post was a little farther on. As far as stars are concerned, three is the highest you can go.

Stars are awarded for what is on the plate, but what about Michelin's *couverts*? In the guides you see them as little pictures of crossed knives and forks, which is why they're known in the restaurant profession as "knives and forks." They are awarded for pleasantness, luxury, aesthetics and ambience. To get five of them, and five red ones rather than black ones, became my new obsession. The Oak Room in London's Meridien Hotel would take me there. It would win not only three stars but also the five red knives and forks, which, according to the guide, made it the finest restaurant in Britain. Others had won stars, but no other restaurant before or since the Oak Room has been awarded a beautiful, complete row of red. Waterside, Gavroche and Tante Claire have only ever managed four.

The room itself has to have been one of the greatest rooms in the world. With its ballroom grandness, majestic mirrors, gentle lighting and generous space between tables, it's like stepping into an illusion. The Oak Room was a temple of gastronomy. It was about perfection rather than creation—making the greatest Oeufs en Nage, the finest Roast Pineapple. It was perfection, from the amuse-gueules to the starter, from the main course to the pre-dessert, the cheese to the coffee and proper chocolates. It was an *event*. The wine list was the finest in Britain. Every available vintage of Mouton Rothschild was there for you to drink, if you had the money. Other three-star restaurants might have had two or three vintages of Pétrus. Here we had Pétrus that went back a century, seventy or eighty different vintages. The wine list included a five-page list of Château d'Yquem, taking you right back to 1850. The vintages and prices were all beautifully written in pencil so that each page was visually attractive. It used to take a wine waiter about three weeks to write out the list.

Dishes were carried from the kitchen on silver platters and the meat was carved at the table. The pigeon, for instance, would be taken out to the table, where the staff had two minutes to put it on the plate before the vegetables came out. Even if you weren't eating pigeon, you certainly got to enjoy the show.

When a lady took her seat, a tiny table was placed beside her for her to put her handbag on so she didn't need to put it on the floor. How many restaurants have a seat for your handbag? If a customer paid in cash, he received his change in brand-new notes and coins. We did not do crushed, creased fivers and dirty fifty-pence pieces. The notes were wrinkle-free, the coins untarnished and sparkling.

I had been inspired by great French restaurants even though I'd never been to one, and with the Oak Room I set out to re-create the sophistication I imagined Parisians experienced. It had to be the ultimate experience, and I was fortunate enough to be given the opportunity to pull it off. In August 1997 I transferred my three stars from the Hyde Park to the Oak Room, where I had six weeks to get the place in shape before opening.

I took the brigade from the Hyde Park, loyal boys who had given me everything and who had traveled with me all the way from Harveys. From one star to three stars and now even further. We became an even stronger team. There were probably twenty-five in the brigade, that's twenty-five cooking for seventy customers. Robert Reid was my head chef and there were five sous chefs. If we had a table of six at the Oak Room, six cooks would do six dishes, so timing was crucial. Front of house, I had six wine waiters, four maître d'hotels and two head waiters in suits—twelve people, six of them in black.

Of the Oak Room, I have only one memory of imperfection. On a Saturday night in December 1997, a customer beckoned Pierre Bordelli, the restaurant manager. He had a complaint. The man pointed toward the ceiling above him and said, "One of the lamp bulbs in the chandelier up there has gone." Pierre looked up and then back at the customer, who added, "It needs replacing."

Pierre was confused. "I'm sorry, sir. Are you saying that a blown lamp bulb is ruining your evening?" The man nodded, "That's precisely what I am saying. What's more, you've got two other bulbs that need replacing in other chandeliers."

Pierre came into the kitchen and told me the story. "Get him out," I said. "Pull him." The customer's foie gras starter was just on its way to the table when Pierre approached the table, pulled it toward him and said, "Mr. White says he is terribly sorry your evening has been ruined. Please go."

Meanwhile, the boys—my brigade—may well have worked hard, but they never lost their ability to play hard too. It was an hour before lunch and I walked into the Oak Room's kitchen, ready for service, only to find the place was virtually empty. There were one or two cooks there from way down the hierarchy, but no sign of the others. "Where the fuck is everyone?" I said. "We're going to have people at their tables in two seconds' time. Where the fucking fuck is everyone?" And then they told me. It transpired that the night before, the boys had finished service and gone off for a few drinks at Break for the Border, one of those overcrowded cattlemarkets where the queue for the bar is ten-men thick and punters scream chat-up lines above the thud of the music. There had been a punch-up. One of the chefs had ended up with a broken arm and the others emerged from the scrap as bruised, bloodied, hobbling invalids. I think they were all still down at ER, being nursed, stitched up and given prescriptions for painkillers. If you were one of the customers who had to wait for your main course that day, then I'm sorry, but the blame lies with the lager at Break for the Border.

Refining, refining. At the Oak Room, I had reached a level where I would start to wonder where refinement of a dish would end. And of course the road to perfection is never ending.

For example, in the kitchen at the Oak Room, every morning we would roast thirty-six chickens just for their juices, rather than for the meat.

We'd roast the birds, take them out of the oven and put them into a colander, then press them so the juices flooded out, which were collected in a tin underneath. Then the chicken went back into the pan and the whole thing—bird and pan—was covered in plastic wrap, because the steam coming from a cooked chicken creates even more juice.

Once all the natural juices were captured, the roasting trays were deglazed, first with a drop of Madeira, which dissolves, and then a splash of water was added and the sediment dissolved into it. The juice extracted by squashing the chickens then went into the pan, together with a tiny spoonful of veal stock—not to give flavor but to add body.

The thirty-six squeezed chickens could not be served, of course, because they were too dry, so they would go in the bin or end up as staff lunches. It might seem like a waste to you, but if you were a customer, that's what you were paying for—pure chicken juices. Thirty-six chickens provided enough juices for thirty portions of freshly cooked chicken. In other words, the customer had the juice of more than one whole chicken accompanying his dish. We'd do the same thing with lamb shoulders, roasting them slowly for sediment and then pressing them just for the juices.

It was extreme. As part of that refinement I virtually stopped using veal stock in sauces like jus blond and jus de volaille because I felt it was too big and strong and dominated everything else.

In January 1998, little more than four months after we had opened the Oak Room, the *Michelin Guide* came out. We had retained three stars and been awarded five red knives and forks. That's not all. The Oak Room received nineteen out of twenty in the influential French guide *Gault Millau* (no restaurant had ever scored twenty out of twenty). Egon Ronay's guide awarded us three (out of three) stars. We got ten out of ten in the *Good Food Guide*, and the *AA Guide* declared that the restaurant was worthy of five rosettes, its highest award. There was not a single British restaurant which had ever achieved such accolades in one year, and hasn't been since. We had won the Grand Slam in British gastronomy. I felt as if I was perched on top of the highest mountain. I could go no further.

TWENTY-TWO

Blue Skies over Leeds, Again

AMID ALL THIS, another great change came in my life. The news came by phone, a call from my brother Clive at about half past nine in the morning. "Dad's had a stroke," he said. The old man was dying. Mati and I put the two boys in the car and headed up the M1 to Leeds and 22 Lingfield Mount. It was Friday, September 12, 1997, a couple of weeks after the opening of the Oak Room. The sense of accomplishment that comes with launching a restaurant was suddenly drowned, of course, by the numbness that accompanies loss.

A sofa bed had been set up for Dad in the front room and he was lying there, dipping in and out of consciousness. He should probably have been in hospital, but he'd always wanted to die at home, in his small two-bed semi, and it seemed as though his wish was being granted. His wife, Hazel, was there, as well as my brothers Graham and Clive and a doctor. "He'd just had his breakfast when it happened," said Clive.

Luciano went up to Dad, kissed him on the cheek and said, "Love you, Grandpa." The old man had been out cold, but at this point he opened his eyes and whispered back to his three-year-old grandson, "You too." He would live to see just another day, but those two words were the last I heard him speak. Mati, the boys and I drove into the center of Leeds and checked into the Queens Hotel, where my father had trained as a chef, starting out as a boy. It was the first time I'd ever set foot in the building (the second and final time was when Granada took me for a tour). The next morning, a Saturday, I wanted a distraction, so I took Luciano for a stroll in the city center to buy the newspapers. I stepped onto the street and looked up. The sky was crystal blue and the sun shone brightly, and I was instantly reminded of that February day—another Saturday—back in 1968 when I last saw my mother. I knew then that this would be the last day of my father's life.

Luciano and I walked along the yellow flagstones and my mind took me back to my childhood and those Saturday mornings when Dad would take me off to Leeds market to do a bit of shopping. For lunch he would buy me pork pie and mushy peas and we'd chop off the pie's lid, chuck in some mint sauce and put the lid back on. Occasionally on those trips we would bump into one of Dad's friends who would hand me ten pence, and as the coin was offered, Dad would nudge me to take it, saying in his dry way, "Don't be shy. Your mother wasn't."

We drove to Moor Allerton to visit Dad for what would be the last time. Others in Dad's position might have wanted a cozy pillow or some soft music to listen to, but a dose of horse racing was the thing that brought him comfort, so the telly was switched on for that day's big race, the St. Leger live from Doncaster. As a lad I had witnessed him crouching in front of the TV, whipping himself with a rolled-up newspaper as the horses charged to the finishing post in "the ITV Seven." Now we all stood around Dad, stretched out on his sofa bed, as the horses galloped along on the screen. I watched him more than I watched the race and I could see life in his eyes, as if he was aware of the dramatic commentary. Come on, my son. Come on, my son. Rather fittingly, the winning horse was called Silver Patriarch.

The doctor gave the old man a final shot of morphine and then he told us, "He won't last longer than two hours. I'm sorry." It was time to go, time to leave Leeds. I wanted to take the boys and Mati back to London and leave my father with his wife, so she could have that last bit of time with him. I can't do anything for the old man, I thought. We said our good-byes and when we were on the M1, driving back down to London, my mobile rang. Hazel said that my father had died. He had passed away at the age of seventy, twenty-six years after a doctor had diagnosed him with cancer and given him six months to live.

We arrived back in London and I asked Mati to drop me off at the Hyde Park Hotel to have a coffee, smoke a cigarette and think things through. As I sat there, I also recalled a night at the Hyde Park, back in January 1995. Michael Winner had come for dinner with some of his journalist friends, who included Rebekah Wade, who went on to edit the *News of the World* and the *Sun*, and Piers Morgan, who was then editor of the *News of the World* and fast becoming the most talked-about maverick in the newspaper industry. Piers would become a good friend and on that first meeting he asked me, "What does your father think of you winning three stars?"

"He doesn't understand," I said. "As far as he's concerned, Michelin makes tires."

When I told Piers that he was, in fact, editing my father's favorite paper, he said he wanted to send a features writer round to interview Mati and me for an article. My dad was delighted when, come the following Sunday, he saw his son taking up the entire center spread—for the right reasons rather than the wrong ones. As far as the old man was concerned, two pages in the *Screws* meant a good deal more than three stars in the *Michelin Guide*. He must be worth something, Dad would have thought.

Our father-son relationship had always been unhinged, I suppose. After I left home and he remarried, there was a period of more than a decade when we didn't see each other and didn't communicate. We did a good job of patching it up after Luciano was born, and unquestionably my father was a very good grandfather.

He adored the boys—he'd send them cards and toys—and from time to time we would travel up to Leeds and take him out for a day. We might go to Bridlington, where the old man loved to walk along the harbor top, looking out at the horizon and taking in the sea air. I'd buy him kippers and fresh crab to take home as a treat, and he said to me once, "I would love to have another ten years just to see the grandchildren grow up." After our day trips and before heading home to London, I would always wait for Hazel to go out of the room and then give the old man five hundred quid—any less than that would have seemed mean; any more would have intimidated him. The money went straight into his back pocket. He didn't call Hazel and say, "Here, love, put that in the teapot." He was very funny, my old man, but he didn't know it.

Two or three days after Dad's death I was in a betting mood. There was a horse called Frank, my Dad's name, racing at Lingfield, the name of the road where the old man lived. I had told myself that I would only have one bet that day and I had already put my money on Cloudy Bay, which was in another race. So I never put anything on Frank, which is a great shame, not least because it would have enabled me to tell you how I won a fortune. Frank, you see, was the first to romp past the finishing post, the lucky winner and home free.

TWENTY-THREE

Rough Seas

SOME CHEFS WANT to own their own restaurant so they can escape the mayhem in the kitchen. Not me. In fact, my growing portfolio of places to oversee just added to the opportunities for good, old-fashioned fun and games. Take, for example, my new project, Quo Vadis. A lively 120-seater in Soho's Dean Street, it was where I'd worked in the mideighties for Italian chef Signor Zucchoni, the man who couldn't work me out because of my long hair. I was to be a partner with Jonathan Kennedy, the PR man; Matthew Freud, the PR guru; and Damien Hirst.

So that meant there was Damien, the rock star artist with a wild, rock 'n' roll lifestyle, and me, the rock star chef known for his temper. From the outset, it had a nitroglycerine whiff about it. There was, however, a big difference between the two of us. Although I was an enfant terrible chef, I was driven by emotion. What I did was not to create effect; it was me being emotional and expressing myself as a person. Damien, however, the enfant terrible of the art world, did everything for effect. He'd make statements or behave in a certain way purely for the shock factor. Anyway, I think I'm correct in saying that he would only do the deal if I was involved, and so that was how it all came about. We had more in common than simply being enfants terribles, though. Damien was a few years younger than me, but he was another Leeds lad and had been to the same school as my older brothers.

We put Damien's paintings on the walls and the restaurant became home to his trademark style of art: on show were two skinned bulls' heads floating in formaldehyde. One day, not long after we'd opened, I got a call from Matthew Freud. He said, "Marco, we've got a problem. You'd better get over here." When I arrived at the restaurant, I was greeted by two hundred animal rights activists, chanting nasty things about Damien, bulls' heads and our restaurant. As I pushed my way through the crowd, one of the protesters screamed, "That's Marco," and they all started spitting at me. The thing is, the bulls were dead long before Damien did his work on them. What's the difference between a head in a tank of formaldehyde and a piece of meat on a plate? I didn't stop to argue this point with them, though.

Inside, Matthew and I stood with the restaurant's staff, gazing onto the street as the activists continued chanting. I couldn't see where it was going so I said, "Why don't we just give them some coffee to calm them down a bit?" The show got tedious, so I headed off, past the gobbing protesters, and soon afterward they stormed the restaurant. The maître d' was chinned, the receptionist attacked. There was a full-scale scrap going on, and among the protesters were three or four undercover policemen who then waded in, fists flying. Furniture was kicked over and telephones were ripped from their sockets. Five of the activists were carted off to Marlborough Street Magistrates' Court. Then the mother of one of the girls who'd been arrested called me to say her daughter was a depressive on tablets. Would I drop charges? I was quite happy to drop the charges but the police wouldn't have it because they treat activists like some sort of terrorist unit. It was a right mess.

Damien's artwork caused further problems and ultimately led to the pair of us suing each other. The restaurant had a deal with Damien whereby it paid him to hang his paintings on the walls. If he wanted to take a painting down, he was obliged to replace it with another—it's what you call rotating artwork. I didn't like paying the rent for the paintings; it didn't seem right. Then Damien started taking the paintings down because he wanted to put them in his house in Dublin, so he'd take out a painting that was, say, eight foot by six foot and replace it with something that was twelve inches by twelve inches. You can't do that. The idea of rotating artwork is that you replace it with something of a similar size, otherwise it just looks stupid.

If you've got a deal where you're being paid an art rent, then you've got to respect that. It wasn't in the spirit in which we'd done the deal. I don't know whether it was Damien taking advantage of a situation or whether it was Damien being Damien, but I wasn't going to tolerate it. I asked him to move all his stuff out and there was no fallout. We needed to replace his artwork and I thought I'd do some pictures myself. It was supposed to be a humorous battle but lawyers ended up getting involved at one stage and there were accusations of plagiarism. For me it was all done with an element of fun. I took myself off to the country and did some conceptual art, painting a canvas black, sticking some cockerel feathers to it and then giving it some weird name like *Oil Slick*. It's quite time-consuming but it's not hard.

I got someone to prepare the canvases. Then I put a black acrylic over a big square canvas, put a glaze to it and stuck feathers on. It looked fantastic, to be honest, but creating a great meal is harder.

I also tried doing a bit of spot painting and then I'd slash up the picture and call it *Divorce*. So that was me being incredibly playful. Damien had done his famous DNA model, so I made a model with bulls' eyes and called it *BSE*. There was lots of publicity as the media followed my entrée into the world of conceptual art. Most people seemed to get my point, that you can scribble all over a piece of paper, frame it, put it on a wall, and now it's art. We were like a couple of kids having a play fight when it suddenly got out of control and lawyers became involved. Terrible really, isn't it? We were two grown men, not a couple of ten-year-olds.

And do you know what encouraged me to try my hand at conceptual art in the first place? One day, when we were still mates, I'd been sitting with Damien and I'd said to him, "Do you remember the world we came from? There was always a fake *Mona Lisa* hanging over the fireplace and three ducks on the back wall, just like in Hilda Ogden's house? I think you should make a really sophisticated version and do three ducks flying across the back wall in formaldehyde." Three months later I picked up the *Telegraph* and there it was: three ducks on the back wall. That's when I thought, it's not that hard really.

Having said that, he is a genius who deserves everything he's got. And that's how I genuinely feel about it. His butterfly paintings were genius, and his spot paintings are fantastic. So you can't take anything away from him. Maybe he just misinterpreted my playfulness.

What was nice about Damien was that while he had an infamous problem with drink and drugs, he managed to maintain a wonderful relationship with his lovely mother. The pair of them would come for lunch or dinner at one of my restaurants and I was always aware that his mother was very proud of her son. I used to think, Maybe he's made his dream come true and his mother has been there to see it, but my mother hasn't been here to see my dream come true.

WE ALL MAKE mistakes. Failure is often the first part of success. Go to the best restaurant in the world and you might still see failure. A sommelier might accidentally knock a bottle of wine onto the table so its contents spill out and onto your partner. Your beef or lamb might be overdone or underdone but certainly not the way you ordered it. These things shouldn't happen in top restaurants, but they do. It's what happens next that decides whether failure is turned into success.

If the maître d' fails to deal with it, then failure prevails, but if the maître d' realizes you are upset and dashes over to your table, a look of genuine concern on his face, he has recognized an inconsistency. Maybe he'll offer you drinks on the house, or perhaps he'll rip up the bill and give you the meal on the house. He walks you to the door and says sorry yet another time. Now, all of a sudden, you're thinking, I'll come back here. The place is great.

That is just one of the ways failure can become success in the restaurant business. With that in mind, look at what happened when the New York Times published a libelous comment about me. It was just a few words but nonetheless defamatory. The paper said that I had had "a well-publicized bout of drink and drugs." I was angry because it was untrue and I asked for an apology. They could have said sorry immediately and turned failure into success. I would have admired that. But they didn't. Nearly two years later I was at the Royal Courts of Justice, in London, with George Carman QC representing me in a historic case of American newspapers being sued in Britain for libel.

I'll start from the beginning. I got a call one day from an American journalist called Florence Fabricant, who said she wanted to write a profile about me for the *New York Times*, a newspaper I thought of as influential and prestigious. I thought it sounded good and suggested we meet up. Then on February 13, 1998, she came for lunch at the Oak Room. She brought her husband, who enjoyed my hospitality but by dessert complained of jet lag and vanished. Florence and I stayed to have a chat and a coffee, and she asked me about my life, as you'd imagine, and I talked to her about cooking, restaurants and my personal background. At no stage did she ask me my views on drink and drugs, and if she had, I could have explained to her that I rarely touched booze and have never taken illegal drugs.

On May 13, 1998, precisely three months after I'd done the interview, a friend phoned to say something like, "My God. Have you seen the *New York Times*?" When I got hold of a copy, I was horrified. Florence's article wasn't a fair interpretation of our conversation, put it that way, and then there was a line about me having "a well-publicized bout with drugs and alcohol." I got on to my lawyers, Schilling & Lom & Partners. I wanted an immediate retraction and apology. A lot of my clients were American, so the piece was unarguably damaging. The *New York Times* didn't respond. Then things got worse: the same untrue and highly damaging allegations were published in an identical article in the *Times*' sister paper, the *International Herald Tribune* a couple of days later.

Libel actions in Britain can take a while to come to court, but in the meantime the *New York Times* set about trying to prove its lie. They hired private detectives in an attempt to dig up some dirt, and Gordon Ramsay, by now an accomplished chef and restaurateur, got a call from someone saying she was a journalist who worked for the *New York Times*. The reporter asked him about the period during which he worked for me at Harveys. Did he have a wild time there? That sort of thing. When she referred to "sex, drugs and rock 'n' roll," he ended the call. Other people I knew also got phone calls.

A couple of weeks before the case was due to start, the two papers conceded that the allegations were false. I wasn't in the mood for settling out of court, and as the hearing drew closer, they reassessed the grounds of their defense and decided they would argue that the piece, though inaccurate, had not affected my reputation.

The most pleasurable part of an otherwise draining experience was meeting George Carman, my QC for the case. Knowing George was one of the greatest educations of my life; he was a huge influence and had that rare combination of intelligence and instinct. Apart from having a good brain, he had a way of speaking that left you, and the jury, mesmerized.

We gathered at the High Court on April 3, 2000—two years after the offending article had appeared in print—and on day one I went into the box. It is customary for the claimant's QC to question you in a relaxing manner before the defendant's QC does a nasty cross-examination. So George was there to warm me up, make me feel settled.

However, his opening questions went like this:

CARMAN: Were you brought up on a Leeds council estate?

ME: Yes, I was.

CARMAN: Did you watch your mother die at the age of six?

ME: Yes, I did.

CARMAN: Did your father get lung cancer and was given just months to live?

He was drawing a picture for the jury, a picture of a boy from humble beginnings who has fought for everything he's got in life and who is a working-class hero, and then here's the *New York Times* trying to run him down. But I was floored. It was harder answering George's questions than it was being cross-examined by Geoffrey Robertson QC.

Geoffrey Robertson was keen to tie me up in knots, but I kept saying, "I don't understand your question," or, "Can you please repeat that?" The jury was amused. I'd chuck in things like, "Could I have some water, please?" Then proceedings would halt while I had a sip to clear my throat.

I'd answer the question really quietly and he'd say, "Sorry?" I was driving him mad. He said something like, "Were you once described as the 'Jagger of the Aga.'"

I said, "Aga?"

He started telling me what an Aga was and I told him I knew what one was—I had one at home—but what did he say before Aga? Cue laughter from the judge and jury.

There were other moments of levity. Geoffrey Robertson button-holed me one morning to say, "I dined in your restaurant Quo Vadis last night. I had the most delicious risotto I've ever eaten in my life." I didn't know how to respond.

George's closing speech was everything you'd expect from a genius. His reputation was one of a master orator. George was a short man, but as his son Dominic said after George's death in January 2001, "With his stage as a courtroom and his audience as the jury, he was a giant among men." The court was hushed, the jury undoubtedly excited about what was to come. Sit down with the popcorn, the lights are dimming, the big movie is about to begin . . .

Ladies and gentlemen of the jury, once upon a time there was a bad, bad boy in the kitchen and the bad, bad boy had the infernal cheek to sue two powerful international newspapers, and they were called the *New York Times* and the *International Herald Tribune*. Of course, it was a claim that should never have been brought because it never was a libel, they had nothing to apologize for, they had no damages to pay and they had done him no harm. They had not hurt his feelings and they had, in fact, done him a great favor. The great favor was to employ private investigators, go round amongst his friends and acquaintances, investigate whether he had, in fact, taken any illegal drugs . . .

Of course, this is a fairy tale. That is what no doubt the *International Herald Tribune* and the *New York Times* would like to publish about this case, as they would like to publish many things, but we can come to the real world and the real case.

. . . I started off with a fairy tale, "the bad boy in the kitchen." Why was that brought out by Mr. Robertson? "You've got a reputation as a bad, bad boy in the kitchen." Was that intended as some kind of slur that would cause you, the jury, to award him less damages in some way? What does it mean, not just "bad" but "bad, bad boy in the kitchen"? It was repeated like you'd say to a small child,

"You naughty, naughty boy" . . . It was all about him,
Marco Pierre White, bawling out the staff to get the food
on the table, which I am jolly sure he does. You cannot say
when six people are paying a lot of money for dinner,
"Would you all mind, please, just getting the plates together, to put them carefully on the table there? Would
you be so kind as to attend to your duties?" Of course not.
Of course he bawls out, with a few emotive words, no
doubt. "Get moving. Get the stuff on the table," or whatever phrase he uses. He would not be the great chef he has
been and is if he was not able to give clear orders and get
his discipline operating on his staff. There is the great discipline of the kitchens involved, kitchens in excellence.

After an adjournment Geoffrey Robertson argued that even if the
story was false, my reputation not been damaged because, as he said,
"You would not dream of refusing his food or his company after reading this article. You might shrink from his bill, but not from Mr.
White himself." He wanted to give the jury an idea of the size of damages awarded in British courts:

Of course, if Mr. White, during his conversation with
Miss Fabricant, she had somehow got angry with him and
cut his hand off, he would get under the current standards, about forty-five thousand pounds. Well, that is a
matter that you may think would cause great anger and
distress and, of course, permanent disfigurement. That is
the sort of money that is the going rate. There is another
personal injury matter that I imagine would be very worrying for a chef: if Miss Fabricant had wielded her knife or
fork in such a way as accidentally to have stuck it in his
nostrils or tongue and destroyed his taste buds so that he
could never as a chef smell or taste again, that would get
him, on the going rate, some nine thousand to twelve
thousand pounds . . .

The jury adjourned on Wednesday, April 5. They were not out for long before returning to announce that they had opted to send George's suggested message across the Atlantic to the editors of the U.S. papers. They awarded me a settlement of £75,000: £15,000 from the *Times* and £60,000 from the *Tribune*. According to Mr. Robertson's figures, that was the equivalent of Florence cutting off one of my hands and chopping off maybe a finger and thumb from the other hand. Plus, of course, costs of about half a million.

TWENTY-FOUR

Letting Go of Status

THIS SLAVE HAD been a slave for twenty-one years. Although I had spent a career questioning the way I cooked; I had never really questioned *why* I cooked; I just did it. When I finally made up my mind that I wanted freedom—wanted out—the chains were released pretty swiftly. For a while I'd been thinking about it, contemplating retirement as I continued to spend long days and nights at the stove or by the passe.

Several factors contributed to my decision to hang up the apron. They included the realization that I had sacrificed everything in order to be in a kitchen, locked away from the outside world. Obviously, I had to give more time to Mati and the kids. Mati was the only person I talked to about retiring, and she was behind my decision, as you might expect of a wife who rarely sees her husband. In the kitchen I had three stars, but at home I had another three: Mati, Luciano and Marco. When I'd get home from work, they would be asleep: we tended to meet when Mati brought them into the kitchen and they would sit on the passe fifteen minutes before lunch service began. We hadn't had the time to build a proper foundation to our life and relationship. Before we knew what we were doing—less than two and a half years into the relationship—we were two young people with two kids. We didn't go off partying and having fun like most young people do. I just worked and worked and worked, and then slept when I had a day off. And Mati would pop into the restaurants. That was our existence. I didn't question it. I was so obsessed with my work, so tunnel-visioned, that nothing else played a part, but I was beginning to accept that I would have to give something back to Mati and the kids.

Meanwhile, ever since I had won the three stars, my relationship with Albert Roux had been a bit unstable. Dear old Albert, the Gavroche general, good friend, first boss in London, mentor and best man at my second wedding. But these days when he phoned it was usually to ask only if I had heard any trade gossip and there was something that made me question his loyalty. We had lunch one day at the Connaught and I decided to check him out. He asked me about a certain issue, which I knew all about, but rather than give him the full story, I told him a little bit of the truth and a few white lies. The following day I got a phone call from a reporter who appeared to know everything I had told Albert, including the fibs. Of course, it's possible Albert may have told someone who, in turn, told someone else who informed the reporter. From then on I believed, rightly or wrongly, that I couldn't trust Albert.

He was a giant in the industry, a man who helped change gastronomy and take it forward. Albert is revered and his influence immense, but I was very close to him for a while and I saw another side to him.

I used to go to his house in the countryside and one year I went to spend Christmas with him and his lovely wife, Monique. Albert and I were fishing for carp when he suddenly turned to me and announced, "Do you know, Marco, nine out of ten people in the catering industry are cunts?" I was stunned. Here was this figurehead, a man I had put on a pedestal, letting me see what lay beneath the statesmanlike exterior.

Our friendship finally came to an end in the late nineties after Albert was invited to be a judge for the Catey Awards, the annual ceremony held by the *Caterer and Hotelkeeper* magazine. I was at Mirabelle when I got a call from Gordon Ramsay, who had a friend at the magazine. Gordon said, "They're quite disgusted at the *Caterer.*"

"Why's that?"

"They had the judging for Chef of the Year and you were going to get it, but Albert started saying, 'We can't give it to Marco Pierre White. It would be bad for the industry to give him Chef of the Year.' You're not going to get the award."

For years I had listened to Albert criticizing other chefs and now he was criticizing me.

So I phoned him and said, "Albert, you were judging Chef of the Year yesterday for the Catey Awards and it has come back to me that you said it would be wrong to give Marco Pierre White Chef of the Year. And you said that Marco Pierre White is bad for the industry. Is that right, Albert?"

Albert came back with, "I signed a confidentiality agreement."

"I didn't ask if you'd signed a confidentiality agreement, Albert. I asked if you said those words."

"Marco," he said, "I don't want to have this conversation with you."

I last saw Albert a couple of years ago, when I arrived at the Sofitel hotel in London for a meeting. Albert and I came face-to-face in the foyer. He looked at me and I looked at him. "Good morning," I said. He froze and didn't say a word, then he looked straight at the door and strutted off. He did a lot for the industry and you can't knock him for that. He also did a lot for me, so I have tremendous regret about the way it ended.

Meanwhile, I had lost respect for Michelin. There was an episode that sounds quite silly now but at the time became something of a preoccupation. Derek Brown had left and been replaced as head inspector by his sidekick, Derek Bulmer, who came to see me one day. When I shook his hand and said, "Hello, Mr. Bulmer," he replied, "Please call me Derek." He was a charming man and meant it in the most friendly way, but I felt myself shudder at the thought of calling him by his first name. It would have been a bit like a pupil being on familiar terms with the headmaster—it just wasn't right. In fact, in my opinion, it was completely wrong and the respect evaporated on that day. It dawned on me that I had spent my whole career being judged by people who had less knowledge than me, be they restaurant inspectors or food critics. Please forgive the arrogance, but can you see my point?

There were other reasons for me wanting to hang up my apron. The nonstop process of refining dishes and striving for perfection was exhausting. I didn't want to push myself anymore. Even when you have three stars, you still have to keep raising your game. People look at you as the top chef and their expectations become greater. It's all about taking yourself as far as you can. It can seem never-ending.

In addition to this disillusionment, my cooks were ready to leave me and become head chefs elsewhere and I didn't like the look of many of the new chefs arriving on the scene. Young men were coming into the industry because they wanted to be famous, not because they wanted to cook. They aspired to be *celebrity* chefs rather than chefs. Forgive the pun, but there was a distinct lack of hunger out there. There wasn't the energy or the passion. I started to ask myself whether I wanted to build up a new team? Disenchantment had set in.

Lots of famous chefs today don't look whacked, because they don't work. They have a healthy glow and a clear complexion. There is blood in their cheeks. They haven't got burns on their wrists and cuts on their hands.

Of the boys who worked for me, they were mostly aged about twenty-seven or twenty-eight and every one of them was a fine chef. Each one of them could walk straight into a job as head chef, and many had acquired enough knowledge to run their own restaurant and become a chef patron. If you look at most large kitchens, there might be two, three, or maybe four who have been there a long time. But now too many of them were talking of flying the nest. Cooks who had come to me as young men were on the verge of launching their own careers and I had to accept that I'd been very lucky to have them, but it was time for them to move on.

I SUPPOSE WHAT I could have done is what so many chefs do these days: stop cooking but pretend to the rest of the world that they are still at the stove, crafting and creating. But that is tantamount to lying, isn't it? They're simply pretending to be in the kitchen, when in fact they're in front of the camera. And if they're in front of the camera, who is at the stove?

Surely, if you go to a restaurant run by a top chef, you can't be blamed for thinking that the chef who has his name above the door is the man who's in the kitchen. Or maybe I'm wrong. Regardless, I am convinced that once chefs win three stars, they become disillusioned, just like I did. Winning becomes a way of life, and once you feel you can go no further, then it becomes nothing more than a job. You see it with boxers. They win the world title and lose their hunger. Why should chefs be any different?

I had lost the passion, so to stay in the kitchen would be the equivalent of lying to myself. By removing myself from the *Michelin Guide*, customers would know that I was no longer the one doing the food. I had lost all sense of direction, but now I was going to do something about it.

Mati was the one who suggested I hand the stars back to Michelin. We had been driving through London late one night when we passed the Hyde Park Hotel and I was reminded of my workload and grumbled. She said, "Why don't you return the stars?" I looked at her quizzically and she continued, "Look, you're not happy and you haven't been for some time. If it is all about the pressure of having the stars, then why don't you get rid of them? No stars, no pressure."

When she asked if a chef had ever returned the stars, I replied, "No, of course not." And then she said, "You made history by becoming the first British chef to win them. Why don't you become the first British chef to hand them back?"

I thought about her comments for a couple of weeks. Then it all clicked into place one morning when I took myself out of the kitchen and onto the banks of the River Test for some fishing therapy.

Test Wood pool is on the Petworth estate and is a rewarding spot for fishing, perhaps the finest salmon pool on the south coast of England. You drive through a rough council estate in Southampton and come to a driveway, and when you get to the end of it—bang—you're in a quiet little paradise. I was introduced to it back in the nineties by Johnny Yeo, the artist and a mate of mine, and it remains one of my bolt-holes. Two other anglers use it: one is called Jumbo and the other is a former gamekeeper known as Toad. We sit there, fishing, thinking, and talking, and at lunchtime Jumbo produces a lunch of fresh crab and lobster with his own potato salad.

It would have been one morning in September 1999, when Mr. Ishii picked me up in the Range Rover at dawn and drove me and my rod from London to Test Wood. Jumbo and Toad weren't around that day, but I sat there for a couple of hours fishing with Billy Webb, my friend and the estate's head keeper. I caught two salmon, put down the rod and wandered up to a nearby lawn for a break. I was standing there, drinking a cup of tea and smoking a Marlboro, when I suddenly thought, "I don't want to be a chef anymore. There has got to be more to life than cooking."

Standing in my waders and looking back onto the calm surface waters of the pool, I fixed a retirement date in my head there and then. My final day in the kitchen, my last day as a professional chef, would be December 23. It seemed the best day, as that's when the Oak Room was due to close for a two-week Christmas break. Having decided that I would no longer be a chef, I knew it would be wrong to keep the Michelin stars. The stars, albeit hard-earned and cherished, would have to be returned. Mati was right: the pressure would be removed. I finished my cuppa, picked up my mobile and phoned Derek Bulmer at Michelin UK. "Mr. Bulmer, it's Marco Pierre White speaking."

"Hello." He was friendly—he didn't know what was coming.

We didn't do "how are you?" or "isn't it lovely weather?" I got straight to the point. "Just to let you know," I said, "I stop cooking on December 23. Please don't include me in your next guide."

There was silence at the other end of the line. Cooks spend their lives working for a mention in the Michelin bible, this little book that has the power to bestow glory on slaves of the stove. Yet here I was, effectively returning the accolade it had taken a career to win. My dream had controlled me for two decades, but now I was in control.

There was a pause, a few seconds of silence, and when Mr. Bulmer eventually spoke, all he could say was, "Oh." There was more silence. He must have hoped I would provide an explanation. He must have been anxious to hear the rationale behind my statement, but he didn't ask why. The only thing I gave him was a very friendly, "Good-bye, Mr. Bulmer."

I heard another "Oh" just as I was pressing End Call. And that was it. All done. It was perhaps the shortest conversation in Michelin history and now I could get on with my day. I put the phone back in my pocket and thought, Glad that's over. There was a feeling of relief and happiness. Happy to be released from my pain, which might sound dramatic, but I think I was in pain. That phone call to Mr. Bulmer felt like the most honest thing I'd ever done. It was, as they say, the end of a chapter.

TWENTY-FIVE

Life Without the Props

THE PROCESS OF doing this book has taught me more about myself than I could have expected. Unlocking my memory bank has been a tough chore at times, and I don't mind telling you that I shed tears on more than one occasion. As the reader, you may well have been startled or shocked by a few episodes (and this is the moment for me to apologize, again, for the language). You're not the only one. I have spent my life thinking, Wow, I can't believe that just happened. Today I am sitting in Luciano, my restaurant in that very posh part of London, St. James's, reflecting on how life has treated me since I retired from the kitchen. A couple of relationships have bit the dust. Some dear old friends are no longer on my Christmas card list. And some beautiful new relationships have begun.

Mati and and I had known each other for eight years and we had two sons, Luciano and Marco. But we had never seriously discussed marriage because my life, of course, was work, work, work. Now that I had left the kitchen, I was free to marry. One night we were at Mirabelle having dinner with Michael Winner, the movie director, when he raised the subject. I had retired from the kitchen partly to spend more time with Mati and the kids—marriage was the right step to take. We were in the romantic surroundings of Mirabelle, Michael shooting Cupid arrows, and we ended the meal with me proposing marriage to Mati.

We married on April 7, 2000, at the Belvedere, my restaurant in

Holland Park, West London. It is in a beautiful setting and has a license that enables couples to tie the knot on the premises. Michael was best man and made a very funny speech, from which I cannot recall a single line. I had thought, who could I choose as my best man without offending anybody else? When you say someone is your best man, you can hurt someone else's feelings. I chose Michael so none of my other friends would get offended, because although he was a great mate, he was out of my regular circle of friends. I never shared him with anybody because he might not like my friends and they might not like him, so I just tended to him alone.

The 170 guests included George Carman, my defender in court, as well as Piers Morgan, Rocco Forte, Fay Maschler and her husband, Reg. Gordon Ramsay and his wife, Tana, were guests, as was Piers Adam, a friend from my days on the King's Road. There was also a smattering of aristocrats, including Lord Coleridge and the Earl of Onslow.

Alan Crompton-Batt had met Mati and a few of her friends to help do the seating plan. When she had asked him, "What shall we do with the lords? What's the tradition?" he'd replied, "Easy. You put two lords on each table." Forty minutes later, when the plan was finished, he stood up, clapped his hands and announced, "Right, it is now customary for everyone to leave the room and I get to fuck the maid of honor."

His two-lords-per-table rule did not suit Onslow and Coleridge. They were pupils together at Eton and apparently one day Onslow accused Coleridge of playing badminton with his yellow canary. I am sure Coleridge would never have done such a wicked thing. The two men hadn't spoken since that day decades earlier and it was only now that they found themselves sitting opposite one another and Onslow's uncomfortable memories of being the Birdman of Eton came flooding back. I remember once going shooting with Lord Onslow and after lunch he said, "Nature calls." He stepped ten paces onto the lawn and got out his cock and relieved himself in the middle of the lawn, facing the trees. He is a beautifully eccentric man and I thought to myself, I wish I had the confidence to do that but to do it facing the shooting party, rather than the trees.

The wedding was a great day and afterward Mati and I flew off to Venice for a honeymoon. We arrived at the world famous Cipriani Hotel and were unpacking our bags when the phone rang. It was the receptionist and she surprised me by saying, "Michael Winner is in reception waiting for you." It's unusual for the best man to join the happy couple on their honeymoon. Some people might be appalled by the intrusion, but Mati and I were touched that he had gone to the effort of keeping it a secret and there were only good intentions behind his decision to join us in Venice. He stayed for just a couple of days and took us sightseeing and to places of historic interest, like Harry's Bar. Our Winner whistle-stop tour lasted forty-eight hours and then he disappeared, leaving us to enjoy the remaining five or six days alone.

The hotel bill must have amounted to thousands of pounds, but when I came to pay, the manager said, "Mr. Winner left instructions that on no account should Mr. White pay the bill." Michael had picked up the entire tab. At least let me pay for the meals. "On no account." Then let me pay for the champagne. "On no account." May I at least pay for the cigarettes? Christ, I've smoked enough of the things. Again, the response was, "On no account." It was a wonderful act of generosity.

Sadly, the warm feelings between us were not to last. Why is it that grooms so often fall out with their best men once the wedding is over? Michael is a very funny man, a brilliant raconteur and very kind, but he gets tetchy sometimes and I think that was the reason we stopped talking back in 2002.

I opened Drones Club with my friend Piers Adam, and Piers decided to throw a party. I didn't invite one person, because as far as I was concerned, it was Piers's thing. I felt it was too early for a party; the place wasn't ready. I thought, Piers can have his party and I might have one at a later date. On the evening of the party I was due to be taking Michael for dinner at Drones Restaurant, my place in Pont Street, so it was unlikely that I would even show up at Piers's bash. Then I got a call from Michael, who was swearing down the phone and going mad. "Why wasn't I invited to the party?" he yelled, though I've cleaned up his language. It was a major bollocking and then the line went dead. He had hung up on me.

I rang him back and said, "Michael, we seem to have been cut off."
He was still ranting away. When I got home, I told Mati about the
bizarre conversation, if you can call it that, with Michael. I was quite
upset by it. He was making a big deal out of nothing. Or rather, to me
it was no big deal but to him it obviously was. Mati took it upon herself
to write Michael a letter, along the lines of: *Dear Michael, it wasn't
Marco's party. He didn't feel Drones was ready. He was going to take you
there next week. This is all a silly misunderstanding . . .*

Michael doesn't live far from us, so Mati walked round with Luciano to drop off the letter. She has never received a response. On that
day I made a decision never to talk to Michael again and our paths
have not crossed since.

AS FOR GORDON Ramsay, I cut the umbilical cord a few years back. I
stopped returning his calls. He had been a protégé at Harveys and he
was always a hard worker and showed tremendous resilience when it
came to my bollockings. Perhaps I created the monster Ramsay, the
monster who ended up as a TV personality screaming at celebrities on
Hell's Kitchen, doing to them what I had done to him.

Anyway, I questioned my friendship with Gordon. I had given a
newspaper interview in which I'd compared chefs to footballers and
had wondered whether footballers made good managers, i.e., can
chefs be successful restaurateurs? Gordon then gave an interview in
which he used the same analogy but against me. In other words, he
suggested that I may have been good in the kitchen but was I a good
restaurateur? I was annoyed about it but he said he had been misquoted. I'd heard him say that before and I think that there's a limit to
the number of times you can be misquoted.

There was another incident when Gordon and I were pulled up for
speeding and the story appeared in the papers. Gordon said his PR
people must have placed it, but I wasn't happy. I think Gordon can't
help himself and he would do it again.

I was also irritated to discover, quite by chance, that he had brought
a film crew to my wedding. They were hiding in the bushes, filming
Mr. Ramsay for his *Boiling Point* program. I had no idea they were

there until about eight months later, when the producers sent me a videotape that contained the outtakes. Mati and I were happily watching it when suddenly we saw the two of us, dressed in our wedding attire, and then there was Gordon, winking at the cameras.

I decided my life would be enriched if I saw no more of him. It's unlikely we shall ever know each other again. When I cut, I cut.

Back in 2001, Mati was shopping in Peter Jones in Chelsea's Sloane Square when she bumped into Gordon's wife, Tana. The pair of them were pregnant and they talked babies. Tana was due to give birth six weeks later, and when Mati asked her if she knew what the sex was, Tana said that she had no idea. Mati then said that we were expecting a girl and that we had already come up with a name: Matilda, to be named after Mati. Tana remarked, "It's a lovely name," and then the pair said good-bye.

A month or so later we heard that Tana had a baby girl and she and Gordon had named their daughter Matilda. Of course, Mati decided that we would have to choose another name, which is understandable. She threw me a book of children's names and I flicked open the pages of names beginning with "M." I came to the name Mirabelle, a variety of plum, and said to Mati, "Why not? We own a restaurant called Mirabelle." Mati objected at first, but shortly after our baby was born, we were watching a movie in which one of the characters, a little French girl, was called Mirabelle. Mati saw it as a good omen and that's how Mirabelle got her name, so I suppose I owe Gordon one.

Heston Blumenthal says I am extremely sensitive about friendship, and perhaps he is right. One Sunday Mati and I went to Heston's restaurant, the Fat Duck in Bray, for lunch with a crowd that included my protégé Philip Howard and Mati's wonderful parents, Pedro and Lali. I wasn't on speaking terms with Gordon, but by coincidence he happened to be in the restaurant on the same day. He arrived with Tana, said hello to Heston and asked, "Any chance of a spot of lunch?" Heston didn't know that we weren't talking and breezily said, "Marco's coming today." Gordon didn't let on that we had fallen out but simply asked where we would be sitting. When Heston said the garden, Gordon asked if he and Tana could have a table inside. Half an hour later

I arrived with my mob. I saw Gordon and said to Heston, "What's *he* doing here?"

Heston was bemused. "Who, Gordon? He's come for lunch."

I said, "You'll have to ask him to leave." Philip Howard, a very nice man, shuffled uncomfortably and said something like, "Oh no."

Heston called Gordon away from the table. "Gordon, Marco says he's not going to stay if you are here. I think you should have a word with him." Heston then scurried away into the kitchen to hide and asked his maître d' to keep him informed of developments.

Gordon came into the garden and said, "Thank you very much, Marco, for ruining a nice day."

I said, "Why don't you sue me for loss of enjoyment?"

He came back with, "You fat bastard. I've always wanted to call you that."

I said, "Is that the best you can do?"

Gordon left. There was silence in the garden. The customers on other tables were gripped by the scene—it was another sideshow worthy of a standing ovation.

AFTER LEAVING THE kitchen, I lost direction. I was hooked on the adrenaline of service and it was extremely hard to kick the habit. It was all very well hanging up my apron on December 23, 1999, and retiring as a chef, but the following morning I woke up to the startling realization that I was unemployed. Incredible though it may seem, it hadn't occurred to me that I wouldn't have a job. I had an income, because I owned or had an interest in a number of restaurants, including Mirabelle, the Belvedere, Drones, Quo Vadis and Criterion, but I felt miserable having deprived myself of that daylong fix of adrenaline. The structure of my life had vanished.

It was cold-turkey time. I escaped for a bit and there were similarities to the way in which I had behaved after my mother's death, going fishing, hunting and shooting. I'd take myself off to the countryside for a day out with those good friends of mine, my thoughts. It seemed strange that I had stopped cooking in order to be happy but found it difficult to boost my spirits. I kept telling myself, I want to develop as a person, not as a chef anymore. Then I resurfaced, filled with the same energy and knowledge that got me three stars, and wanting to use that knowledge, skill and understanding to move forward. I just needed a direction.

One night in the spring of 2004, Mati and I went for dinner with my manager, Peter Burrell, who also represents the jockey Frankie Dettori. Peter wanted me to meet Frankie, so I suggested he come along with his wife, Catherine. The five of us went to my restaurant Drones, and Frankie and I got along very well. He moaned about the starter, carpaccio, and I said, "Frankie, what do you know about food?" To which he replied, "Actually, I know quite a lot about food. Being a jockey I need to watch my weight, so I'm very specific and fussy about everything I eat." I took his point.

He then wanted my advice. "Can you suggest a restaurant where I can go with Catherine and the kids? A place where I can have good food but also feel happy that the kids are eating well." He didn't want a fast-food joint, in other words. I thought long and hard about the question but was unable to answer it. I simply could not think of a single restaurant that would meet his requirements. When I said, "No, I'm sorry. You've got me there," he replied, "Then why don't we open one together?"

I promised to sleep on it. A day or two later I phoned him to say yes, I was in. Four months later, in September 2004, we opened Frankie's in Yeoman's Row, Knightsbridge. Unlike the jockey it was named after, Frankie's is growing. The first one in Knightsbridge was followed by another in Chiswick. There's a Frankie's in Putney, and the Criterion, that monster of a restaurant in Piccadilly Circus, changed its name to become the flagship Frankie's.

Having stepped away from the stove, my understanding of food is far greater. It sounds odd, but when you've been engrossed in cooking, you become, to a certain extent, lost in what you are doing. Seventeen or eighteen hours a day in the kitchen not only stunts your growth socially; it can also stunt your growth in cooking terms. You become blinded. You are just working, working, working. Routine. Standards, standards, standards. Now that I'm no longer under that pressure, I find I can look at a dish, mentally dissect it and see a way of improving it far better than I could then. I can sit down and work things out more easily. I reflect well and am better at simplifying, working out concepts and understanding food.

A young chef has a habit of overworking things and it takes great confidence to believe in your produce and yourself. I have discovered that I didn't need to put that much effort in. For instance, in the old days I would have put a huge amount of effort into designing a Dover sole dish, but now that I'm out of the kitchen, I know that it should be served plain and simple, with only a little bit of lemon juice and perhaps a splash of olive oil. Delicious. I no longer want complicated food. If I decided to cook again tomorrow, I would do uncomplicated dishes. My menu would contain things I like to eat, and if that's whelks with a bit of malt vinegar and white pepper, then that's what I'd do. It might be fresh crab, seasoned nicely, with a bit of olive oil and some hot toast. Or red mullet with sauce vierge—olive oil, lemongrass seeds, tomatoes and basil. Perhaps, it would be a top-quality medium-rare steak, hung properly (which is for twenty-eight to thirty days, in my opinion), pan-fried and seasoned properly, then served with a great salad. The problem with a lot of chefs today is that they don't have a classical foundation. If food is that good, you don't have to do that much to it.

Of course I like to indulge and eat something quite rich occasionally. I love classical food and adore a big bowl of choucroûte or daube de boeuf. In the summer of 2005, I bought a pub, the Yew Tree Inn, not far from Highclere Castle in Berkshire. Logs blaze in the inglenook fireplace, the ceilings are low, the wooden beams are four centuries old. There are even six bedrooms for customers who have let the mood take hold of them and don't fancy the drive home. The menu is good. There might be venison (brought in by yours truly after one of my shoots), and not overhung or overcooked, but sliced thinly like roast lamb and with the same texture too. The menu changes daily, but there could be a risotto of local crayfish, or Brixham mussels, roast fillet of brill or maybe a fillet of beef. But the menu also includes one or two dishes that were served at the Connaught during those twenty-six years when the brilliant chef Michel Bourdin oversaw its kitchen until his retirement in 2001.

Michel served the Connaught's old-money clientele a superb dish, Oeufs de Cailles Maintenon, which is on the Yew Tree's menu for three reasons. First, it tastes magnificent—a blanquette of pastry, on top of which is a druxelles (minced mixture) of sautéed mushrooms and shallots, on top of which are five gently boiled quails' eggs, soft and runny in the center, on top of which is hollandaise sauce. Second, it enables you to taste Michelin-standard food that was being served in the Parisian restaurants of the fifties and sixties, restaurants where Michel had trained before coming to England. Eating this dish is a bit like stepping back in time—one mouthful and you are in the golden age of gastronomy, the Escoffier style of cuisine. It's fattening, of course, but if you want to indulge yourself, then this is comfort on a plate. Third, this dish is on the menu as a small tribute to Michel. I never worked for him, but I admired him tremendously. In my own little way, its presence on the menu says I haven't forgotten the world that I came from, in the same way that he did not forget his roots. He didn't forget where his passion was born.

MATI SHARED MY dream of reaching the top. I risked my marriage to pursue that dream, and once I had achieved it, I realized how wonderfully supportive Mati had been. I sometimes think about where my life could have gone seriously wrong. It was back in the days of Harveys, during the recession of the late eighties. The restaurant business was struggling, but my rivals reacted to the dire economic situation in a completely different way to me: they put their prices down. They reckoned that to reduce the price of a meal would bring in the punters, and when that tactic failed, they reduced their prices even further. They were searching desperately for the right price to appeal to customers. In contrast, I put my prices up. My rationale was simple: like it or not, fewer people were eating out, but the ones who were going to restaurants were the ones who could afford to pay more. My rivals sank. Their ever-reducing prices took their losses higher and higher. They went bust and chefs disappeared to do God knows what. Meanwhile, I stayed in business and saw out the recession. I went on to achieve that dream and open thirty more restaurants.

However, there must be more to success than seeing out a recession. For instance, without Mati at my side, I don't know how I would have fared. I have always said that winning three stars was a monument to my mother, but now I wonder if I could have done it all without my father? Surely, he is responsible for my success. He is the one who made me the person I am, a driven man who keeps on pushing. Gambler that he was, the old man managed to turn me into his own thoroughbred.

There were two other men who played a significant role in my life: Alan Crompton-Batt, my publicist, who died a couple of months before I started this book, and Bob Carlos Clarke, the photographer who took those great shots for my first cookery book, *White Heat*, and who died as the final pages of this book were being written. Alan and Bob were like my props, supporting me through the rough times.

Bob was one of those friends who pop in and out of your life, rather than being a constant presence. Six months might pass before we saw each other, but when we spoke, we could pick up where we had left off. A lot of people in the fashion business found him difficult to deal with, but I never had a problem with him. Shortly before his death we had seen quite a bit of each other and enjoyed a good lunch at Luciano. Then I got a call to say that he had died. Desperately depressed, he had thrown himself in front of an oncoming train.

Although Bob was a big part of my life, I can't recall him ever meeting Alan Crompton-Batt, that other influential figure who helped my career. I think I kept them apart and I don't know if they would have mixed well.

In the autumn of 2004 Alan went to stay with a friend in South Africa and that is where he died of pneumonia. I have never cried so much for one person since my mother's death.

Then this book came along.

A year and half of introspection is not a bad thing for a man who had previously found it hard to focus for more than a few minutes. Of course, I have been forced to go back to the difficult periods of my childhood, as well as two failed marriages. Recounting my days with Roux, Koffmann and Blanc—what they gave me, what they instilled in me—has been mostly blissful and made me smile. Today I can say confidently that I am happier than I have ever been. I think back to my teenage days at the Box Tree, when I would be in the kitchen, slaving away, and waiting for those swing doors to fly open so that I could catch a glimpse of the glamorous customers in the soft light of the dining room, laughing and clinking glasses, enjoying the wine. Loving the food. Now I am with them. And if you'll excuse me, I must go. I have a slow lunch to enjoy.

Acknowledgments

First off, I owe a sincere debt of gratitude to the thousands of people who helped my kitchen dream come true. The kitchen brigades, the front-of-house teams, the cloakroom attendants. And special thanks to the kitchen porters, who spend their lives washing up but never see gratitude. Without you, the staff, I would not have achieved success in gastronomy, and it follows that this autobiography would not exist. My wife, Mati, was my constant companion and without her I'd have nothing.

Other special people are due credit: Malcolm Reid, Colin Long, Michael Lawson, Nico Ladenis, Albert Roux, Raymond Blanc and Pierre Koffmann. I also want to acknowledge Robert Reid, my right-hand man for many years, as well as Lee Bunting, Thierry Busset, Tim Payne and Roger Pizey.

There were memory joggers who took me back in time and helped me recall anecdotes for this autobiography. They included Piers Adam, Heston Blumenthal, Pierre Bordelli, Martin Blunos, Peter Burrell, Eric Chavot, Keith Floyd, Mr. Ishii, Nicky and Juanita Kerman, Bernard Lawson, Nick Munier, Jean-Christophe Novelli, Andrew Regan, Morfudd Richards, Egon Ronay and Jean-Christophe Slowik (my maître d' who taught the staff, "Rule number one—zee boss is always right. Rule number two—if zee boss is wrong, go back to rule number one"). I owe a lunch to Charlie Day-Williams.

My literary agent, Jonathan Lloyd of Curtis Brown, has done more than enough to earn a mention here. And I truly appreciate Kim Witherspoon and Eleanor Jackson at Inkwell Management, the U.S. agents who brought me together with Bloomsbury.

At Bloomsbury, Nick Trautwein steered and guided the manuscript toward a better place. He was meticulous, fastidious and . . . patient. The copy editor, Maureen Klier, saved me from looking like a complete idiot. Alan J. Kaufman, the libel lawyer, devoted hours to poring over the pages with aspirin at his side. Sticking with the legal side of things, Beverley Nunnery, of the eponymously named company of shorthand writers, kindly gave permission to publish transcripts of my High Court action against the *New York Times* and *International Herald Tribune*.

I am particularly indebted to Karen Rinaldi, who was confident the Americans could do with a hefty dose of me and my bizarre existence. Karen backed me, believed in the dream and admired the story.

To James Steen, my ghostwriter, I want to say a million kind things. But he's probably sick of my voice, so let's leave it at this: Thank you, thank you, thank you, matey.

Recipes

If I had to think of my life in food as a collection of favorite recipes, then they would be the ones that follow. To me, each one was an epiphany, either in terms of taste, refinement or, quite simply, perfection.

If I were to choose any one recipe above the others, then it would be the braised pig's trotters. When Pierre Koffmann was not whacking chefs on the arse with his palette knife, he taught me how to make them. My preferred dessert would have to be the Harveys Lemon Tart, which, like the trotters, has been on the menu at many of my restaurants over the years. This tart, I promise, will win you smiles and respect from your friends and loved ones.

I have worked with chefs who have put blood, sweat and tears—and pure aggression—into creating the lightest, most divine dessert, and I have worked with the most intelligent chefs who have put decades of knowledge into the creation of a sandwich. I have worked with the best and taken the best and now I am giving them to you.

CLUB SANDWICH OF CRAB AND TOMATO

The vinaigrette:
5 tablespoons white wine vinegar
$^{1}/_{2}$ cup peanut oil
$^{1}/_{2}$ cup olive oil
Salt and freshly ground white pepper

The mayonnaise:
2 egg yolks
1 tablespoon Dijon mustard
2 tablespoons white wine vinegar
1 teaspoon salt
A dash of Tabasco sauce
2 cups plus 1½ tablespoons peanut oil

The tomato coulis:
7 ounces good-quality ripe cherry tomatoes, roughly chopped
3 tablespoons red wine vinegar
2 tablespoons tomato purée
A dash each of tomato ketchup and Tabasco sauce
3 tablespoons extra virgin olive oil
Salt and freshly ground pepper

The sandwich:
20 even-sized beefsteak tomatoes, peeled
1 head iceberg lettuce
1 bunch watercress, leaves separated from the stems
4 teaspoons vinaigrette
2 Golden Delicious apples
1 avocado
Juice of 1 lemon (about 2 tablespoons)
8 ounces fresh white crab meat
3 tablespoons mayonnaise
½ cup tomato *coulis*
8 chervil leaves

TO PREPARE THE VINAIGRETTE:
Place the vinegar in a bowl and add a pinch each of salt and pepper. Stir to dissolve. Add both oils and whisk to an emulsion. Taste and adjust the seasoning, if necessary. This keeps well for up to a week in the fridge. Whisk or shake well before use.

TO PREPARE THE MAYONNAISE:
Place the egg yolks, mustard, vinegar, salt and Tabasco sauce in a bowl and whisk together. Add the oil drop-by-drop to start with, constantly whisking so that the yolks absorb the oil. When about half of the oil has been incorporated, you can start adding the remaining oil in slightly larger amounts, whisking continually. Once all of the oil has been added and the sauce is thick, creamy and just a little stiff, it is ready for

use. The mayonnaise can be stored in the fridge, covered well, for up to a week.

TO PREPARE THE TOMATO *COULIS*:
1.   Place all the ingredients except the oil in a food processor and blend to a purée. Add the oil and blend for an additional 30 seconds.
2.   Pass through a fine sieve three times to make a very smooth *coulis*. Taste and adjust the seasoning.

TO PREPARE THE SANDWICH:
1.   Cut a thin slice off the stem-end of each tomato, and place the tomato cut-side-down on the work surface. Cut a vertical slice off each side of the tomato, scoop out the seeds and flesh, and flatten each slice so that it forms a rectangle. You should end up with 20 rectangles, which will form the layers of the sandwiches. Be sure that they are uniform in size and, if necessary, tidy them up with a sharp knife.
2.   Separate the lettuce leaves. Take several leaves at a time, roll them into a cigar shape and slice very thinly with a very sharp knife to give you fine ribbons (*chiffonade*). Do the same with the watercress leaves. Keep the lettuce and watercress separate and dress each with a small amount of vinaigrette.
3.   Peel and core the apples, then cut into $^1/8$-inch cubes. Peel, stone and dice the avocado similarly. Keep the apple and avocado separate and sprinkle both as quickly as you can with lemon juice to prevent discoloration.
4.   Shred the crab meat and mix with the mayonnaise and shredded lettuce. In a separate bowl, combine the watercress, chopped apple and avocado.
5.   For each sandwich, lay a base tomato rectangle on a cutting board. Place a little of the lettuce and the crab mixture on the rectangle and top with another tomato rectangle. Top this with more lettuce and crab, and then another tomato rectangle. Cover with the watercress, apple and avocado mixture. Finish off with a final layer of tomato.
6.   Using a very sharp knife, slice the layered rectangle diagonally to transform it into two triangles.
7.   Place a small amount of tomato *coulis* in the middle of each plate. Place a club sandwich in the center and garnish with a chervil leaf at each end.

> **TIP:** If you are not very confident in your knife work, you could also use a very sharp circular cutter to shape the club sandwich, which would look just as pretty.

WHITE ASPARAGUS WITH TRUFFLE VINAIGRETTE

The truffle vinaigrette:
3½ tablespoons sherry vinegar
⅓ cup truffle juice (the liquid in jarred truffles)
⅓ cup olive oil
1 cup heavy cream
1 small whole truffle, roughly chopped

The asparagus:
24 medium white asparagus spears
Salt
A dash of lemon juice
Sprigs of chervil

TO PREPARE THE TRUFFLE VINAIGRETTE:
Whisk together all of the ingredients.

TO PREPARE THE ASPARAGUS:
1.   Snap off the tough bottoms at the ends of the asparagus spears. Asparagus spears snap naturally at the point at the bottom where they become woody and inedible. Cook the spears in salted boiling water, with a squeeze of lemon juice added, for 4–6 minutes until just tender but still slightly crisp.
2.   Warm 6 plates. Drain the asparagus and place 6 spears on each plate. Pour the dressing over the asparagus and garnish with fresh chervil.

GRILLED LOBSTER WITH SAUCE VIERGE

The stock:
1 carrot, peeled and roughly chopped
1 onion, roughly chopped
1 celery stick, roughly chopped
1 bay leaf
A sprig of thyme
A small handful of parsley stalks
20 white peppercorns
2 cups white wine
2 cups white wine vinegar
Sea salt

The lobster:
4 1¼-pound lobsters, preferably alive
Sauce vierge
A few sprigs of chervil

The sauce vierge:
⅓ cup olive oil
2 tablespoons lemon juice
1 teaspoon coriander seeds, crushed
8 basil leaves, cut into fine julienne strips
2 tomatoes, peeled, seeded and diced

TO PREPARE THE STOCK:
Put all the stock ingredients into a large pot with 10 quarts of water and simmer until all of the vegetables are cooked. Remove from the heat and let stand for one hour. Strain the stock through a fine sieve into a clean pot and season with salt to taste.

TO PREPARE THE SAUCE VIERGE:
1. Heat the oil gently in a small pan, and then add the lemon juice. Remove from the heat.
2. Add the coriander and basil and let it infuse the warm oil for a few minutes.
3. Add the diced tomato and serve immediately.

TO PREPARE THE LOBSTER:
1. Using a cooking thermometer to check, heat the stock to 175°F. Carefully take the bands off of the lobster claws and then plunge the lobsters into the stock to cook for 3½ minutes. Remove from the pan, wrap individually in plastic film and set aside in a warm place for 45 minutes to relax and rebalance the juices in the lobsters.
2. Remove the claws from the lobsters. Crack them open and carefully remove the meat in whole pieces. Do the same with the knuckles of the lobsters. With a large, sharp chopping knife, cut the body of each lobster in half lengthwise, from the head through to the end of the tail, taking care to preserve the shells. Remove the meat. Discard the brain sac, which is at the front of the head. Wash and clean up the lobster shells.
3. Cut each portion of body/tail meat into 3–4 pieces and place them in the shell so that the red edge is visible. Put the knuckle and claw meat into the head cavity. Lightly cover the lobster with the sauce vierge.
4. Arrange on plates and garnish with parsley or chervil.

GRILLED DOVER SOLE NIÇOISE

4 1-pound whole Dover sole, skinned and left on the bone
Sea salt and freshly ground white pepper
1 teaspoon chopped shallot
¼ teaspoon crushed garlic
5 tablespoons extra virgin olive oil, plus extra for frying
8 medium vine-ripened tomatoes, diced
12 black olives
8 very large canned anchovies, drained and rinsed
1 lemon, halved
A large handful of cilantro sprigs

TO PREPARE:
1.   Panfry the fish in a little olive oil for 6–7 minutes, turning halfway
through (you may have to do this in batches). Season with salt and
white pepper. Remove from the pan and keep warm.
2.   While the sole are frying, gently cook the shallots and garlic in 1 tablespoon of olive oil in a saucepan; do not allow to brown. Add the tomatoes
and cook until all of the water from the tomatoes evaporates, which should
take about 2 minutes. Remove from the heat and keep warm.
3.   Using a small sharp knife, slice a petal from each side of each olive.
You should end up with 24 small ovals. Cut each anchovy into quarters
on a slant.

TO SERVE:
Place the fish on warmed plates. Spread the tomato dressing lengthwise
down the center of each fish, following the spine from head to tail. Top
the dressing with a crisscross of anchovy pieces, again working from
head to tail. Put a petal of black olive into the center of each crisscross.
The garnish should resemble a lattice. Drizzle about a tablespoon of
olive oil on the plate, down each side of the fish, and top with a very
light squeeze of lemon.

BRAISED PIG'S TROTTERS PIERRE KOFFMANN
Makes 6 servings

The veal stock:
6 pounds veal knuckle bones
½ cup olive oil
1 onion, roughly chopped

3 carrots, roughly chopped
3 celery sticks, roughly chopped
$^{1}/_{2}$ bulb of garlic
4 tablespoons of tomato purée
1 pound button mushrooms
$^{1}/_{2}$ bottle of Madeira
10 quarts of hot water
A sprig of thyme
1 bay leaf

The trotters:
6 pigs' trotters (from the back legs only, as they are bigger)
Olive oil
2 carrots, peeled and cubed
1 celery stick, cubed
1 onion, cubed
$^{1}/_{2}$ cup dry white wine
3 cups veal stock
A sprig of thyme
$^{1}/_{2}$ bay leaf
Salt and freshly ground white pepper

The chicken mousse:
$^{1}/_{2}$ pound skinless, boneless chicken breast, sinews removed
A pinch of ground mace
1 tablespoon chopped tarragon
1 egg
2 tablespoons salt
1 cup heavy cream

The filling:
$1^{1}/_{2}$ ounces dried morels
$1^{1}/_{2}$ pounds veal sweetbreads
$^{1}/_{2}$ onion, diced
Chicken mousse

The sauce:
2 chicken legs
Sweetbread trimmings, reserved from the filling
$3^{1}/_{2}$ ounces mushrooms, sliced
$3^{1}/_{2}$ ounces shallots, chopped
$^{1}/_{2}$ bulb of garlic, sliced across to halve each clove

A sprig of thyme
$\frac{1}{2}$ bay leaf
$1\frac{1}{2}$ tablespoons sherry vinegar
$1\frac{1}{2}$ tablespoons cognac
$1\frac{3}{4}$ cups Madeira
$2\frac{1}{2}$ cups veal stock
1 cup chicken stock
4 dried morels
Lemon juice
A few drops of heavy cream
72 fresh wild mushrooms
2 tablespoons of butter

> **TIP:** You need to start cooking this at least a day in advance, to
> have enough time to soak your trotters adequately. I would sug-
> gest making the various stocks and sauces well ahead.

SERVING SUGGESTIONS:
Basic mashed potato (recipe follows)
Roast button onions (recipe follows)

TO PREPARE THE VEAL STOCK:
1.   In a large Dutch oven, cook the veal knuckle bones in 4 tablespoons
of olive oil until golden brown, stirring and turning occasionally.
2.   Simultaneously, in a separate pan, cook the onion, carrots, celery
and garlic in 2 tablespoons of oil until soft, but not brown.
3.   Add the tomato purée to the vegetables and stir in, then allow it all to
cook gently and color lightly. Be very careful not to burn the ingredients.
4.   In another pan, cook the button mushrooms in the remaining oil,
then deglaze with the Madeira. Boil to reduce down to almost nothing.
Add the syrupy mushrooms to the rest of the vegetables.
5.   When the veal bones are golden brown, place them in a large stock
pot and cover with the hot water. Add the vegetables and herbs and bring
to a boil. Skim, reduce heat, and allow to simmer for 8–12 hours, top-
ping up with water as required to keep the bones covered.
6.   Pass the stock through a fine sieve into another pan (preferably tall)
and boil to reduce by half. Cool, then store. This can be kept in the
fridge for up to a week or frozen for 3 months.

TO PREPARE THE TROTTERS:
1.   Soak the trotters in cold water for 24 hours, then drain and pat dry.
Singe off any remaining hairs, particularly between the toes. Scrape off
the singed stubble and any stray hairs with a sharp knife.

2.   Slit the underside of each trotter lengthwise, starting at the ankle end. Cut the main tendon and then start to work off the skin by cutting around it with a sharp knife close to the bone. Remember that the skin is essentially going to form a sausage skin, so be careful not to tear it. Pull the skin down and cut through the knuckle joint at the first set of toes. Continue to pull the skin off to the last toe joint. Snap and twist off the bones and discard them.

3.   Preheat the oven to 425°F.

4.   Heat 1 tablespoon of olive oil in a heavy casserole dish and fry the carrots, celery and onion over moderate heat for about 2 minutes. Add the trotters, skin-side-down, and the wine and boil until the wine is reduced by about half.

5.   Add the veal stock, thyme and bay leaf. Bring back to a boil, then cover and place in the oven to cook for about 3 hours. During that time, shake the casserole from time to time to keep the trotters from sticking to the bottom of the pot. Remove the trotters from the cooking liquid and let cool. They should be a wonderful oak-brown color.

TO PREPARE THE CHICKEN MOUSSE:

1.   Roughly chop the chicken breast. In a blender, process the chicken with the mace and tarragon for 1 minute or until smooth. Add the egg and salt and process the mixture for another minute. Chill the mixture for 10–15 minutes (this will prevent it from separating later).

2.   Add the cream, and then force the mixture through a sieve to make it a velvety texture. Taste and adjust the seasoning. Store the mousse wrapped in plastic film in the fridge until needed.

TO PREPARE THE FILLING:

1.   Soak the morels in cold water for 10 minutes; drain and rinse. Repeat this process once more.

2.   Remove the sinew and membranes from the sweetbreads (save the trimmings for the sauce). Cut the sweetbreads into cubes and fry these in a little very hot olive oil in a large frying pan until they are golden brown with a crunchy texture.

3.   Add the soaked morels and the onion and cook for 1 minute only (this mixture is to be cooked again once it is used to stuff the trotters). Season with salt and white pepper. Drain the mixture thoroughly in a colander and let cool.

4.   When the mixture is cool, stir in just enough chicken mousse to bind the ingredients together. Taste and adjust the seasoning again, if necessary.

TO PREPARE THE SAUCE:

1.   Heat some olive oil in a large frying pan over medium heat and fry the chicken legs and sweetbread trimmings until they are golden brown but not cooked all the way through.

2.   Add the mushrooms, shallots, garlic, thyme and bay leaves and stir well. Deglaze the pan with the sherry vinegar, allowing it to bubble to get rid of the acidity. Deglaze in the same way with the cognac. Add the Madeira and reduce until it looks caramelized. Pour in the veal stock and the chicken stock and add enough water, about $1/2$ cup, to cover the chicken legs and vegetables. Drop in the dried morels and simmer for 20 minutes.

3.   Strain the sauce, then pass through a fine sieve or muslin cloth several times, saving the morels for a garnish for the mashed potatoes if you wish. Just before serving, reduce the sieved sauce just a little to give a coating consistency, like a thin cream. Add the butter, a few drops of lemon juice, 1–2 drops of cream and freshly ground pepper. Taste the sauce, while adding these final ingredients, and adjust the seasoning to suit you.

TO FINISH THE TROTTERS:

1.   Cut out 6 large squares of kitchen foil big enough to wrap and seal a stuffed trotter. Butter one side of each square of foil, and then place a trotter on it, skin side down. Pick out the little pieces of fat on the inside of the skin.

2.   Divide the filling equally among the trotters. There should be enough filling to give the trotters enough bulk to retain their original shape. Roll the foil tightly around each trotter, making a sausage shape, and twist the ends to seal them securely. Put the parcels in the fridge to set for about 15 minutes.

3.   Poach the trotters in a large pan of boiling water for about 12 minutes.

4.   Meanwhile, prepare the garnish. Cook the wild mushrooms in half of the butter in a large frying pan over high heat until they produce liquid. Drain the mushrooms in a sieve then cook again for 1–2 minutes in the remaining butter. Keep warm.

TO SERVE:

Remove the trotters from the poaching water, unwrap them and carefully place one, intact-skin-up, on each warmed plate. If using the roast button onions, arrange them on each plate in lines above and below the trotter. Scatter the wild mushrooms over the trotters. Place a pool of mashed potatoes, about the same width and length as the trotter, alongside it at the top of the plate and dot it with sliced morels left over from the sauce. Coat the trotters with the sauce and spoon more sauce onto the plate.

BASIC MASHED POTATOES
Makes 4–6 servings

2 pounds Desirée potatoes
$^1/_2$ tablespoon salt
7 ounces unsalted butter
6 tablespoons heavy cream

TO PREPARE:
1. Peel the potatoes and cut into one-inch cubes.
2. Put 1 quart of water in a pan, add the potatoes and salt and bring to a boil. Poach the potatoes for 4–5 minutes. Drain well and pat dry with kitchen paper.
3. Purée the potatoes in a food processor, then add the butter and cream. Serve hot.

ROAST BUTTON ONIONS
Makes 8 servings

48 button onions
7 tablespoons butter
Salt and freshly ground pepper

TO PREPARE:
1. Preheat the oven to 425°F.
2. Top and tail the onions. Blanch in boiling salted water for 3 minutes. Drain the onions and then cool them in a cold-water bath. Pop the onions out of their skins.
3. Melt the butter in a small, heavy-bottomed, flameproof pan over moderate heat and add the onions and seasoning. Sauté for 3 minutes. Cover with buttered paper, roast in the oven for 5 minutes until the onions are caramelized. Serve hot.

HARVEYS LEMON TART

The pastry:
18 ounces plain flour
6 ounces confectioner's sugar
9 ounces unsalted butter, at room temperature

Grated zest of one lemon
1 vanilla pod, split open
1^1/$_2$ eggs, beaten

The lemon filling:
9 eggs
14 ounces superfine sugar
Grated zest of 2 lemons
Juice of 5 lemons
1 cup heavy cream

The decoration:
2^1/$_2$ ounces confectioner's sugar
Sprigs of mint

TO PREPARE THE PASTRY:
1.   Sift the flour and confectioner's sugar onto a work surface and work
in the butter. Make a well in the center and add the lemon zest and
seeds scraped from the vanilla pod. Add the eggs. Knead the mixture
with your fingers, working as quickly as you can, until everything is
combined to form a smooth dough. Wrap in plastic film and set in the
fridge for at least 30 minutes.
2.   Preheat the oven to 350°F.
3.   Grease a flan tin with a removable base that is 8 inches in diameter
and ^{1}/$_2$ inches deep. Roll out the pastry on a lightly-floured surface to
form a disc large enough to line the tin and to allow an overhang of not
less than ^{1}/$_2$ inch. Lay the pastry gently into the tin.
4.   Line the pastry shell with greaseproof paper and fill with enough
dry beans or lentils to ensure the sides as well as the bottom are
weighted. Bake for 10 minutes. Remove the beans and greaseproof paper and trim off the overhanging pastry, then return the shell to the
oven to bake for a further 10 minutes.

TO PREPARE THE LEMON FILLING:
Whisk the eggs, superfine sugar and lemon zest in a large bowl until
smooth. Stir in the lemon juice, and then add the cream. Continue to
whisk until all of the ingredients are thoroughly combined. Skim any
froth from the top.

TO ASSEMBLE THE TART:
1.   Reduce the oven temperature to 250°F. Pour the cold filling into the
hot pastry shell (this will ensure that the shell is sealed). Bake for 30
minutes. Remove from the oven and let cool and set for about an hour.

2.   When ready to serve, preheat the broiler to very hot. Sift the confectioner's sugar over the top of the tart and place in the broiler to caramelize the sugar to a light golden brown. Alternatively, you can just sprinkle the tart with confectioner's sugar without caramelizing it. Cut the tart into slices and decorate each slice with a sprig of mint.

TIP: The secret of a really good lemon tart is that the filling should be firm and clear and the pastry light and crisp. It should never be cut immediately after it is cooked as it needs time to cool and set for at least an hour or the filling will be too runny.

PEAR TART TATIN

The puff pastry:
1 pound bread flour
1 tablespoon salt
1 pound unsalted butter, softened slightly
3/4 cup water
2 teaspoons of white wine vinegar

The tart:
3 1/2 ounces unsalted butter
3 ounces superfine sugar
A pinch of ground cinnamon
2 pears, peeled, cored and halved
1 cinnamon stick
3 1/2 ounces puff pastry

TO PREPARE THE PUFF PASTRY:
1.   Sift the flour onto a work surface. Make a well in the middle and add the salt, 2 ounces of butter, the water and the vinegar. Mix and knead until the dough is smooth and elastic. Mold the dough into a ball and lightly slice a cross across the top with a knife. Cover the dough with a cloth and let it rest in a cool place for about an hour.
2.   On a lightly floured surface, roll out the dough into a sheet of about 8 inches, rolling the corners a little more thinly than the center.
3.   Place the remaining butter in a block in the center of the dough. Bring up the four corners of the pastry over the butter to make an envelope.
4.   Roll this out into a rectangle of about 10 inches by 6 inches. Fold in three and turn by 90 degrees. This constitutes a "turn."

5.   With a rolling pin at right angles to the folds, roll out the dough
again into a rectangle of the same size as before. Fold in three as before
and, again, turn the pastry by 90 degrees (in the same direction as the
previous turn). Two turns have now been completed. Cover the dough
and let it rest in the fridge for an hour.
6.   Repeat the procedure to complete two more turns, and then set the
dough in the fridge for another hour.
7.   Make two more turns. A total of six turns have now been completed. Let the dough rest for another hour in the fridge, after which
time it is ready for use. The dough will keep in the fridge for 1–2 days,
and it also freezes well.

TO PREPARE THE TART:

1.   Preheat the oven to 350°F.
2.   Spread the butter on the bottom of a copper pan measuring 6
inches in diameter and sprinkle evenly with the superfine sugar and
cinnamon. Place the pear halves, rounded-side-down, symmetrically in
the pan. Place the cinnamon stick diagonally in the center.
3.   Roll out the puff pastry into a disc with a diameter of 7 inches. Trim
the edge neatly, then lay the pastry over the pears and tuck the sides
down between the pears and the pan.
4.   Place the pan on the stovetop and cook over medium heat, watching carefully, until the butter and sugar make a light brown caramel.
You will see it bubbling up around the edges of the pan. This will take a
few minutes.
5.   Transfer the pan to the oven and bake for 30 minutes until the pastry is golden brown.

TO SERVE:

Set the pan on medium heat until the caramel starts to bubble again.
Give the pan a shake then flip it over, turning the tart out and onto a
serving plate. Serve with whipped cream.

> **TIP:** I have made this tart with apples and pears—both work
> equally well. The apple variety I like to use is English Cox's
> Orange Pippin, as they are good, firm apples that don't collapse
> during the cooking process and have a great aromatic flavor.

Index

A Note on the Authors

Born in Leeds in 1961, **Marco Pierre White** was the first British chef (and youngest chef anywhere) to win three Michelin stars. His gastronomic empire—Luciano and Marco's restaurants, among others—is rapidly expanding to include ventures in Las Vegas, Shanghai, Jamaica, and Dubai, with more in the works. Though he retired from the kitchen in 1999, White recently returned to the stove to serve as the host of the reality television show *Hell's Kitchen*. He lives in West London with his wife, Mati, and their three children. He also has a daughter by his first wife.

As a gossip columnist in the late eighties, **James Steen** phoned Harveys to speak with Marco Pierre White. A maître d' answered the phone and ranted on in a strong French accent about how White was "a monster, a crazy man, a lunatic to work for." The "maître d'," it transpired, was White himself. The relationship went from there. Steen, a freelance journalist, lives a short stroll from what was once Harveys, with his wife, Louise, and three children, Charlie, Billy, and Daisy.